WHAT PEOPLE ARE SAYING ABOUT

THE AGE OF NIXON

This is a wonderfully informed and enlightening exercise in cultural and political analysis, in which Freedman tackles the problem, just what was this man who was vice president, then a two-term president of the United States. It examines how Nixon's flaws – and his considerable strengths – fitted into, reflected, and finally illuminate philosophy, novels, and films, to produce, what, for better or for worse, can reasonably be called the Age of Nixon. Given the U.S.'s recent turn toward the conservative, it's amazingly timely and informative about the nature of such forces.

Samuel R. Delany, author of *Dhalgren, Dark Reflections,* and *Times Square Red/Times Square Blue*

Richard Nixon was real, for all that he seems like a fictional character concocted in the course of some strange literary collaboration between Fyodor Dostoyevsky, Theodore Dreiser, and J. G. Ballard. And Nixon continues to fascinate us, and to haunt our dreams, even these many years after his death. Carl Freedman's compelling book takes the full measure of Nixon the man, Nixon the media image, Nixon the myth, and even Nixon the ideal type, the quintessential expression, and the most capacious representative of the political and economic system under which we continue to live today.

Steven Shaviro, author of *Connected, Without Criteria,* and *Post-Cinematic Affect*

The Age of Nixon

A Study in Cultural Power

The Age of Nixon

A Study in Cultural Power

Carl Freedman

zero books

Winchester, UK
Washington, USA

First published by Zero Books, 2012
Zero Books is an imprint of John Hunt Publishing Ltd., Laurel House, Station Approach, Alresford, Hants, SO24 9JH, UK
office1@o-books.net
www.o-books.com

For distributor details and how to order please visit the 'Ordering' section on our website.

ISBN: 978 1 84694 943 2

A CIP catalogue record for this book is available from the British Library.

Design: Stuart Davies

Printed in the UK by CPI Antony Rowe
Printed in the USA by Offset Paperback Mfrs, Inc

CONTENTS

Dedicated to:

My wife Annette, now and forever—

Also dedicated to:

Chip Delany

Chris Kendrick

Steve Shaviro

—valued friends and ideal readers of this book

I believe the second half of the twentieth century will be known as the Age of Nixon. Why was he the most durable public figure of our time? Not because he gave the most eloquent speeches, but because he provided the most effective leadership. Not because he won every battle, but because he always embodied the deepest feelings of the people he led. - Robert Dole

Nixon's entire political career—and in fact his whole life—is a gloomy monument to the notion that not even pure schizophrenia or malignant psychosis can prevent a determined loser from rising to the top of the heap in this strange society we have built for ourselves in the name of "democracy" and "free enterprise." For most of his life, the mainspring of Richard Nixon's energy and ambition seems to have been a deep and unrecognized need to overcome, at all costs, the sense of having been *born guilty*—not for crimes or transgressions *already* committed, but for those he somehow sensed he was fated to commit as he grappled his way to the summit. . . .Nixon really *was* "one of us"—not in Conrad's sense of that term, or my own, but as an almost perfect expression of "the American way of life" that I'd been so harshly immersed in for the past eight or nine months of traveling constantly around the country. . . .Jesus! How much more of this cheapjack bullshit can we be expected to take from that stupid little gunsel? Who gives a fuck if he's lonely and depressed out there in San Clemente? If there were any such thing as true justice in this world, his rancid carcass would be somewhere down around Easter Island right now, in the belly of a hammerhead shark. - Hunter S. Thompson

Always give your best, never get discouraged, never be petty. Always remember: Others may hate you, but those who hate you don't win—unless you hate them. And then, you destroy yourself. - Richard Nixon

Preface

In the fall of 1960, I possessed—it is, probably, still somewhere to be found in my parents' home—a large lapel button that said, "If I Were 21 I'd Vote For Kennedy." I proudly wore it every day to my elementary school. I did not then know a great deal about John Kennedy, except that he was a United States senator from Massachusetts, and a Roman Catholic, and the Democratic nominee for president. Above all, I knew that he was running against Vice-President Richard Nixon. I didn't know a great deal more about Nixon, though I had a somewhat more specific impression of his political profile. Essentially, I regarded him as one of the most evil creatures ever to slither across the American political landscape. This was my parents' view, but not only theirs: somehow it was generally in the air around me (in Chapel Hill, North Carolina, where I grew up). Evil is often fascinating (and not only to children), and I soon became quite interested in Nixon—though I eventually discarded "evil" as (for most purposes) a useful political category, and came to see that Nixon was far too complex to be encompassed by any simple moral label. My interest in Nixon continued to grow over the decades. I have been reading and otherwise learning about Richard Nixon—and thinking about him—for half a century: that is, for most of my life and for a period of time equivalent to more than half of his.

I am not a professional historian or biographer. I have read the major, and many of the minor, historical and biographical works about Nixon, and I could never have written this book without them. But this volume is not intended as primarily a work of political history or biography, though it naturally contains a good deal of historical and biographical material. By both training and practice, I am a cultural critic and theorist, and this book, as its subtitle, I hope, makes clear, is meant to be a contribution to cultural studies. Though culture is most certainly interconnected with politics in many complex ways, the two categories are not identical; and I am primarily interested in the *cultural* significance of Richard Nixon's political career, above all in the way that his political profile and political success are paradigmatic of many of the most important currents in American culture. Cultural critics have rarely taken a detailed interest in electoral politics, but I believe it is vitally important to do so. If we can understand Nixon, we will learn a great deal not only about the political history of the second half of the twentieth century in America, but, even more important, about the very character of this country of ours—which is to say, we will learn a great deal about ourselves, even if that knowledge is not necessarily flattering.

Cultural studies is a thriving section of American (and British) academic scholarship today and one of which I myself am proud (on most days) to be a part. But this book is not intended solely, or even mainly, for my fellow scholars (though I naturally hope it will interest them). I am convinced that the so-called "intelligent general reader" is, despite some rumors to the contrary, still alive and well; and it is this reader whom I have kept in mind from the first to the last word of this volume. I believe that there are many readers who enjoy serious conceptual analysis of important social and cultural issues, even though they may lack the kind of specialized training that most academic writing tends to assume in its readership. Though I hope that, in content, this book never falls below proper scholarly standards in matters of fact or interpretation, I have tried to make it, in form, as accessible and enjoyable as possible for the lay reader: hence the avoidance of a technical theoretical vocabulary and of formal systems of documentation—both frequently essential in strictly academic writing, but often felt to be distracting and otiose by more general readers. I have been especially determined to write the book in this way precisely because sophisticated cultural analysis in the academy has very seldom chosen to focus on electoral politics. Since I am in this way breaking largely new ground, it seems sensible to do so in such a way as to reach the widest possible audience.

Chapter 1, "The Age of Nixon," provides an overview of Nixon's career—in effect, a refresher course in his political biography for readers with some previous familiarity with the subject, or an introductory course for other, especially younger, readers, for whom Nixon may already be just a dimly glimpsed figure from the history books. The chapter also offers a basic statement of the cultural significance of Nixon, and attempts throughout to make clear what is explicitly stated at the chapter's close: that in America *every* age is the Age of Nixon.

Chapter 2, "The Meaning of Cultural Power," is *directly* concerned with Nixon in only a minor way. Since cultural analysis and US electoral politics are so infrequently found in the same book, many readers may reasonably wonder just what they could have to do with one another. This chapter provides my answer—it lays out the major conceptual presuppositions of the book as a whole—and it amounts to a sort of *apologia* for the serious study of culture in general. I have envisioned the reader as beginning the book and then taking a little time out for theoretical sustenance before returning to further and more elaborate analysis of Nixon—hence the chapter's placement. But some readers may prefer to skip the second chapter until they have read the rest of the book, while others may want to start with it. The book is designed so as to place no obstacles in either path.

Chapter 3, "Marx/Nietzsche/Freud/Nixon," is in many respects the conceptual core of the book. Here I take one key concept from each of the pre-eminent modern masters of the human sciences—the concept of the petty-bourgeoisie from Marx, the concept of *ressentiment* from Nietzsche, and the concept of the anal-erotic character from Freud—and demonstrate how these categories are linked in Nixon and in American culture generally. The following two chapters then extend this analysis in two closely related and interlocking ways. Chapter 4, "Nixon and the Other: Elements of Anti-Semitism and of Racism," traces Nixon's extremely complicated relationship to social marginality, specifically examining how he felt marginalized while heavily involving himself in the stigmatization of the two classic victims of marginalization, the Jew and the black. Chapter 5, "Nixon as Liberal?", traces Nixon's equally complicated relationship to American liberalism, considering the senses in which he might be regarded as one of its most emphatic exponents. This chapter also offers an appreciation and critique of Garry Wills's *Nixon Agonistes,* the book which first put the question of Nixon's liberalism on the agenda and which remains, in my opinion, the most important single work in the entirety of Nixon studies.

Chapter 6, "America's Nixon, Nixon's America," weaves together many themes discussed earlier in the book, doing so by way of considering four major modern tendencies in American culture and politics that all had a big impact on Nixon's career and to which he, in turn, significantly contributed. The chapter also balances the detailed analyses, in previous chapters, of earlier major events in Nixon's political life—notably the Checkers speech of 1952 and the race against Kennedy in 1960—with some discussion of the episode that still looms largest in the public understanding of Nixon, namely Watergate.

There follows a substantial epilogue on "Nixon in Art." No full-length examination of Nixon should omit some consideration of the way he has been represented by novelists, filmmakers, and many other creative artists. That Nixon has inspired the artistic fancy of so many talented people, and that so much of the most penetrating work on Nixon is to be found in fictional and semi-fictional products of the creative imagination, both testify to just how deeply fascinating he has always been, and remains.

This book then concludes with a brief bibliography which, though selective, includes the bulk of the volumes on which I have most directly drawn. It is intended mainly as a guide for further reading.

I will say a few words about my epigraphs. It would, I think, be impossible to find two more violently contrasting evaluations of Nixon than the quotation from Robert Dole's funeral oration, with its solemn and effusive praise, and the quotation from one of Hunter Thompson's journalistic pieces, in which Nixon is abused with a ferocity notable even by the standards of this most robustly (and brilliantly) Nixon-hating of all the journalists who covered the thirty-seventh president. But what seems most striking to me is that Dole and Thompson, despite their vastly different perspectives, ultimately *agree* on what is the fundamental point for both and is also the point that forms the central thesis of this book: that Nixon was deeply typical, in many ways, of his country. If the Dole and Thompson quotations thus provide the essential clue to Nixon's success, the final epigraph, from Nixon himself, gives a clue to his ultimate downfall. Surely the most eloquent public statement Nixon ever uttered, the quotation is taken from the speech to his staff on his final morning in the White House, and describes the origins of his political destruction as succinctly as anyone has ever done.

I will confess to an additional and more personal reason for giving Nixon the last word on the epigraph page. Whatever else he may have been, Nixon was the president of my youth—indeed, the single most dominant American politician of my lifetime from childhood until young adulthood—and I am loyal to my president, in my fashion.

ACKNOWLEDGEMENTS

One bit of this book has seen print before: the section of "Nixon in Art" that deals with Oliver Stone's biopic about Nixon, which appeared, in somewhat different form, in *Film International*. I am indebted to the journal's editor, Daniel Lindvall (to whom I also owe a good many other debts unrelated to the current volume).

The three friends and ideal readers to whom this book is dedicated (listed here and on the dedication page in alphabetical order) read each of the chapters in draft as they were being produced, and the book has gained a great deal from their wise and witty criticism. Chip Delany, with extraordinary—but, for him, characteristic—generosity, has taken time from his own work as one of the finest novelists and critics of our time to offer extremely prompt and detailed comments. I am grateful for his many useful suggestions on matters large and small, and no less so for the enthusiasm he has consistently expressed for this project—enthusiasm that frequently sustained me during the writing process. Chris Kendrick, whom I have identified elsewhere as, intellectually, my "closest comrade in arms," has continued to function as such while I was composing this book. Over the years he has taught me as much as Murray Chotiner taught Nixon, though as a peer rather than a mentor; and, if there is somewhere a parallel universe where I am John Ehrlichman, I trust that there he is H. R. Haldeman. Of all the friends with whom I have discussed Nixon, Steve Shaviro's interest in the thirty-seventh president is most similar to my own, in both kind and intensity. I owe a great deal to his specific comments on the drafts of this book, but perhaps even more to the many conversations we had years and decades ago, long before I had any notion of writing about Nixon. For example, the chapter on Marx, Nietzsche, Freud, and Nixon originated in one particular conversation we had many years ago on a bright sunny day outside the

Cross Campus Library of Yale University. It is quite probable that there are ideas in this volume that were Steve's before they were mine.

Yet my most profound debt of all is surely to my parents, who, perhaps without quite meaning to, began teaching me about Nixon at roughly the same time that they were teaching me how to cross the street and how to tie my shoelaces.

I. The Age of Nixon

1

Richard Nixon once described himself as "an introvert in an extroverted profession." Among those who have written about the enduringly fascinating thirty-seventh president of the United States, points of near-universal agreement are few. But this, I think, is one. Very few students of Nixon would be likely to contradict Nixon's own insight that he was oddly suited by personality and temperament for the profession—electoral politics—in which he scored so many successes.

For electoral politicians do, of course, tend to be extroverts. They are glad-handers and back-slappers, exuberantly outgoing men (or, more rarely, women) who enjoy nothing so much as "working a room" full of people they scarcely know. They seem to crave human contact, but in the most superficial, limited, distanced ways. Often they feel more comfortable, more "at home," in the middle of a giant rally than sitting in a room with one or two members of their own households.

Such is the general personality type. But the very greatest electoral politicians take things a big step further. They possess the rare and baffling talent of being able to project the illusion of emotional connection—even emotional intimacy—to millions upon millions of total strangers. They are able to convince us, on some sub-rational level, that they actually know us and that we somehow know them too—even though this is patently, obviously false. Among modern American presidents, Franklin Roosevelt and Ronald Reagan displayed this talent supremely. Bill Clinton had it too, though to a somewhat lesser extent (partly because Clinton's streak of insecurity, his evident yearning to please at all costs, always contrasted badly with the effortless self-confidence of a Roosevelt or a Reagan). In varying ways and to various degrees, Dwight Eisenhower also had this ability, and so, brilliantly, did John Kennedy, and so even, for a very brief time, did Lyndon Johnson. Even Gerald Ford, never one of the masters of our politics, knew how to convey the impression of the affable, gregarious, clean-cut football hero (unfortunately for him, he couldn't help also conveying the closely related stereotype of the dumb jock). Even Jimmy Carter, whose mind sometimes seemed capable of grasping almost any subject—from nuclear engineering, to peanut farming, to English poetry—*except* US electoral politics, nonetheless knew how impressive it could be simply to carry his own suitcase or garment bag onto Air Force One.

But Nixon? Despite an intense lifelong desire to be a "leader," Nixon was always reserved and studious rather than brash and outgoing. In law school, he was noted not for any potential courtroom magnetism but for the "iron butt" that enabled him to slog through volume after volume in the library. Throughout his political career, his public appearances tended to be reserved and formal at best, awkward and undignified at worst. Attempts to seem winningly spontaneous usually made matters worse, as with the almost frighteningly mechanical smile he sometimes flashed, or the famous walk on the beach he once staged as president for the benefit of news photographers—while wearing a pair of expensive dress shoes. The shifty-eyed and badly shaven appearance he made during the first debate with Kennedy in 1960 became widely known as the perfect example of how a politician should *not* appear on television. Marshall McLuhan, the first great theorist of television, was mightily struck by the polls that revealed that, though most people who heard that debate on radio thought Nixon the winner, most people who saw it on TV gave the victory to Kennedy.

This is not to say that Nixon was incapable of being an effective public performer, which, in our age, mostly means an effective television performer. On the contrary, and as we will see, he could be, in his own way, superb. The Checkers speech of

1952 (which Nixon himself always referred to as "the Fund speech") established him as the first important politician who really understood and exploited the power of the then-new medium; and, though the televised debates with Kennedy turned out to be unhelpful to the Nixon campaign, Nixon would never have agreed to meet the much lesser known Kennedy on equal terms had he not had good reason to be confident of his performing skills. Yet, even when he used television well, he used it with none of the expansive warmth with which Reagan and Clinton later used it, or with which Roosevelt had earlier used radio. His speaking style was clipped and quasi-academic, devoted, it seemed, not to establishing emotional bonds but simply to making things "perfectly clear," in the phrase he used so often during his presidential speeches that it became a national joke (and the title of a biography of Nixon written by one of his fiercest political opponents). He could speak persuasively in a debating-society sort of way—fittingly enough for one who as a student had excelled in formal debate. But, when it came to establishing any feeling of emotional empathy with his audience, he superficially appeared to be less gifted than the average president of a high-school student council.

And yet, despite all obstacles, Nixon *did* succeed in establishing the (fictional) emotional connection with the masses that the highest success in electoral politics demands. How he did so—and, correlatively, the *cultural* significance of Nixon's career—will form the main theme of this volume. But first, I will maintain that the ultimate measure of how well he connected with voters is simply the record of his popular triumphs. The fact that Nixon's political career ended in disgrace (in addition to the reputation of being a "two-time loser" that haunted him, though unfairly so, for a while in the 1960s) has tended to obscure just how brilliantly successful he was for so long. So it is worthwhile, in this chapter, to recall just how well he did, though gifted neither with independent wealth, nor physical charm, nor obvious personal magnetism (the advantages, of course, that he so admired, envied, and resented in John Kennedy).

2

Nixon considered his first political victory to be his happiest, and it was probably his most remarkable. As the 1946 elections approached, Nixon, then 33 years old and a small-town lawyer (and a soon-to-be-discharged Naval officer), was unknown in most of the 12th Congressional district of California, let alone beyond it. Jerry Voorhis was the wealthy and very popular five-term incumbent Democratic representative. The district itself was regarded by the Democrats as one of their safest seats in the entire country. On election day, Nixon not only defeated Voorhis, but scored something of a landslide, winning by a margin of 57 per cent of the vote to Voorhis's 43 per cent. Nixon even took Voorhis's home town. This triumph was achieved mainly by consistently outstanding public performances before small and medium-sized audiences, most notably in a series of debates with Voorhis himself. Nixon's basic theme was simply to question—falsely but convincingly—Voorhis's patriotism and even his fundamental loyalty to the country in whose national legislature he served. It was Red-baiting at its most effective.

Of course, 1946 was a very good year for the Republicans nationally. They took control of both houses of Congress and seemed perfectly poised to recapture the White House in 1948. It is also true that Nixon hardly invented the demagogic Red-baiting that played such a large role in the elections generally and in his own victory specifically. On the contrary, Red-baiting had been a staple of right-wing demagoguery in America since at least the Russian Revolution. It was especially potent in the years following the Second World War, when its reactionary scapegoating and promises of restored stability had considerable appeal for Americans feeling dislocated by the shocks and changes wrought by the Great Depression and by the war itself.

Though the Communist Party had never been more than a tiny numerical presence in American political life (even as compared to the old Socialist Party of Eugene Debs), various factors had given it an importance and prominence disproportionate to its numbers: its popularization (and vulgarization) of the Marxian critique of capitalism during the Depression, when capitalism seemed to so many Americans to have failed so disastrously; its pioneering anti-racism, which was almost unparalleled among predominantly white political organizations at the time; and the prestige it gained from its ideological association with America's most important wartime ally, the Soviet Union. Accordingly, with the launching of the Cold War and the general political shift to the right, the CP's relative prominence combined with its small numerical base to make it especially vulnerable to persecution. What the historian David Caute has termed "the Great Fear"—the postwar era of anti-Communist mobilization—was on, and the targets included not only actual Communists, but also anyone else (Trotskyists, anarchists, old-line Socialists, liberal Democrats, and sometimes even liberal Republicans) who could be plausibly or even *implausibly* associated with the Communists. Nixon was one of a large Red-baiting company.

Indeed, in one of the cutest historical ironies of Nixon's whole career, Jerry Voorhis had already established himself as one of the more enthusiastic Red-baiters and anti-Communist zealots among non-Southern Congressional Democrats. Still, even if Nixon in 1946 was doing much the same kind of thing that many Republicans and some Democrats across the land were doing, few, if any, candidates did it as well as he; and few, if any, achieved such a stunning come-from-behind victory. Two years later, in 1948, Nixon's popularity had only increased. In the district that had very recently seemed safe for the Democrats, Nixon managed to capture both the Republican *and* Democratic nominations, and so coasted to re-election unopposed—despite the fact that nationally the Democrats retained the White House and retook the Congress.

During his first term, Nixon attained a prominence (mainly on foreign policy and on the Communist issue) then all but unheard of among freshmen congressmen (largely thanks to the patronage of the Republican House Speaker, Joe Martin, as well as to his own furious efforts). Nonetheless, he almost immediately became impatient with the long wait that he calculated would be required before attaining serious power in the House. He wanted to move up to the Senate, and was able to do so chiefly because of one of the most storied episodes of his entire pre-presidential life: the case of Alger Hiss.

This is not the place to rehearse the extremely complex merits of the Hiss case, about which opinion today remains very nearly as divided as half a century ago. There is a respectable, though far from conclusive, body of scholarship that holds Hiss to have indeed been lying under oath when he denied Whittaker Chambers's allegations that he had been a Communist and a Soviet agent. At the very least, it should be recognized (as Nixon's opponents have generally failed to do) that Nixon's successful pursuit of Hiss was somewhat less reckless than many of the other charges made during the great anti-Communist purge that dominated so much of American politics during the later years of the Truman Administration and the early years of the Eisenhower Administration. But, for the political story, the legal merits of the case against Hiss are largely beside the point anyway. According to those around him, Nixon took an instant dislike to the handsome, well-dressed, well-spoken, Ivy League patrician Hiss; and he determined to pursue Hiss *before* he could, on any view, have known any incriminating facts. For over a year beginning in August 1948, Nixon set himself against Hiss, not only through the investigative machinery of HUAC (the House Un-American Activities Committee) but in a series of highly effective public appearances that included speeches both in and out of the Capitol and, interestingly, the very first televised

Congressional committee hearings. Nixon came across as earnest, hard-working, and professional. By the time it was over, he had made himself the most prominent apostle of anti-Communism among American electoral politicians: no small achievement in the time of the Great Fear, when anti-Communism was the primary defining fact of American political life. To most, Nixon was a hero. The young congressman who a few years earlier was unknown beyond his immediate acquaintances was now on the front page of every newspaper in the country.

Nixon's status as America's premier anti-Communist politician was short-lived, however. Less than a month after Hiss was convicted of perjury in January 1950, a hitherto little-known Wisconsin senator named Joseph McCarthy delivered his first anti-Communist tirade in Wheeling, West Virginia, ushering in what has generally come to be known as "the McCarthy era." It is worthwhile pausing to compare these two very different Red-baiters. Nixon could not match McCarthy in histrionic flair. Indeed, for pure demagoguery McCarthy may have been the most talented figure in American history (with the exception, perhaps, of Huey Long). But he was also one of those curious politicians (the Russian president Boris Yeltsin was another) who combine a genius for tactics with an imbecility for strategy. For a while, McCarthy seemed incapable of putting a foot wrong. Nearly every fresh charge, no matter how ludicrous, produced a bonanza of publicity and prestige. But he never seemed to have any long-range plans, and soon began to get sloppy, to overreach, to make mistakes, and even to lose interest in the whole thing. Within a few years McCarthy had burned himself out. Nixon was far more skillful. Whereas McCarthy never appeared to have any goals beyond generating more and more headlines, Nixon was already aiming at supreme executive power, i.e., the presidency. Though impatient, he was not recklessly so. He made no attempt to rival McCarthy's showmanship, but bided his time, repeatedly stressed the importance of the Hiss case, avoided the kind of wilder charges in which McCarthy specialized, quietly assisted McCarthy when that seemed the shrewd course, quietly betrayed McCarthy when *that* seemed the shrewd course, and survived to be a major force in American politics long after McCarthy was first politically and then biologically dead.

McCarthy's intensification of the political importance of the Communist issue was, however, certainly useful to Nixon's 1950 campaign for the U.S. Senate against his fellow California representative, Helen Gahagan Douglas. This race is remembered mostly as the paradigmatic instance of Nixon's highly effective Red-baiting, in which he was assisted by Murray Chotiner, Nixon's early mentor who is today generally recognized as the godfather of modern negative campaigning. With Chotiner's help—but also remaining firmly in control of his own campaign—Nixon unleashed the full fury of his Red-baiting talents against Douglas, attacking her patriotism; linking her with Alger Hiss; linking her with the American Labor Party congressman from New York, Vito Marcantonio; printing broadsides against her on pink paper (a touch especially dear to Chotiner); and occasionally combining Red-baiting with prurient titillation, as when he described the physically gorgeous Douglas as "pink right down to her underwear." It was during this campaign that he acquired the nickname that followed him ever after, Tricky Dick.

In retrospect, perhaps the most striking thing about Nixon's tactics is that they may have been unnecessary. Though good-looking, articulate, and personally engaging, Helen Douglas was irrevocably alienated from the deeply reactionary political climate that gripped America in 1950. Unlike Jerry Voorhis (whose only honest complaint against Nixon would have been that Nixon was simply a better Red-baiter than Voorhis himself), Douglas was a (usually) *principled* liberal who had given little aid or comfort to the Cold War abroad or to the anti-Communist frenzy at home. She took stands for racial equality that were extremely rare in American politics outside of explicitly Communist circles, and was widely reviled in California as a "nigger-lover." There were also anti-Semitic slurs because of her Jewish husband, the actor Melvyn Douglas, whose original surname had been Hesselberg. Indeed, many of the virulent attacks on Helen Douglas in 1950 came not from the Nixon campaign but from conservative elements of the California Democratic Party, up to and including the retiring incumbent Democratic senator for whose seat Douglas and Nixon were contending. Given the general anti-Communist hysteria—which was naturally augmented by the outbreak of the Korean War during the summer and then by the entry of Chinese troops into the war about a week before the general election—it is difficult to imagine how the *echt* anti-Communist Nixon could have lost.

But Nixon, as ever, took no chances. He was rewarded not just with victory but with a stunning margin of roughly 680,000 votes out of 3.7 million cast—proportionately the biggest win attained in any Senate race that year. In 1951 he became the youngest member of "the world's greatest deliberative body," as the U.S. Senate likes to style itself—and almost immediately began working for yet higher office.

Not even an ambition the size of Nixon's could have cast him as a plausible presidential contender in 1952, when he would be only four years beyond the Constitutional minimum age of 35. And, then as now, there was no very clear way to run for vice-president. But Nixon did what he could, which turned out to be quite a lot. He traveled across the country almost incessantly, establishing connections with local Republican Party bosses and grass-roots activists everywhere. During the Lincoln's Birthday weekend of 1951, for instance, he was the keynote speaker at party rallies in four different states. He also began cultivating a number of national party elders, most notably former New York Governor (and a two-time presidential nominee) Thomas Dewey, who was deeply impressed with Nixon and almost instantly saw him as a possible vice-president.

Dewey was also working to make General Eisenhower the Republican presidential nominee, and this was a fortunate conjuncture for Nixon. During the 1952 political season, the three major contenders for the Republican nomination were Eisenhower; Senator Robert Taft of Ohio, the evident front-runner; and Governor Earl Warren of California, who hoped to become the compromise candidate if the convention deadlocked between the other two. It was clear that, of the three, only Eisenhower was likely to choose Nixon for the vice-presidential spot. Nixon was effectively barred, Constitutionally, from serving with his fellow Californian Warren; while Taft was generally expected to choose someone much senior to Nixon—possibly Warren (who had been Dewey's running mate in 1948), or possibly William Knowland, California's other senator and a close personal friend of Taft's. So, as the convention approached, Nixon went to work for Eisenhower. Though the California delegation was supposed to hold firm for its favorite son, Nixon betrayed Warren (and Knowland, Warren's campaign manager) by influencing a number of California delegates to support the Eisenhower position on a series of crucial procedural votes. This service helped to bring about Eisenhower's victory. It also combined with the support that Nixon already enjoyed with the Republican grass roots and with elder statesmen like Dewey—as well as with the evident "balance" Nixon would bring to the ticket: his youth against Eisenhower's age; his California political base against the East Coast orientation of the Eisenhower forces; and his record of extremely partisan Red-baiting against Eisenhower's studied aloofness from such things—to guarantee Nixon the second spot on the ticket that seemed (and was) certain to sweep the country in November. Barely six years after emerging from provincial obscurity,Nixon was moving to within the proverbial heartbeat of the most powerful office in the world.

The most important and sensational political event of Nixon's eight years with Ike occurred only a couple of months after the Republican Convention of 1952. Journalists revealed that Senator Nixon had been supplementing his government salary with a private slush fund provided by California business interests. The total amount of money involved was relatively small—much too small to maintain Nixon in the "luxury" that some accounts suggested (not that Nixon had displayed much taste for fancy living anyway). Nor was the fund either technically illegal or unique in American politics at the time. But it was nonetheless a major political embarrassment, especially given Eisenhower's plans to lay great emphasis on the financial scandals of the Truman Administration. Many of Ike's closest supporters wanted Nixon to be dropped from the ticket. It looked as though Nixon's almost unbelievably rapid political rise might come to a sudden and ignominious end.

Everything, of course, depended on Eisenhower, and Ike at first seemed undecided as to what to do. While his running mate became the target of savage heckling and editorial attacks, he at first carefully avoided issuing any statement of confidence or support. Eventually, he suggested (through Dewey) that Nixon should make a television broadcast to explain the whole matter to the American people; and he promised that, if the response seemed sufficiently favorable, Nixon would be allowed to remain as the vice-presidential candidate. But then, less than an hour before Nixon was to go on live national television, Ike had Dewey instruct Nixon to end the broadcast by resigning from the Republican ticket. Nixon, of course, disobeyed this order and went on to deliver one of the most completely successful speeches in the history of electoral politics and the first major political speech ever televised. Response to the Checkers speech was so overwhelmingly and intensely pro-Nixon that Eisenhower was left with no good choice but to keep Nixon after all.

I will later examine this speech, which is often remembered as the one occasion on which Nixon *did* make a powerful emotional connection with his audience, in greater detail. For the moment, it is worth noting that, despite the speech's undeniable emotional impact, most of it was delivered in the emphatic, straightforward style of the debating society or the lecture hall—the style, that is, that Nixon normally favored. There was very little folksiness or warmth of the Rooseveltian, Reaganite, or Clintonian sort. Indeed, many of the most important parts of Nixon's speech had nothing to do with the famous sentimental references to his wife's cloth coat and his children's dog ("Checkers"), but were instead devoted to the clipped, deliberate attacks that one expected from Nixon. Having defended his financial probity to his own satisfaction, he went on to question that of the Democratic candidates Adlai Stevenson and John Sparkman and, in a veiled way, even that of Eisenhower himself—who was by no means eager to reveal his personal finances as Nixon suggested the candidates should do. Ike, the five-star general, was one of the great strategists of the century, but with the Checkers speech Nixon had out-maneuvered him.

After the Checkers speech, the rest of the 1952 campaign and even the whole two terms of Nixon's vice-presidency were something of an anti-climax. In 1952 and again in 1956 Eisenhower's own popularity was so great that it is difficult to identify any decisive contributions that Nixon made to the Republican landslides. But vice-presidential nominees seldom add much strength to their tickets anyway, and, contrary to what many liberal-to-moderate Republicans once suspected, there is no convincing evidence that Ike would have done better with a different running mate. Like any other vice-presidential candidate, Nixon (post-Checkers) campaigned in more-or-less the way that his chief wanted him to. Eisenhower was attached to the nonpartisan ethos in which he had lived as a professional military man, and he left it to Nixon to deliver the partisan tirades that kept the core party faithful happy. Nixon gladly obliged, especially in 1952, when he Red-baited Stevenson and Stevenson's allies in the Truman Administration with much the same fierceness that he had attacked Voorhis and Douglas.

Nixon's greatest political achievement as vice-president (the youngest but one in American history) was the radical transformation he helped to effect in the office itself. Today it seems natural, and sometimes even inevitable, that the vice-president should be one of the major figures of the president's administration, and for some purposes his real (as opposed to merely nominal) second-in-command—as well as his heir apparent. But this conception of the office is little more than half a century old and was created by Richard Nixon more than by any other individual. Hardly anyone thought of Nixon's immediate predecessor, Alben Barkley, as a possible president or an important power of the Truman Administration—just as Truman himself, when Roosevelt's vice-president, was so marginal that he was not even told about the Manhattan Project. Yet every vice-president since Nixon has been considered presidential timber, even such unpromising specimens as Dan Quayle or Nixon's own first VP, Spiro Agnew. Furthermore, the most influential vice-presidents after Nixon have depended heavily on a close personal and professional trust with their respective chiefs: Walter Mondale with Carter, George H. W. Bush with Reagan, Al Gore with Clinton, Dick Cheney with George W. Bush. Yet Nixon, who in a sense made those vice-presidencies possible, was forced to refashion the office *without* any such trust, the fund crisis and the Checkers speech having forever rendered genuine closeness between Nixon and Eisenhower impossible.

Beyond the constant factors of Nixon's own ambition, drive, and studious intelligence about political matters, there were several factors that enabled him to reshape the office that its first occupant, John Adams, had famously called "the most insignificant that ever the invention of man contrived or his imagination conceived." Probably the most important was Eisenhower's unusual distaste for party politics. Ike liked to surround himself with people from the military and business worlds, and he had little time for professional partisans. In 1956 he even briefly toyed with the idea of running for re-election as a Democrat, or without a party affiliation. So he was happy to let his VP take over the duties of party leadership that normally fell to the president: thus enabling Nixon vastly to expand his already extensive connections at all levels of his party. In many ways Nixon became the actual, while Ike remained the titular, leader of the Republican Party. At the same time, Eisenhower, though personally not much impressed with Nixon's foreign-policy skills, also allowed him to do a good deal of the foreign travel that the innovations of jet technology had recently made far more feasible than ever before. These trips enabled Nixon to balance his reputation as a partisan gut-fighter with the very different persona of the reflective geopolitical statesman and strategist—and at least to *appear* to be assuming diplomatic responsibilities unprecedented for a vice-president. Toward the end of his vice-presidency, he scored particular political triumphs when he faced a hostile crowd in Venezuela in 1958, when he made a successful good-will visit to Britain later the same year, and when he engaged Soviet Premier Nikita Khrushchev in the famous "kitchen debate" in Russia in 1959. Finally, Nixon's good fortune included Ike's two serious illnesses of his White House years—the heart attack of 1955 and the stroke of 1957—that allowed the vice-president to function, for a time, more "presidentially" than any of his predecessors had done.

The greatest prize of Nixon's vice-presidency was, of course, the Republican presidential nomination in 1960, when Ike was ineligible to run again. Though other ambitious Republicans with national followings had arrived on the scene—notably Governor Nelson Rockefeller of New York and Senator Barry Goldwater of Arizona—Nixon had spent eight years positioning himself so well that he sailed to the nomination against only token opposition. Perhaps never before had a non-incumbent secured a major-party presidential nomination quite so easily. Now he had only to defeat a relatively obscure senator from Massachusetts in the general election in order to capture the summit of American politics.

3

In many ways, the campaign against Kennedy in 1960 seems the pivotal event of Nixon's career—the incident toward which all that came before led up and from which all that came after flowed. Nixon himself, near the end of his life, remembered the 1960 election as "probably the greatest election of this century because the candidates were both outstanding." It was certainly the closest presidential election ever, and it is hard to resist speculating on how things might have happened differently. Had Nixon won, he would have been the fourth-youngest man ever elected to the presidency and the second-youngest (after his hero Theodore Roosevelt) of the century. If he had gone on to serve two full terms, his career might well have counted as the most completely and unambiguously successful in the history of American electoral politics. He would have become not just a hero but virtually an icon to Republicans, and the object of much grudging respect from Democrats. His worst problem might have been leaving office while still in vigorous middle age and with no more worlds to conquer.

It didn't turn out like that, of course. And any sort of defeat must indeed be counted as a serious setback for a politician who had previously experienced nothing but overwhelming victories. But the margin of defeat was so razor-thin that it is impossible to see in the 1960 results any decisive rejection of Nixon by the voters. According to the official tallies, Kennedy's popular vote surpassed Nixon's by just over 112,000 votes out of 68.8 million cast. The state-by-state breakdown is even more heartbreaking from the Nixon point of view; for a shift of just 27,000 votes—

23,000 in Texas and 4,000 in Illinois—would have given those states and, with them, an Electoral-College majority to Nixon.

Nixon and his admirers have always maintained that the election was not just close but fraudulent. Though no major formal challenge was ever mounted, the quasi-official Nixon line, retailed again and again over the years, has it that an honest count would have made Nixon probably the popular winner and almost certainly the winner in electoral votes, which are Constitutionally all that matter; but that Nixon was simply too good a sport, and too patriotically concerned with the country's stability, to demand a recount. In this view, Nixon preferred to relinquish the prize he had ardently craved and honestly won rather than plunge the nation into the uncertainties of a disputed presidential election. In pro-Nixon circles the notion that the 1960 election was illegitimate has become something of an obsession, and has even survived the deaths of both principals. At Nixon's funeral in 1994, Governor Pete Wilson of California, one of the main speakers and a long-time Nixon protégé, saw fit to use the solemnity of the occasion to make (or imply) yet one more charge that President Kennedy, himself then dead for 31 years, had stolen the White House.

The self-serving nature of the Nixon claims does not necessarily make them false. But an impartial evaluation is difficult, and agnosticism about the technical legitimacy of the 1960 election is probably the only fully honest position. The Nixon claims are strongest with regard to the Texas and Illinois results. No one familiar with the workings of Lyndon Johnson's political machine in Texas or Mayor Richard Daley's in Chicago can dismiss the notion of widespread irregularities as at all implausible. The Illinois situation is especially suspicious, not only because of the extreme closeness of the statewide margin, but also because there is evidence that Daley deliberately held back vote tallies until he knew with some precision how large a Democratic margin Chicago would have to produce in order to carry the state for Kennedy. On the other hand, the immense amount of attention that Nixon and his allies have managed to focus on the possibility of Democratic fraud in 1960 has distracted attention from the fact that *Republican* vote fraud was (as Nixon himself was well aware) by no means unknown then either, particularly in Illinois. Indeed, the head of Daley's Chicago Election Board once suggested to a journalist that, though his people naturally stole votes for the Democrats, in statewide elections "the Republicans are stealing so much downstate that all we do is balance it out." This claim is also self-serving and hard to test, but it too is far from implausible. As for Nixon's fairly weak interest in recounts (he did quietly ask for a few here and there at the time, contrary to the legend that he himself successfully promoted), he must have known, as a minute student of American politics and elections, that recounts very rarely overturn an announced result. He must also have calculated that a too visible refusal to accept Kennedy's apparent victory would have painted him as an unpatriotic sore loser and likely killed forever his presidential prospects.

Nixon's pre-occupation with the 1960 results and with the Kennedys in general are matters to which I will return. For now, the main point is that, though we will probably never know whether Kennedy or Nixon got more genuine votes, the election was in all but strictly arithmetical terms a draw. The electorate was simply unable to make a clear choice between the two nominees. A draw is, obviously, not as good as a landslide win; but it is not the worst result in the world either. Especially in view of Nixon's previously unbroken record of stunning success, the notion that the 1960 election revealed him to be an essential "loser" is wildly unfair. To some degree, this idea was the product of wishful thinking among the legion of Nixon-haters. But it was greatly enhanced by the authentic loss that Nixon suffered two years later.

The California gubernatorial campaign of 1962 was, without

question, a bad political mistake on Nixon's part, by long odds the worst of his pre-Watergate career. Nixon lost, and by a substantially larger margin than that by which he had lost the presidency. His loss was also fairly predictable, despite some early polls that had had him ahead. The incumbent Democratic governor, Pat Brown, was hugely popular and successful, and the Nixon campaign gave California voters very little reason to replace him with a former vice-president who displayed little interest in actually governing their state. Nixon would in any case have been suspected of wanting Brown's job only in order to prepare for another run at the White House. But he did much to aggravate the problem, for instance by talking a good deal about foreign policy—always Nixon's primary interest, of course, but an issue that sways few votes in gubernatorial races. When the crushing defeat came, Nixon reacted with a gracelessness that became legendary, announcing his "last press conference" and blaming his failure on everyone but himself, from Governor Brown, to the journalists who covered the race, to his own campaign workers. The nearly unanimous conventional wisdom was that Nixon's career was finished. ABC News aired "The Political Obituary of Richard Nixon," complete with an appearance by Alger Hiss.

But the California race was a mistake also because Nixon had little to gain even if he had won. If he had become California's governor, he would have been stuck in Sacramento for at least four years, doing a kind of work for which he had never displayed much aptitude or interest. He may have felt that it was necessary to be holding an important office in order to mount a credible presidential bid in the future—an assumption then much more common in American politics than it is now (and one that was urged on him by Eisenhower). Still, the wiser course would have been to keep a lower profile, practicing law and making occasional speeches, and above all expanding and reinforcing the excellent network of contacts he had established throughout the Republican Party. This is exactly what he actually did between 1962 and 1968.

Nixon's long march to the White House during these six years is justly regarded as one of the great comeback stories of American political history. But its exact nature has not been generally appreciated. The loss in California was considered so devastating because of the assumption, then generally accepted, that a politician who fails to win office in his home state can never hope to win anything beyond. But (as we will see in some detail in chapter 6) Nixon understood that the state- and region-centeredness of American presidential politics was weakening; and his strategy for 1968 was the most *national* that any presidential aspirant had yet devised. Of course, he was immeasurably aided by being already a fully national figure. He moved his residence to New York and, while also engaging in a lucrative law practice, began cultivating (or further cultivating) Republicans throughout the country, with special attention to the South.

Most important of all, he had to navigate his way around the Goldwater debacle of 1964, and he did so almost flawlessly. He foresaw the magnitude of the defeat that Goldwater's candidacy would bring on the Republican Party; and he knew that, for the foreseeable future, no Republican who was closely associated with Goldwater's brand of hard-right conservatism could expect to win national office. But—unlike most politicians and political observers at the time—he also understood the depth of Goldwater's ideological hold on the party, which would never give its nomination to anyone perceived as a traitor to the Goldwater cause. While the intensity of the intra-party fight in 1964 led almost all other prominent Republicans to line up either for or against the Arizona senator, Nixon adopted Eisenhower's policy of strict neutrality. After the nomination, however, he enthusiastically introduced Goldwater to the Republican Convention and campaigned tirelessly for him in the fall.

Goldwater, whose candidacy was openly spurned by Rockefeller, Michigan Governor George Romney, and others, was grateful. Despite considerable personal mistrust for Nixon, Goldwater, after his own crushing defeat, felt he had little choice but to offer Nixon his prompt and open support for the 1968 contest. With that, Nixon was, so far as the Republican nomination was concerned, already more than halfway home.

In 1966 he emerged in his old role, familiar from the 1950s, as the all-purpose Republican campaigner and the person who knew and befriended more Republicans in more places than anyone else. Although there is statistical evidence that Nixon's campaigning did indeed contribute significantly to the big Republican gains that year, the election was bound to be fortunate for Nixon in any case. Lyndon Johnson's landslide of 1964 was the last U.S. presidential election (with the partial, but only partial, exception of the Reagan victory of 1980) with a major coat-tail effect: Johnson not only rolled up an immense margin for himself, but brought with him numerous other Democrats at all levels of government—"from the White House to the courthouse," as the saying used to be. Many of these newly elected Democrats were from normally Republican areas, and Nixon knew they would be vulnerable when they had to stand for re-election without a popular presidential nominee at the top of their ticket. With or without Nixon working against them, many were bound to fall in 1966; and Nixon, as always leaving nothing to chance, concentrated his efforts against these freshman Democrats. Accordingly, by plunging into his customary around-the-clock travel-and-campaign mode, Nixon was almost assured that, when the votes were counted, he would look like the Republican savior—even though not necessarily as *much* of a savior as he actually turned out to be.

Having campaigned sleeplessly for Goldwater in 1964 and for Republicans everywhere in 1966, Nixon spent the early part of 1968 campaigning for himself, and won an impressive series of victories in the Republican primaries. But primaries were much less important in selecting nominees than they are now, and, though Nixon was certainly the front-runner from the start, the 1968 convention did not look like being the cakewalk that 1960 had been. Instead of only token opposition, he now faced serious challenges from Rockefeller and from Ronald Reagan, whose election as California's governor had been one of the most sensational Republican gains of 1966. Many of the more moderate delegates admired Rockefeller's personal abilities and his ten-year record as governor of New York; and the conventional journalistic wisdom of the year regarded Rockefeller as the most formidable Republican candidate for the general election. (Nixon's surrogate victories of 1966 and his primary victories of 1968 had not entirely erased the "loser" stigma he bore from 1962.) As for Reagan, the Goldwater faithful—still the decisive force in the party—tended to regard him, much more than Nixon, as the authentic heir to the Goldwater mantle, despite Goldwater's own endorsement of the former vice-president. Journalists who walked the floors of the 1968 convention were convinced that Reagan was the sentimental favorite. Both Reagan and Rockefeller were incomparably better-looking than Nixon; both spoke much more expansively than he did; and both projected immediate personal magnetism in ways that Nixon never could.

But Nixon's exquisite positioning of himself vis-à-vis the Goldwater movement of four years earlier continued to serve him well. Rockefeller had his following and his political sex appeal. But the right-wingers hated him so bitterly for his anti-Goldwater stance that most of them, probably, would rather have seen the Republican Party splintered into a thousand pieces than led by the man they had tried to boo off the convention stage in 1964. Conversely, the enthusiasm for Reagan was tempered by doubts about his relative inexperience and, even more, by fears that nominating such a hard-core Goldwaterite could easily lead to a

Goldwater-style electoral disaster in the fall. Nixon inspired less raw enthusiasm than either Rockefeller or Reagan, but he was *generally* acceptable as they were not. This general acceptability combined with the immense collection of political IOUs that he had been amassing for almost two decades to give him a fairly comfortable first-ballot victory at the convention. Actually, the configuration of forces there provided Nixon with a kind of insurance policy. For if the vote *had* threatened to tip toward Rockefeller, most of the Reagan delegates would have abandoned their first choice in order to support Nixon and block their bête noire. Contrariwise, if the Southern delegates had started a stampede toward Reagan, the Rockefeller forces would have cut it off by making common cause with Nixon. By deftly establishing himself as the centrist alternative to two exciting but unacceptable extremes, Nixon could not lose.

4

Nor did Nixon look like losing the general election. The Democrats, who four years earlier had attained a dominance unprecedented since the glory days of Franklin Roosevelt, were now in a shambles caused by Johnson's massive escalation of the Vietnam War; and Robert Kennedy, the one Democrat who still might conceivably have put together a winning presidential coalition, was dead by an assassin's bullet. The actual nominee, Vice-President Hubert Humphrey, was crippled by his own ineptness, by his ambiguous relations with the president he served so fawningly, and by the implacable hatred for him felt by much of the party's antiwar wing (there are, in fact, some interesting formal resemblances between the attitude of the Democratic left toward Humphrey and that of the Republican right toward Rockefeller). Humphrey was hardly even in the same political league as Nixon, who was more lavishly funded and was campaigning more skillfully than ever before.

But Nixon still faced one serious obstacle: the independent

candidacy of Alabama Governor George Wallace. The core of Nixon's appeal lay in the so-called "Southern Strategy" that he devised in collaboration with his campaign manager (and law partner), John Mitchell. Smooth, somewhat covert race-baiting had largely replaced the old rough and overt Red-baiting in Nixon's repertoire of demagoguery. But, when it came to playing the race card, no politician in America could possibly out-perform Wallace, who had made himself into the very symbol of white resistance to the civil-rights movement. Nixon could easily have beaten Humphrey in a head-to-head contest. But if Wallace could draw enough racist votes from Nixon, then Humphrey might win plurality victories in enough states to achieve an Electoral-College majority. Nixon's task, then, was to marginalize Wallace as much as possible without attacking him in ways that might offend white racist sensibilities. This he achieved. He avoided Wallace's openly fascistic crudities as he had once avoided the wild-man style of Joe McCarthy. Nixon let Humphrey flounder, repeatedly presented himself as the respectable, "moderate" face of racism and reaction, and pretty much ignored Wallace, only occasionally criticizing the Alabama governor in very mild terms. In appealing to the most zealously racist voters, i.e., those most tempted by Wallace's savage charm, Nixon was greatly and perhaps crucially aided by the all-out support of Senator Strom Thurmond of South Carolina, who had also been a key ally in gaining the Republican nomination. Thurmond, after all, had been crusading against racial justice much longer than Wallace, and was second only to him in the pantheon of segregationist heroes. In this fashion, the 1968 nominee of the Party of Lincoln finally won the White House.

There was more than racism to Nixon's self-presentation in 1968—but not, in truth, so very much more as might superficially appear. Nixon's specialty had always been the right-wing demagogic appeal to fear of change and the concomitant yearning for stability and restoration. During the time of the anti-

Communist Great Fear, such feelings could most efficiently be mobilized against the Communists and their presumed allies or dupes among liberals and Democrats—as Nixon's campaigns against Voorhis, Douglas, and Stevenson had so brilliantly illustrated. But, by 1968, conservative America was less obsessed with the Red and more concerned with an older and even more durable scapegoat—the black. The appeal to white hatred of African-Americans had been the most reliable form of American demagoguery since at least the several decades preceding the Civil War; and it was especially effective in the late 1960s. It was black demands for racial equality that most disturbingly threatened the American status quo in the 1960s: and (as both Nixon and Wallace were quick to understand) not only in the South but through huge areas of the North as well, especially among the white petty bourgeoisie.

There were, indeed, other factors too in the restless resentment of the constituency to which Nixon and Wallace (and sometimes even Humphrey) appealed: moralistic disgust at the sexual openness of the youth counterculture; outrage at the politics of the antiwar movement; and fear that the judiciary was too sensitive to the rights of criminal defendants. Yet these concerns were not only secondary in importance to the specifically racial issue but also closely related to it. For crime, as law-and-order politicians like Nixon meant it, was understood to connote black street crime against white victims; while white cultural and political radicals appeared to right-wing eyes largely as "white niggers," who emphatically supported black political demands and extravagantly admired black culture. It is significant that, during the late 1960s and early 1970s, the term *nigger* was widely used generically by both black and white radicals to signify the outsider, the Other, the opponent of the status quo. If one were to summarize Nixon's 1968 campaign in a phrase, one could not do better than to call it the campaign against the niggers.

For the rest, all Nixon really had to do was to avoid talking too precisely about the war in Vietnam. He repeatedly advocated "peace with honor"—a something-for-everyone sort of slogan—but wisely declined to give any very clear idea of how this was to be achieved. (Contrary to what many people believe they remember, Nixon never did explicitly claim to have a "secret plan" to end the war.) To have advocated prompt withdrawal of U.S. troops would have seemed to align him with the antiwar movement that he meant to stigmatize. But the war was not, in truth, very popular even among those most furiously opposed to the antiwar protests. If Nixon had said that he intended to expand the war and to prolong it for another four years—which is what he actually did after being elected—he would have angered and disturbed many of his most natural constituents. It may seem astonishing that a national election could be held in the middle of a major and intensely controversial war without the war's becoming a substantive campaign topic. But Nixon had no motive to discuss the subject, and, since Humphrey had his own (even more compelling) reasons to avoid it, the war became a non-issue.

Nixon's 1968 campaign was excellently crafted in form as well as in content. Above all, Nixon used television more professionally than any politician had ever done before. In place of the debates of 1960, the Nixon campaign relied heavily on what today might be designated as "town meetings"—that is, question-and-answer sessions between the candidate and members of the general public from various places around the country. Though the questions (contrary to what some suspected at the time) were genuine enough, the questioners' lack of training or experience in interrogating politicians meant that few queries posed any real difficulty for so skilled a candidate as Nixon. One index of the brilliance of Nixon's media campaign is that it inspired one of the major literary events of 1969—Joe McGinnis's *The Selling of the President 1968*, which became the most talked-about political book of the year and a bit of a cultural phenomenon in its own right. McGinnis was a previously little-known journalist who somehow persuaded the Nixon campaign staff that he was sympathetic to their cause. Accordingly, they allowed him fairly free access to their media operation, from which the press in general was barred. When the volume appeared shortly after the election, the Nixon people were outraged: for—although McGinnis's account of the making of the Nixon commercials is told in a quite low-key, dispassionate tone—the book was generally received as a devastating and slyly satiric exposé of just how manipulative the Nixon campaign had been and how "packaged" had been the candidate. But the book is seldom read anymore; for, save as a purely historical document, it would have very little point for readers today. What may have been an outrage to McGinnis is now routine, the Nixon media operation of 1968 having served as the model for nearly all serious candidates since.

After moving into the White House, Nixon instituted another important innovation that has also become routine: the permanent campaign. Of course, most presidents had generally desired to serve more than one term and hence necessarily gave some thought to the possible electoral consequences of their policies. But with Nixon the next election became not one factor among others but the central organizing principle of the executive branch. After more than a quarter of a century of experience with campaign organizations, Nixon recognized that the White House could be the mightiest campaign organization of all; and he meant to use it as such from day one, in ways legal and illegal. (One might argue, however, that Nixon kept his law-and-order pledges of 1968 in the sense that few, or maybe none, of the crimes of the Nixon Administration were committed by African-Americans.) A second term became the overriding goal of the first term, and the Nixon White House sought it in every possible way: by raising unprecedented amounts of money for the Nixon campaign fund; by violating Nixon's own neoclassical economic principles to stimulate the economy and to produce what at least looked like prosperity during the 1972 election season; by announcing (through Henry Kissinger) the imminent end of the Vietnam War just before the 1972 vote (though some have claimed, implausibly, that Kissinger was acting strictly on his own); most famously, of course, by instituting an intricate series of crimes and dirty tricks against the Democrats, especially Senator Edmund Muskie, whom conventional wisdom held through most of Nixon's first term to be his strongest potential opponent; and, above all, by structuring nearly every decision, great or small, on the basis of public relations. It was no accident that H. R. Haldeman, the first chief of staff of Nixon's White House and his most trusted adviser, had his professional background not in law or scholarship or government or the military, but in advertising.

Curiously enough, Nixon himself often seemed to signal the political basis of his policy decisions—although by way of negation, that is, by elaborate *denials* of his electoral calculations. In announcing the invasion of Cambodia in 1970, for example, he spoke at odd—and, one might have thought, unseemly—length about the effect this military operation might have on his own political career. He claimed that the invasion could result in his being a one-term president: just as two decades earlier he had sometimes prefaced his attacks on Helen Douglas by saying, absurdly, that he knew that talking about Communism was not the popular thing to do. It was all as if Nixon's political yearnings were so strong, his desires to make contact with the electorate so intense, that he *had* to talk about them, even if in inverted and preposterous ways.

Furthermore, it seems highly probable that, as 1972 approached, Nixon's lust for one last big win must have been especially keen. He had not, after all, enjoyed a landslide that was unambiguously his own since the victory over Douglas in 1950.

The landslides of 1952 and 1956 obviously belonged much more to Eisenhower than to him; 1960 was a loss, though a close and arguably an unfair one; 1962 was a loss indeed; the results of 1966 were gratifying, but he himself had not been on any ballot that year; and in 1968 the Wallace candidacy had deprived him of the overwhelming victory he would otherwise have won. But 1972 would be different, and his strategy could not have been more successful—though helped along, it must be said, by much bumbling amateurism within the Democratic campaign of Senator George McGovern. Nixon took over 60 per cent of the popular vote, winning the biggest numerical landslide and the third-biggest percentage landslide in history. He carried every state but Massachusetts, and became the first Republican nominee to win a majority of such traditionally Democratic (if admittedly overlapping) groups as blue-collar workers, Roman Catholics, and members of labor-union households. His triumph was—or seemed—complete.

It was a spectacularly *personal* triumph, and quite deliberately so. One constant factor in Nixon's career had been his identity as a party man, as the ultimate Republican partisan. But in 1972 he pretty much abandoned his party. Perhaps he reckoned that, as this was his final race, he would not need the GOP again. Perhaps he could not bear to have his own victory in any way diluted. Whatever the reasons, he took nonpartisanship and personality cult much further than Eisenhower had ever done. He marginalized and even humiliated the regular party machinery of the Republican National Committee, while concentrating resources in his own Committee to Re-elect the President (which Senator Robert Dole, the chairman of the RNC, promptly dubbed CREEP in retaliation). When faced with the choice of helping a Republican candidate in a tight race or just rolling up a bigger margin for Nixon in a state he was certain to carry anyhow, the Nixon campaign again and again chose the latter. This policy turned out to be rather short-sighted during the depths of Watergate—not only because the Democrats had retained secure control of both houses of Congress, but also because many Republicans in those bodies began to doubt that they owed Nixon any greater loyalty than he had recently displayed toward them. But, in the short run, Nixon achieved exactly what he intended.

5

The foregoing summary of Nixon's electoral career, though necessarily brief, has proved, I trust, what many people still find difficult and uncongenial to grasp: that Richard Nixon, despite what might have appeared to be fatal disadvantages, was one of the most successful and popular electoral politicians of our history. When Senator Dole, speaking at Nixon's funeral, described the second half of the twentieth century as the Age of Nixon, he seems to have been thinking mainly of geopolitical trends, and doubtless he exaggerated, as funeral orators often do. But if one were to seek a term to describe American domestic politics from the end of the Second World War until the middle 1970s, one might indeed choose Dole's felicitous phrase. Astonishing as it will sound to many, Nixon was the most durable hero of our politics between the era of Roosevelt and that of Reagan.

There is a further point to be made here. The depth of attachment that Nixon established between himself and the American electorate can be gauged not only in his many successes but in elements of his ultimate failure as well. Nixon, as everyone knows, left the political scene in disgrace. The movement against him in Congress was no narrowly partisan effort like the impeachments of Clinton or Andrew Johnson, but an overwhelming and fully bipartisan *tsunami*. Had he not resigned before the final votes were taken, he would have been impeached by the House with only three dissenting votes, and removed from office by the Senate with probably no more than about a dozen votes for acquittal. And yet, even as this ultimate political catastrophe approached—as the likelihood of his having used the powers of his office to commit serious felonies against the nation's Constitutional order rose from high probability to mathematical certainty—as the nation's political and journalistic establishment turned decisively against him—as much, even, of his own White House staff decided that there was no way Nixon could or should survive politically—*still* he inspired widespread loyalty and love in the country. Contemporary polling data are difficult to interpret with precision, but they suggest that even at his most unpopular he retained the allegiance of something between a quarter and a third of the nation. For ordinary political purposes, this is, of course, a disastrously low approval rating for a president (though comparable to the lowest ebb of Truman's popularity). Yet, in absolute numbers, it represents a huge minority of Americans, tens upon tens of millions of them. It also highlights a gulf, at the end, between popular and elite opinion of Nixon, whose standing with the people was thus roughly *thirty times* as high as with the House of Representatives.

Furthermore, there is reason to believe—though the point is hard to prove—that a great deal of Nixon's support was just as intense as any hatred for him on the other side. Very little of this love for Nixon during the depths of Watergate came from people who were in a position to make their views generally known; and those few who were often struck an almost comically weird note. There was the Indiana representative who, as he watched all but two of his colleagues decide for impeachment, declared that he would stand with Nixon "even if he and I have to be taken out of this building [the U.S. Capitol] and shot" (not an unappealing image for many on the anti-Nixon side). There was the Massachusetts rabbi who began agitating full-time for "fairness" to the president, because, as he told Nixon, "In my heart, Mr. President, you have grown tall like the cedars of Lebanon." But such public silliness was just froth at the top of a deep, constant sea of intense pro-Nixon feeling. As newspaper after newspaper editorialized that Nixon should go, a significant percentage of letters to the editor pleaded even more strongly that he must stay. In taverns across the nation, there was never a lack of amateur pundits who pounded their fists on the bar and declared their support for the president. At no time was there less than a huge slice of the American middle class who identified Nixon's deepest aspirations with their own and who felt with certainty that Nixon's opponents were just the sort of people who most despised them. Whatever else one may say of the hard-core Nixon following, they were certainly not summer soldiers or fair-weather friends—unlike those who had been Nixon's more influential supporters in politics and journalism. On the contrary, the disgraced and tormented Nixon of 1974 may have been, in the eyes of his most devoted supporters, an even lovelier figure than the triumphant landslide winner of 1972.

Adapting the words of Nixon's favorite predecessor in the White House, one might say that he was deeply in tune with most of the people most of the time and with some of the people all of the time. Long before Watergate, the journalist Tom Wicker quoted Joseph Conrad's Marlow on Lord Jim to proclaim that Nixon was "one of us." This insight has been generally ridiculed and misunderstood, and was at one point somewhat repudiated by Wicker himself. But it was profoundly right. The record proves that Nixon was one of us. But how, exactly, was he one of us? If we can answer that question, we will learn a good deal about Richard Nixon but even more, perhaps, about ourselves as Americans—perhaps more, indeed, than we really want to know. For we may discover a sense in which, for America, *every* age is the Age of Nixon.

II. The Meaning of Cultural Power

1

First, however, it is necessary to clarify the meaning of the term and the concept through which we will revisit the career and the era of Richard Nixon: *cultural power*. It is not a familiar phrase, and to many people its two components will seem to make little sense when joined together. We tend to think of power as something raw, solid, and above all practical: whether it be the economic power of a large corporation, the political power of a president or prime minister, or the military power of an armed force. Power may not be pretty or edifying, but it is, we feel sure, inescapably actual. Power does real things in the real world.

Culture, by contrast, is often considered to be refined, insubstantial, and far removed from the world of gritty realities. Culture—especially in the sense of poetry, art, music, dance, and the like—is, we generally suppose, above all *impractical*: gloriously impractical, as some (but by no means all) would add. People who otherwise hold very different attitudes toward culture frequently agree on this particular point. On the one hand, there are those who cherish culture precisely because it does seem to them to exist on a different and higher level from the mundane practicalities of getting and spending. They might acknowledge that such practicalities are necessary to sustain life itself, but they would immediately add that culture gives life a value beyond the scope of the merely practical. T. S. Eliot, for instance, once defined culture simply as that which makes life worth living. On the other hand, there are those who also see culture as impractical but think that its impracticality is sufficient reason not to take it seriously. They may grant it a certain decorative value, but they feel certain that anything so insubstantial as culture, anything so evidently lacking in urgent claims upon the here-and-now, is nothing worth the full attention of a really grown-up person, and especially not of a really grown-up *man*. Culture, from this viewpoint, is not just refined but probably "soft" and effete as well, the province of ineffectual and pathetic "culture vultures". The phrase "cultural power" may therefore seem like a contradiction in terms.

Yet is that really the whole story? Our modern political history is littered with clues that strongly suggest the opposite. Even if we restrict culture to the narrow meaning already suggested—"high culture," or the fine arts—we find it turning up in the political news surprisingly often. Consider the "culture wars" over which so much journalistic ink has been spilled and so many partisan speeches made. One prominent concern here has been a matter hitherto unsuspected of being a question of widespread or burning public interest, namely the literature curricula in institutions of American higher education. One briefly well-known study, for example, claimed to show that the African-American novel *Song of Solomon*, by the Nobel laureate Toni Morrison, was more widely taught in the English departments of American universities than *Paradise Lost*. The claim turned out to be false—the product of a right-wing disinformation campaign, in fact—but the really interesting thing is that so many people seemed to care so passionately about the issue: including (indeed mainly) people not generally distinguished by a profound concern with literature or education, and who, indeed, were frequently ignorant of *both* texts. Or recall the ferocious controversy that raged (and to some extent still rages) over the grants given by the National Endowment for the Arts to support, in one way or another, such works as the homoerotic pictures of the gay photographer Robert Mapplethorpe; or *Piss Christ*, Andres Serrano's celebrated photograph of a plastic crucifix immersed in urine; or the often sexually charged performance art of Karen Finley, best known for appearing on stage with chocolate smeared over her body. It is easy enough to understand why many—or most—Americans might find such art not particularly to their taste. But why all the political *outrage* over it, generally from citizens not previously known for their interest in contemporary avant-garde art: outrage so intense that calls for the abolition of the NEA itself have become commonplace?

The answer certainly does not lie in the sums of government money involved. The total amount of cash disbursed to Karen Finley and other controversial recipients of NEA patronage has always been vanishingly tiny, not only as compared to the overall budget of the federal government but even as compared to that miniscule percentage of it allocated to the NEA itself (the overwhelming majority of whose grants have never upset anyone, save perhaps unsuccessful applicants for those same grants). Nor does a somewhat different answer often suggested—the principle that, regardless of the sums at stake, Americans should not be taxed to support art they find morally offensive—hold water. The main problem with this superficially plausible logic is simply that the federal government spends an almost unimaginably large amount of money every year on an almost uncountable number of diverse activities. As several wits have pointed out, if your government is not daily spending more money than Finley and her colleagues ever dreamed of on projects that deeply offend your moral standards, then that can only be because you *have* no moral standards at all. If Congress declined to appropriate money for purposes deemed objectionable by any significant number of citizens, then the federal budget would shrink to a small fraction of itself pretty quickly (and the entire *military* budget would be wiped out overnight).

If neither money, then, nor fiduciary principle is really the issue at stake here, neither even is art itself—in that what we are looking at has almost nothing in common with aesthetic controversy in any strict or usual sense. Of all those whose blood boiled at the thought of Morrison being taught in more college classrooms than Milton, how many, for instance, could retrieve from memory even a half dozen consecutive lines of *Paradise Lost*? One can imagine a genuine argument about which text should have priority over the other in the college English curriculum, with plenty of rigorous and interesting things said on each side. But this argument never took place, not, at least, on anything like the scale on which the public furor was played out.

Or again, what, really, is the meaning of *Piss Christ*? If you look into the critical literature on the matter, you find that Serrano's picture has been seriously and rather persuasively celebrated as a deeply religious work, which aims to peel away the veil of familiarity through which we habitually look at images of the Crucifixion, and so to restore a sense of shock at that terrible act by protesting against the world's filthy ruination of Christ's teaching. In other words, the title signifies not, "Let's piss on Christ," but rather, "How awful that the world constantly pisses on Christ"—a message exactly congruent with that of the New Testament. Of course, this interpretation can be challenged. An art critic *could* argue that the picture is indeed the deliberate blasphemy that most journalistic accounts automatically assumed. For that matter, it could also be maintained that it is just in the impossibility of deciding between the pious and the blasphemous meanings that the main significance of *Piss Christ* lies. The real point, though, is that hardly any of those who reacted to Serrano's vision by carrying signs saying, "Defund the NEA"—or who, watching the news at home, identified with the sign-carriers—ever displayed the least interest in participating in actual debate over such rival interpretations.

Despite superficial appearances and claims, then, the hot political disputes of the culture wars have little or nothing to do with either economics or aesthetics. What has been at issue is neither money nor art, but cultural *values*. Mapplethorpe's photographs and Finley's performances both actively challenge the received sexual norms in which tens of millions of Americans try to believe, and which they desperately wish to be placed forever beyond dispute: Mapplethorpe by implicitly asserting the legitimacy (and indeed inevitability) of homoerotic masculine desire, Finley by forcing awareness of the symbolic and physical violence visited upon women when they are constructed as objects of male lust. As for *Piss Christ*, it may be an emphatically religious or an emphatically irreligious picture—or even both at once—but in any case it upsets the bland, unreflective, semi-Christian religiosity that constitutes the quasi-official creed of mainstream America and that it is generally considered the most offensive breach of good manners to transgress. As for the controversy over the teaching of *Song of Solomon* and *Paradise Lost*, it seems clear that the Morrison text functioned simply as a figure for an "alien" and threatening blackness, an "intrusive" presence in an increasingly multicultural America that many Americans ardently wish to think of as still essentially white and Eurocentric. Contrariwise, Milton's epic, as a long established British classic by a white male author, functioned as a reassuring reminder of conservative white male dominance—ironically enough, to be sure, since, in his own time, Milton was far more radical and politically subversive than Toni Morrison has ever come close to being.

It is clear, then, that, however marginal culture may superficially seem to be, huge numbers of people do care about it passionately: not because they are genuinely worried about the government money spent on cultural projects, or because they are interested in participating in real aesthetic debate about the meaning of particular works of art, but because they often feel—very strongly—that cultural productions can outrage (or, conversely, reassure) their deepest emotions on such considerable matters as race, religion, gender, and sexuality.

We need, in fact, to move beyond the merely aesthetic meaning of culture with which we have been working thus far—the meaning by which culture is more-or-less synonymous with the fine arts—and embrace a more anthropological sense of the term, a sense that encompasses nothing less than the totality of intellectual and emotional frameworks that groups and individuals use to orient themselves toward the world. To be sure, the aesthetic and anthropological meanings of culture are interrelated in complex ways. It may well be that—as the controversies about Mapplethorpe and Serrano and others tend to suggest—works of "high" art are often capable of challenging or confirming our most deeply held beliefs and prejudices with a special force and intensity. Indeed, many aestheticians would argue that much of the value of great art resides precisely in this ability to condense common emotions with uncommon power, to articulate (in Alexander Pope's words) "what oft was thought but ne'er so well expressed." But we need to be clear that culture, in the larger sense, is not *only* something that happens (for instance) in art galleries and opera houses and classrooms. It is equally something that takes place in churches and shopping malls, on baseball diamonds and in movie theatres. Culture speaks in the sort of sexual desire we feel, in our preferences for casual television viewing, and in the impulses that move us in raising children. We provide clues to our culture in the food we eat, in the games we play, and in the design of the houses in which we live. Even those departments of life that are primarily something other than cultural—the economic production that takes place in a factory, for instance, or the military destruction wrought by an army at war—are always heavily influenced by the culture of those who produce or fight. Our culture is, in the end, very nearly the same as our way of life in general—or, more precisely, the conscious *and* unconscious ways that we adapt ourselves to our way of life and our way of life to ourselves. Culture, in this sense, is roughly synonymous with "ideology" as used by the French philosopher Louis Althusser, and with "discourse," as used by his most famous pupil, the historian Michel Foucault.

2

Given these considerations, it is plain that the political power and significance of culture are enormous. We have already examined several prominent political controversies that are essentially cultural in nature, and it is easy to think of many others that, though they may not involve particular works of art, are predominantly cultural in the big anthropological sense. Burning a copy of the American flag that you yourself own is, for example, very obviously an act protected by the free-speech clause of the First Amendment to the Constitution (as, indeed, even the extremely right-wing Justice Scalia pointed out in the pertinent Supreme Court case). But the act is so culturally repugnant to so many Americans that the Constitutional point usually counts for little in the public controversies on the matter that flare up from time to time. During one such controversy in the late 1980s and early 1990s, *every* nationally prominent American politician—save one—who took a position on the issue supported some sort of political action (whether by statute or by Constitutional amendment) against flag burning. The lone exception was Senator Bob Kerrey of Nebraska, a Navy veteran who had been awarded the Congressional Medal of Honor in Vietnam; for the cultural aura surrounding the Medal of Honor protected Kerrey from the patriotic opprobrium that so terrified other politicians.

Or, to take another example, consider the controversies that frequently turn up in the political news over the teaching of evolutionary biology in the public schools. Among those scientifically qualified to have an opinion on the matter, there is no controversy at all. Though biologists do indeed differ sharply among themselves as to the precise mechanisms by which evolution operates, the fact of evolution itself is as well established as any scientific finding can be. But, of course, the controversies are sparked not by science but by culture—specifically, by the prominent role (unparalleled in the industrialized world) played by a Fundamentalist reading of the Book of Genesis in the religious culture of America.

Or, yet again, consider the whole network of legal and political issues designated by the term "gay rights." Opponents are notoriously unmoved either by informed speculation on the origin of homosexuality (which, according to nearly all current scientific hypotheses, is either innate or acquired within the first two or three years of life) or by empirical research into the actual behavior of homosexuals (such research indicates that, for instance, gay men are measurably *less* likely to sexually molest children than are heterosexual men). Nor, even, does precise legal reasoning about whether homosexuals should be a "protected class"—that is, whether sexual orientation should be, like race or religion, one of those exceptional categories by which it is illegal to discriminate in matters such as housing and employment—dominate public discussion of the matter. Again, it is really a cultural issue that is at stake: in particular, the issue of what sort of roles (if any) homosexuality should be allowed to play in the public culture of America at large.

Despite the persistence of such controversies, however, it is still not widely appreciated just how politically powerful culture can be. There is a widespread body of thought (which, as we will later consider, does *not* include Marxism, contrary to what is believed by many who have not read the works of Karl Marx and his followers) holding that the great majority of people are reliably motivated, as political beings, primarily by their economic interests. "It's the economy, stupid," as the political consultant James Carville neatly encapsulated this conventional wisdom during the presidential campaign of 1992. Though it cannot be denied that what American journalists commonly call "pocketbook issues" are of considerable electoral significance, what is in many ways more impressive is how often culture manages to trump personal finances at the ballot box.

An especially clear example is provided by the 2000 presidential race in West Virginia. The state is heavily unionized (by American standards), and working-class poverty is more pervasive in West Virginia than in almost any other state in the union. Accordingly, the state had been overwhelmingly Democratic in modern times: before November 2000, it was generally considered one of the three or four states most likely to vote for the Democratic nominee in any presidential race. Pre-election projections in 2000 nearly always put West Virginia in Al Gore's column. But on election day George W. Bush took the state and, because of this victory, the White House. As with any concrete political event, there were multiple causes at work here, for instance pocketbook-centered fears that the environmentalism with which the vice-president was rhetorically identified might cost jobs in West Virginia. But it seems clear that one specific and easily identifiable factor made the decisive difference between victory and defeat—namely, an intense and sophisticated propaganda campaign waged by the National Rifle Association against Vice-President Gore and on behalf of Governor Bush. What makes this result especially striking is that Gore (who had himself been allied with the NRA during an earlier phase of his career) did not, in fact, advocate any actual policies that, if implemented, would have materially inconvenienced gun owners. But he was more favorably inclined to certain very mild forms of gun control than was Bush. Out of this slender reed of fact the NRA constructed an image of the vice-president as deeply alien and at least vaguely threatening to the robust culture of gun ownership in which so many West Virginians had emotionally invested (and continue to invest) so heavily. Culturally, the vice-president just *seemed*—or was made to seem—somehow "anti-gun". On such matters can the occupancy of the mightiest political office in the world turn.

A more complex instance of the way that culture and economy can relate to one another is provided by the presidential election of 1984, in which the incumbent Republican Ronald Reagan won a 49-state landslide against the Democratic nominee Walter Mondale—one of the most decisive victories ever achieved in a presidential contest. Most commentators generally accept that Reagan had originally won the presidency four years earlier, in 1980, mainly because of widespread unhappiness with the state of the American economy during the later portion of the Carter Administration—when fairly high inflation rates combined, astoundingly, with extraordinarily high interest rates. By 1984 economic prospects seemed much sunnier to most Americans, and contemporary polling data tend to confirm what is suggested by the actual vote: namely, that a substantial majority of voters felt that Reagan was better equipped than Mondale to deal with the economic issues over which the president has influence. Is, then, the 1984 election a relatively pure example of a "pocketbook" contest, in which culture had little importance? Can we conclude that the electorate, though of course it may have misunderstood its own economic interests, did at any rate vote strictly according to what it *believed* those interests to be?

Not exactly. For there are some fascinating polling data that strongly suggest that in 1984 Mondale's economic policies were actually a good deal more popular than Reagan's. When asked by pollsters to choose between the two sets of recommendations for the American economy—but with neither set explicitly labeled as belonging to either candidate—voters preferred Mondale's by a significant margin. It thus appears that voters only *thought* they believed Reagan to be the better economic manager. What they actually chose on election day was not really Reagan's economic policy but just *Reagan*. Reagan, indeed, was—as we noted in the preceding chapter—one of the supreme American political masters at establishing what felt like links of personal intimacy to masses of voters. But, of course, the voters could never completely forget that, on a straightforward factual level, they did *not* know Ronald Reagan personally: so that the best way of describing Reagan's achievement here (and, by extension, the similar achievements of other great electoral politicians, including Richard Nixon) might be to say that he established the feeling of a shared culture between himself and the voters—a commonality of emotions, values, and fundamental working assumptions about life in general—so powerful as to outweigh every other electoral factor. By a kind of Orwellian doublethink, voters could know, in one sector of their minds, that they disagreed with Reagan's economic ideas and still, because of their mighty cultural attraction to him, feel Reagan to be the superior candidate *even on specifically economic issues*.

The meaning—and political importance—of what I am calling "cultural power" should, then, by now be clear. In the remainder of this chapter I will sketch out a few theses in order to give a somewhat fuller and more concrete sense of just what cultural power is and how it operates. It is obvious that what follows amounts to only a tiny fraction of all that could be said on the subject, about which a good many important books have already been written. To many readers, it will also be obvious just how much my analysis owes to the Marxist concept of ideology as analyzed in the works of Marx and Engels themselves and of such later Marxist thinkers as Georg Lukács, Antonio Gramsci, Theodor Adorno, Jean-Paul Sartre, Louis Althusser, Raymond Williams, and many others—and also to the non-Marxist thought of such figures as Nietzsche, Freud, Jacques Lacan, Michel Foucault, and Jacques Derrida. But, both here and throughout this volume, I have developed my arguments in such a way that they can be followed without any prior acquaintance with any of this material.

3

Thesis: *The power of culture derives in large part from the fact that it is deeply interwoven with all other social activities.* We may begin here by noting that culture and hence cultural power belong to what the literary critic F.R. Leavis called the "third realm": by which he meant an arena of activity that is neither fully public nor fully private. For Leavis, the public realm is the "objective" world studied by the natural sciences, where meaning is practically invariable from individual to individual. A typical public statement would be, "Water boils at 212 degrees Fahrenheit," or perhaps, "Paris is the capital of France". Conversely, the private realm is the purely "subjective" realm of individual feelings and whims that are of no particular interest or importance—indeed, perhaps of no definable meaning—to anyone other than the private individual and those intimately connected with him or her. A typical private statement might be, "I enjoy eating sliced mangoes". A "third realm" statement, then, would be one fundamentally different from *both* these private and public examples; and for Leavis the primary homeland of such statements is literature—which Leavis always maintained to be the paradigm and the most consequential instance of culture in general.

The concept of the third realm appears to make pretty good rough-and-ready sense, and is a useful way to *begin* locating culture and cultural power on the continuum of human activities. Recall the political controversies mentioned above that concern the teaching of evolution. In the public realm proper—that is, the realm of verifiable (or falsifiable) scientific inquiry—there is, as we have noted, no significant disagreement at all. Scientifically, to say that human beings did not evolve from a lower order of animals is simply *wrong*, as wrong as saying that water freezes at 212 degrees or that Paris is the capital of Bulgaria. If we all discussed the matter purely as scientists, there would be no controversy. But there would *also* be no controversy if the notion that humanity was specially created by God on the sixth day in the life of the world were merely the fancy of an isolated individual. The controversy depends upon the fact that the doctrine of special creation—specifically, the statement, "So God created man in his own image, in the image of God created he him; male and female created he them," in the King James translation—derives from the Bible, which is not only a major work of literature but also the most influential single artifact in the religious culture of America today. Neither sheerly public nor sheerly private, the sentence from Genesis thus seems a precise example of a statement emanating from the Leavisite "third realm." To this extent the concept is genuinely illuminating.

But we should also note that the opposition between objectivity and subjectivity on which the viability of the concept of the third realm depends is philosophically a great deal more slippery than superficially appears (or than Leavis himself ever seems to have noticed). In actual human practice, object and subject are not only interrelated but are constantly determining one another, so that neither ever exists in pristine form. Look again at the sentences offered above as examples of objective and subjective discourse respectively. Even leaving aside the inevitable ambiguities of language in the statements about water and Paris—for in fact the boiling point of water varies depending upon atmospheric pressure, and there are plenty of towns named Paris that are *not* the capital of France—these apparently "objective" statements have an irreducible subjective content. When I utter them, I implicitly assert, for instance, that I speak with a certain authority and interest in matters of chemistry and political geography. In many contexts I might also be implying that boiling water is more common and familiar in my life than boiling mercury, or that I find France more appealing than Mongolia as a place to spend a holiday. Contrariwise, to say, "I enjoy eating sliced mangoes," is not entirely private or subjective. The utterance indicates that you and I both know that mangoes exist, that we at least roughly agree as to what they are, and that we both acknowledge that one may or may not have a taste for them. I may even be speaking the sentence in order to help you plan the menu for a perfectly "public" and objective dinner party to which I am invited.

The distinction between objectivity and subjectivity is not, indeed, meaningless. On the contrary, it seems to be an indispensable tool of thought. But it is always a somewhat simplistic abstraction from a more complex material reality. Though, "Water boils at 212 degrees Fahrenheit," is certainly a *more nearly* objective sentence than, "I enjoy eating sliced mangoes," full objectivity and full subjectivity remain chimeras. The problem with the idea of the third realm is therefore that the "first" and "second" realms turn out to be inextricably bound up with one another all the time—which is to say that they are not, strictly speaking, "realms" at all (the metaphor, after all, derives from the concept of discrete political sovereignties).

What, then, becomes of the notion of culture as a category of the third realm? We can conclude that this designation, "the third realm," though it may serve an important preliminary function in understanding culture, finally limits the concept of culture much too narrowly. If strict objectivity and strict subjectivity are just convenient (and necessary) fictions in the first place, then culture is far more than a third alternative distinguishable from both. If culture, as the concept of the third realm suggests, exists somehow "between" object and subject, then the dialectical interaction of object and subject means that culture is the most broadly encompassing of all human activities—and that it is complexly interwoven with the most nearly objective processes and the most nearly subjective alike. Culture is—literally—everywhere. It is possible to go even further (as some have done) and proclaim that culture is not only everywhere but every*thing*, that is, to define culture as simply the sum total of all human processes whatever. But this move is self-defeating. For such a global definition of culture must empty the concept of all specific meaning and render it a useless term for rational analysis. If everything is culture, then all power is cultural power, and cultural power in the more particular sense that this volume employs does not finally exist. If culture is to be a really usable category, then it must be possible to point to important non-cultural activities; and it is indeed possible to do so, most clearly,

I think, by pointing to economic production, to politics, to military force, and to science. At the same time, however, it must be stressed that these activities are "non-cultural" *only* in the sense (to be discussed later) that they cannot be usefully *reduced* to their cultural aspects, as religion, or journalism, or entertainment can be. They are not non-cultural in the sense of being unconnected to culture. On the contrary, they are, as we have already seen with regard to some particular examples, intimately linked to cultural realities at point after point.

The interface between culture and economy, for example, is worth some further consideration. We have already seen that it is possible for cultural factors to trump economic ones in a political contest. Certain forms of cultural identification—for instance, with the public persona of Ronald Reagan—can lead citizens to vote against their own economic interests even as they themselves perceive those interests to be. But cultural power can partly determine the economic in even subtler ways too. An example especially pertinent to the understanding of Richard Nixon is the fact that the actual economic practice of American capitalism has long been accompanied by a culture of American capitalism, a culture often (though somewhat misleadingly) summed up by the name of the novelist Horatio Alger—who is generally taken to incarnate the belief that in America anyone who possesses exemplary diligence and moral virtue together with an appealing personality and an ordinary share of intelligence and good luck should be able to make a fortune.

This is, for instance, the idea classically dissected and left for dead in Arthur Miller's *Death of a Salesman*. Indeed, Miller's play is especially relevant in this context. For it is not a particularly anti-capitalist work in any direct or economic sense. The play levels no criticisms against the actual economic facts of American "free enterprise"—which, after all, have made Uncle Charlie, the real moral center of the drama, into a rich man—but instead takes aim at the *promises* of American capitalism, at the mendacious culture of opportunity for upward mobility that Charlie expressly rejects but that confounds and finally kills Willy Loman. It is the cultural power of American capitalism, not the economic power, that constitutes Miller's real target. And yet the play is a deeply anti-capitalist work: for the capitalist cultural power it attacks has been of enormous importance in securing the continued dominance of American capitalism. It has been even more important, in some ways, than capitalism's economic power (e.g., the ability of those who own or control vast reserves of capital to determine the economic destinies of others) or political power (e.g., the use of police forces, courts, administrative agencies, and other political bodies to aid corporations and impede labor unions). As we will see, the cultural power of the Horatio Alger myth was crucial to the formation of Nixon's political personality and was in turn used by him to major political effect—so much so, indeed, that Nixon often pretended that his own success, his own achievement of "the American dream," had been attained despite initial economic obstacles more formidable than any he ever really faced.

The omnipresence of culture must, then, help to make it an enormously potent enemy or ally in any socio-political battle. Since culture is everywhere, there is no place where it cannot intervene, including the most minute nooks and crannies of personal—and social—feeling.

4

Thesis: *The power of culture is a predominantly conservative power; for culture tends to change more slowly than any other major aspect of society.* This thesis is a corollary of the preceding one, as is, indeed, clearly suggested by the immense conservative force of the Horatio Alger myth in American political and economic history. The omnipresence and subtlety of cultural power not only give it huge scope and influence but also (as Edmund Burke, the intellectual founder of modern conservatism, clearly recognized) help to make it a power that operates, for the most part, against change.

The key point here is related to the principle that—insofar as such a sweeping generalization can ever be valid—the available evidence seems to indicate that human beings are naturally conservative creatures. Inertia is as important a factor for the human sciences as for the physical ones. Serious change, of almost any sort and on almost any scale or level, is almost invariably difficult and usually at least somewhat painful for the overwhelming majority of people. It should be stressed, of course, that to recognize this fact is not to endorse conservatism as a political philosophy. For the properly political question is always whether change is *desirable,* or even necessary, not whether it is hard. Logically, the fact that changing the status quo generally seems to cut against the grain of human nature implies precisely nothing about whether any particular status quo *ought* to be conserved or overthrown. Furthermore, the situation is especially complicated as regards what is typically but confusingly called "conservatism" in our own time and place. Modern American conservatism nearly always specifies the defense and preservation of capitalism as one of its central goals—logically enough, on one level, since capitalism is the economic status quo in the US today. Yet such conservatism is thus structured on an immense self-contradiction. For capitalism is itself the most thoroughly disruptive, the most emphatically *anti*-conservative, social force in the history of the world: a truth integral to the thought of Burke, for whom conservatism was by definition the defense of a pre-capitalist old order against the revolutionary innovations of the new middle-class regime. Capitalism, after all, is the force that razes historic buildings in order to construct shopping malls, that prizes "growth" over stability, that destroys traditional ways of life wherever there is money to be made by doing so. It melts into air all that was apparently solid, as Marx and Engels observed. In some instances, accordingly, it may well be a left-wing, anti-capitalist position that is in one sense most genuinely "conservative." In his novel *Saints and Scholars*, the Marxist author Terry Eagleton gives this line to the Irish revolutionary-socialist leader James Connolly: "Revolution isn't a runaway train; it's the application of the emergency brake."

Change, then, can be of various sorts, and it operates in various directions: so that conservatism in the widest meaning of the term has many more different political connotations than the term's ordinary polemical use today would suggest. At the same time, it remains a legitimate working assumption that *all* change, whether destructive and purely pragmatic, or whether constructive, progressive, and principled—whether it's the pressing on the accelerator of a train already wildly out of control, or the socially useful braking and steering of the same train, to extend Eagleton's figure—necessarily operates against a degree of conservative resistance that is intrinsic to the human organism itself. William Buckley, the most influential popular exponent of conservative political thought in modern America, famously defined conservatism as "the politics of reality." The definition may be accepted in this sense: that, short of death itself, inertia is quite possibly the most inescapably real of all realities.

Nowhere does the conservative force of inertia make itself felt more emphatically than on the level of culture. Precisely because culture is so multivarious and subtle, because it functions in so many different places and in so many different ways at once—because culture is both nearly objective and nearly subjective, and in a sense even supplies the glue, to speak, that binds objectivity and subjectivity into a concrete social totality—cultural change is bound to be even more intimate and wrenching than change in general. So it is that conservative thought from Burke onwards tends to praise the wisdom supposed to be crystallized in tradition and custom, in the ordinary use of language, in commonsense modes of knowledge, and in inherited attitudes towards life in general: that is, in the dominant culture. For if wisdom really is necessarily to be found in such places, then no sane person would ever attempt to mobilize the immensely difficult and complex forces needed to change them radically. Cultural processes take place so variously and in so many subtle, intimate ways that, when it comes to changing culture, it is often difficult to know even where to start.

One way to frame the problem is by contrasting culture with the economic and political structures of society. A good deal of significant political and economic change takes place by way of comparatively discrete and expeditious events. Elections are held, governments are formed or dissolved, wars are waged, prices are set, new technologies of production are adopted, union contracts are won, labor strikes are begun or ended, and so forth. But on the cultural plane "events" of this sort hardly even exist. An exception might be made for culture in the most narrow sense—that is, the fine arts—for there it is possible to identify genuinely punctual phenomena of major consequence: for example, the original exhibition of French Impressionist paintings in 1874, the controversial first performance of Stravinksy's *The Rite of Spring* in 1913, or the publication of Joyce's *Ulysses* in 1922. Clearly, each of these events (all of which took place, remarkably enough, in Paris) exercised a significant impact on the development of aesthetic modernism. But for culture in the wider and more anthropological sense there is nothing truly comparable. At most, one might point to certain incidents that can be taken to symbolize and perhaps summarize much larger, more complex, and more gradual movements of cultural change. For instance, the Woodstock rock festival of August 1969 is often taken as a figure for the whole hippie culture (or counterculture, as it liked to style itself) centered on music, drugs, nonviolence, and free sexuality. But nobody supposes that Woodstock *caused* the emergence of the flower children in anything like the same way that, say, the Wagner Act of 1935 really did create new opportunities for the economic and political organization of American labor.

The point, however, is not only that cultural power changes more slowly and hence generally exercises more conservative effects than other major forms of social power. Because different forms of power within the same society are always dialectically interrelated, the conservative force of cultural power can often retard change on the political and economic levels; and, conversely, the development of something like a new cultural consensus can often be one of the preconditions for radical economic or political change. We have already noticed the cultural power of the Horatio Alger myth—particularly the notion that a relatively untrammeled American capitalism, whatever its shortcomings, provides almost anyone with the opportunity to get rich—that has played such an enormous role in forestalling serious political challenges to the rule of capital in modern America (and despite a series of strictly economic capitalist disasters stretching from the Great Depression of the 1930s to the Great Recession that began in 2008). A different example is provided by the narrative of progress towards a greater degree of racial justice in the US during the past half century (a story in which Nixon played a complicated role, as we will see in the fourth chapter of this volume).

The most important specifically *political* events in this story are the Civil Rights Act of 1964 and the Voting Rights Act of 1965; both deserve a place on any list of the most socially consequential laws in American history. But it is impossible to explain the passage of either bill solely in terms of the pertinent political factors (e.g., Lyndon Johnson's mastery of legislative tactics combined with the extraordinary political leverage he enjoyed in the wake of the Kennedy assassination) or economic factors (e.g., the increasing impatience of modernizing business interests, North and South, with the regressive system of racial segregation dominant in the Southern states). At least equally important was the development of a culture of racial equality that was the chief accomplishment of the Civil Rights Movement during its heroic period (which can be conveniently dated from the Montgomery bus boycott led by Martin Luther King between 1955 and 1956). The tactical wizardry of Johnson in the White House (and of Hubert Humphrey on the floor of the Senate) would have counted for little—indeed, would never even have taken place—had it not been for the cultural sea change regarding racial attitudes that developed in response, for instance, to the photographic and televisual images of anonymous black Southerners voluntarily risking brutality and murder in order to protest against officially sanctioned bigotry. Conversely, actual implementation of progressive laws often had to wait for further cultural change. This was most clearly the case with the provisions about gender discrimination in the 1964 act, provisions that evidently originated in a legislative practical joke by Southern reactionaries (who intended to mock the idea of equality by extending it from race to gender) and that were effectively ignored for years after the law's passage. If any social project moves, almost by definition, at the speed of its slowest essential component, this component is most often cultural in nature.

As we have already begun to see in the preceding chapter, the conservative tug that culture generally exercises was indispensable to Nixon's political success. For it was largely through demagogic appeals to Americans' strong fear of cultural change—with regard to the Communist issue in the 1950s and the race issue in the 1960s—that he scored his most important electoral triumphs.

5

Thesis: *Culture is not, however,* invariably *conservative; and the project of an emancipatory cultural power should have a high priority for any progressive politics.* The story of the civil rights movement serves to remind us that cultural change, however slow and difficult it may typically be, is by no means impossible. But cultural change is much easier to recognize than to explain. If it is clear, for example, that Woodstock was not the cause of the hippie culture that so upset Richard Nixon and his admirers, but just the unusually emphatic expression of a cultural phenomenon that had been taking shape for years—or even, by some reckonings, for decades—it is far less clear what the cause actually *was*. It is easy enough to point to various contributing factors: the postwar economic boom; the new African-American assertiveness with which white hippies generally identified; the many intellectual critiques of "alienation" and feelings of *ennui* in middle-class American life during the 1950s and after; the upsurge of creativity in Anglo-American rock music typified especially by Bob Dylan and the Beatles; the increasing accessibility of oral contraceptive devices; and so forth. But to identify the precise mechanisms by which the hippie culture emerged as something decidedly new and strange in American life is much more difficult. So it is with other instances of cultural change. Despite some valuable contributions, perhaps most notably by Gramsci and Raymond Williams, the theory of cultural change—the way, that is, to conceptualize the specific dynamics by which cultures are born, change, and fade away—remains one of the most underdeveloped sectors of cultural theory generally. This is especially true in comparison with—and contrast to—change on the political and economic levels. Indeed, it is not even evident that we can identify a plausible paradigm of cultural change, in the sense that the paradigm of political change is the overthrow of a state by those opposed to the class interests represented by it, or that the paradigm of economic change is the supersession of one mode of production (slaveholding, feudalism, capitalism, socialism) by another as the dominant economic force in a given society. Once again, culture looks rather nebulous compared to polity or economy.

Of course, the greater difficulty of explaining cultural change is precisely what we should expect in view of the especially multivarious, ubiquitous, and subtle character of culture and cultural power. The further point here, however, is that the importance of cultural change is especially pronounced in dealing with the Age of Nixon. For the latter portion of Nixon's career—the portion inaugurated by his re-emergence as a major political force in the 1966 Congressional elections and concluded by his forced resignation from the presidency in 1974—is contemporary with one of the most exciting, creative, and atypical periods of cultural change in American history. In a way perhaps unparalleled during the entire twentieth century, and certainly unparalleled since the advent of the culture of the "Roaring Twenties" that followed World War One, the mid-to-late 1960s and the early 1970s witnessed an extraordinary degree of cultural change. This change was unusually rapid (by the normal standards of cultural change, that is). It made itself felt in several distinct though certainly not unrelated departments of American life; and it was oriented overwhelmingly in a progressive or "left" direction. Instances include the general loosening of received sexual mores and the greater acceptance of (and even, to some degree, insistence upon) racial equality, and also the development of a specifically political culture increasingly skeptical of anti-Communism and of the supposed beneficence of American global power; and, a bit later, the burgeoning cultures of protest against gender inequality and against the degradation of the natural environment (and, a bit later still, against the ferocious stigmatization of homosexuality). I noted in the preceding chapter that Nixon's 1968 presidential campaign can be neatly summarized as the campaign against the "niggers," using the term in its specifically racial sense but also in its then-common generic meaning of the minority outsider in general. The enabling condition of the campaign's success was the widespread conservative response to an unwelcome assertiveness—of almost unprecedented speed and volume—by the outsiders. It was overwhelmingly on the cultural plane that so many right-wing Americans felt bewildered, angry, and resentful in the face of anti-conservative change.

Indeed, so powerful were the cultural shifts that had been accomplished by the time that Nixon wrote out his one-sentence letter of resignation in August 1974 that we still live in their backwash today. Most of the cultural division on which Nixon played so masterfully in 1968 remains with us, though in some instances it is typically expressed in terms somewhat different from those most current in the 60s and 70s. For example, lip service is almost always paid to formal racial equality nowadays, despite the persistence of racism on many more implicit levels, cultural and otherwise. Even such hypocrisy marks genuine progress, of course, since, before the 1960s, the etiquette of public discourse in the US did not by any means require avoidance of overtly racist formulations. Indeed, the cultural progress achieved during the past half century or so is, by almost any reckoning, considerably more substantial and profound than the total of either political or economic advance during the same period; and this asymmetry suggests an important general principle about cultural change in general. We have seen that culture is most often a predominantly conservative force, because the rather amorphous shape of culture makes it difficult and time-consuming for those who seek progressive change to gain the sort of decisive purchase on which such change demands. Yet this same amorphousness can also mean that, in some instances, the conservative roadblocks to change likewise function with less precision and effectiveness than equivalent roadblocks on the political and economic levels.

Many, of course, would argue that resistance to cultural change may seem less forceful than to political or economic change simply because the latter areas of society are of much greater importance to the ruling order. It may be claimed, in other words, that the consolidation of the economic power of increasingly globalized capital and the persistence of the political power of deeply antidemocratic electoral arrangements (e.g., in the US Senate, where members representing less than 20% of the American population can usually block any legislation) are accompanied by, say, the partial but still spectacular successes of gay liberation mainly because the ruling elites of our society care far more about the smooth flow and reproduction of capital, and also about the containment of political democracy, than they do about what people do with each other in bed. There is much truth in this claim. But it is also true that the same ubiquity and subtlety of culture that can make progressive change so difficult to launch may also mean that, once such change *is* launched, the mechanisms with which to resist it can be difficult for the conservative order to come by. The imposed structural weaknesses of American trade unionism are generally sufficient to prevent radical challenges to the rule of capital. Likewise, immense political suppression of dissenting voices is achieved by the Democratic-Republican duopoly through (for example) so apparently simple a device as the first-past-the-post system of vote-counting (whereby citizens vote for only one candidate each, as opposed to the instant-runoff system of weighted votes, which allows voters to express second and third as well as first choices). There do not appear to be any really comparable devices with which conservatives can block, say, not only toleration of sexual minorities but also the considerable cultural influence wielded by gay sensibilities and gay aesthetics (for instance, in "Camp") since the 1960s. This difficulty in resisting cultural change accounts, indeed, for the tone of weary frustration that cultural conservatives today often adopt.

Accordingly, progressives—most of whom are still inclined to underestimate the importance of cultural as opposed to economic or political power—should recognize not only the extent to which culture is a consequential battlefield but also the unusual degree to which it happens to be a particularly favorable one in our time and place. Though generally the most conservative level of society, culture has in modern America provided those working for emancipatory change with a disproportionate share of their victories. Indeed, sometimes even specifically political or economic progress can be most efficiently advanced through cultural means: a point to which we will return in chapter 5 when we come to consider how Nixon's presidential administration counts in some (though by no means all) ways as the second most politically liberal (after Lyndon Johnson's) between that of Franklin Roosevelt and that of Barack Obama.

6

Thesis: *While mightily important, the power of culture does have limits.* Though usually underestimated, cultural power can be exaggerated too, and indeed frequently *is* exaggerated in the precincts of academic cultural studies. Such exaggeration may well be little more than the tendency of any discipline to overstate the importance of its own object. At all events, even a survey of culture as brief and synoptic as this would be incomplete without some consideration of its boundaries, and therefore of those forms of human activity that partly lie beyond the cultural and cannot be reduced to it.

Existing somewhat in a category of its own is science. To be sure, the notion that scientific research is simply and solely a straightforward, disinterested pursuit of objective truth has long been exposed as an illusion of nineteenth-century positivism—and not only in the most general conceptual terms, by the major modern philosophers of science (of whom Thomas Kuhn, author of *The Structure of Scientific Revolutions*, remains the best known in the US), but also, and more recently, by those working in "science studies," who have sought to demonstrate the detailed impact of cultural and other social forces upon the actual work of professional scientists. It is now pretty widely understood that scientists discover only what they are in some sense already looking for and what their intellectual tools permit them to grasp. Science thus has an irreducible subjective aspect *not* (necessarily) because of accidental moral or intellectual failings on the part of individuals (though of course those may play their part) but because of the intrinsic nature of research. This is true in terms of the most abstract frameworks in which scientific knowledge is organized—on the level of what Kuhn called the paradigm or what Althusser called the problematic—but in much more specific terms as well. Funding decisions provide an obvious example, since today a scientific research project that fails to attract corporate or government money is unlikely to progress far (the controversies surrounding stem-cell research are an obvious instance). But more subtle factors are also at work. Few, for instance, would any longer deny that the fact that most research into human contraception has aimed at controlling female rather than male fertility is at least somewhat related to the fact that most of this research has been performed by male scientists working within an overwhelmingly male-dominated society.

Nonetheless, however important it is to appreciate the extent to which science interacts with cultural and other extra-scientific factors, it is equally important to understand that the cognitive integrity of science cannot simply be *dissolved* into the social forces that determine it. In certain (always compromised) ways and to certain (always limited) degrees, science *does* discover truth and thus does enjoy a relative autonomy vis-à-vis cultural power, however unfashionable this recognition may be in certain philosophically naïve circles. To be sure, the only ultimate tests of scientific validity do seem to be essentially statistical. Bridges constructed on certain physical and mathematical assumptions are more likely to remain standing than those constructed on different assumptions, and children given certain vaccinations are less likely than other children to sicken and die of particular diseases. But such statistical validation is, in the long run, the only philosophical alternative to returning to the eighteenth-century subjective idealism of Bishop Berkeley, who denied the existence of matter itself; and it is thus sufficient to establish science as an activity that cannot be reduced to culture, despite the undeniable importance of culture for science.

Nor can political or military power be reduced to cultural power. Since the central purpose of this volume is to explore the importance of culture in the political career of an American politician, I am not tempted to understate the extent to which culture and politics interact. Even so, here too it is important not to overstate the impact of culture. Political institutions can enjoy remarkable autonomy, especially in inertial ways for both good and ill. For instance, the core political institutions of the US are those established by the nation's founding political and legal document, the US Constitution; and this document was designed to be extremely difficult to change. The effects of this difficulty are often conservative in the bad sense of retarding genuine progress. For example, one specific line (the final clause of Article Five) makes it almost impossible—even if the necessary popular consensus developed on the cultural level of "public opinion"—ever to change the rule that all states, regardless of population, are entitled to equal representation in the Senate. On the other hand, sometimes the effect is to block reactionary change. During the national flag-burning controversy discussed above, the cultural hysteria on the subject was so intense that restrictions on free expression would almost certainly have been written into law had it not been for the purely political obstacles to amending the Constitution.

Furthermore, the power of political factors can be decisive in active as well as passive ways, even against considerable cultural resistance. An excellent example is provided by the Voting Rights Act of 1965. As we have discussed, this law could never have been passed had it not been for the momentous cultural changes wrought by the Civil Rights Movement. But specifically political and legal factors made enforcement of the act difficult for the white political oligarchies of the South to evade. The act was thereby directly responsible for enormous electoral change throughout the Southern states, leading to the emergence of the first significant body of African-American office-holders—and the first real experience of political democracy in the region—since Reconstruction. And this electoral change—on the political level it amounted almost to a revolution—in turn accelerated the cultural trends in favor of greater racial equality that had been primarily responsible for the law in the first place.

As for military power, many would regard it as a subset of politics. Indeed, the German military theorist Clausewitz superficially seemed to suggest as much when he famously defined war as "nothing but the continuation of politics with the admixture of other means." Carefully read, however, Clausewitz's maxim actually categorizes war as the *breakdown* of politics—for the "other means" are by definition extra-political—just as the point of Mao Zedong's complementary thesis, "Political power grows out of the barrel of a gun," is to locate the origin of politics beyond itself. The inner character of military power that establishes its relative autonomy with regard to culture inheres in something that is even further removed from cultural power than are the documents and institutions that define politics: namely, plain physical force.

To be sure, the military is, like the political and the scientific, always complexly interwoven with the cultural. For instance, in the legally undeclared "war against terror" launched by George W. Bush, enormous military blunders have been committed for specifically cultural reasons. One of the first was that, during and after the collapse of the Taliban regime in Afghanistan, US policy allowed numerous al-Qaeda militants (supposedly the prime targets of the war in the first place) to escape: *not* because the US lacked the military means to capture them, but (mainly) because doing so would have been physically dangerous for American ground troops, and because the Bush Administration bowed to what it perceived to be a cultural consensus among the electorate that large-scale US military casualties were unacceptable, even after the mass murders of September 11th. One can hardly imagine a clearer example of cultural feeling trumping military logic and force. Still, when all such allowances have been made, the power of guns and bombs remains. When Stalin rhetorically asked how many divisions had the Pope, he doubtless intended an ignorant, philistine devaluation of the cultural dimension, in this case the cultural power of Roman Catholic religiosity in Europe. But there is nonetheless a considerable element of truth in his words.

Finally, we come to the power of economic production. Marx was the first thinker to define with precision the special role of the economy in the structure of societies. But his basic point has been generally misunderstood as not only different from but in many ways opposed to what he actually said and wrote. Marx never argued that individuals invariably pursue their own economic interests (or even what they perceive to be their own economic interests) above all other matters. This proposition is about as patently false as a proposition can be, and Marx himself provides a perfect example of someone who subordinated his own financial welfare to much else. Nor did Marx maintain that, on the level of social conflict, economic factors necessarily trump all other factors in each and every instance. As we have seen, numerous counter-examples, like the 2000 presidential race in West Virginia, could be cited against such a thesis. What Marx *did* argue is that, on the whole and in the long run, economic factors tend to exercise a more powerful determination upon social processes than factors of any other sort. Extra-economic factors, like cultural power, enjoy their own autonomy. They exert an impact upon one another and upon the economy itself, and can even prove more decisive than economic power in particular cases. But, ultimately, economic production sets the basic agenda for the human narrative as a whole.

Ontologically—that is, on the level of social being itself—economic production owes its privileged position within the social totality to the simple and irreducible fact that human beings must produce the means of their own physical survival before they can do much of anything else. A society capable of producing only just enough wealth to provide for the biological subsistence of its members is in effect a society where *only* the economy fully exists. Only in such a society could the simplistic economic determinism often confused with Marxism actually be true. In such a society stories might be told, prayers might be said, and primitive leadership structures might be established. But such activities are likely, in such a society, to be totally, directly, and immediately subordinate to the practical economic tasks of physical survival—mainly the hunting, gathering, and growing of food. When a society begins to produce an economic surplus beyond what is required for pure subsistence, this surplus can be directed to the maintenance of extra-economic processes—like culture—which thus begin to assume an autonomous existence and a history of their own. Yet it is never possible to jump off one's own shadow completely. As societies become wealthier and more developed, the determining force of economic production may somewhat recede into the background and function in increasingly subtle, qualified, long-term, and indirect ways. But the ontological priority of the economy never entirely ceases to function, no matter how wealthy and complex a society may become. The economy of the capitalist United States, for example, allows for an uncountable number of political and cultural possibilities. But it does set certain limits. We can state with as much certainty as science can ever muster that, for ultimately economic reasons, America during the next decade will not be governed by a hereditary absolute monarchy, nor will its dominant literary form become alliterative sagas in the style of *Beowulf*. Though the economy, like every other extracultural process, is certainly influenced by cultural power, it can least of all ever be *reduced* to culture.

It has been necessary to describe the limits of cultural power not only for the sake of a realistic intellectual modesty, but, more important, in order to highlight the significance of culture itself. Like anything else, culture cannot be fully understood without some contrast with what it is *not*. To appreciate the boundaries of culture should help us to study the awesome and usually underestimated importance of cultural power. We are, indeed, now in a position to deploy the conceptual tools sketched out in this chapter, and so to continue with our primary task of examining, in detail, the cultural significance of the career of Richard Nixon.

III. Marx/Nietzsche/Freud/Nixon

It is, I think, something more than pure accident that the three thinkers commonly regarded as having made the most original and important contributions to the human sciences during the past two centuries or so—Karl Marx, Friedrich Nietzsche, and Sigmund Freud—should each have developed a particular concept crucial to understanding the cultural significance of Richard Nixon: I mean the Marxian concept of the petty bourgeoisie, the Nietzschean concept of *ressentiment*, and the Freudian concept of the anal-erotic character. Though the centrality of Marx, Nietzsche, and Freud to cultural studies is a commonplace, what the collocation of this Germanic triad with Nixon tends to suggest is the very different centrality of America's thirty-seventh president: his centrality to American culture, as I am arguing throughout this volume, but probably beyond as well. In any case, to engage each of these pioneering ideas in a specifically Nixonian context is indispensable for the analysis of Nixonian cultural power.

1

The context for understanding Nixon as a member of the petty bourgeoisie is, in fact, as classically and traditionally Marxist as it could possibly be. By the middle of the twentieth century, the theory of the petty bourgeoisie had, of necessity, been much complicated beyond its Marxian origins by the unprecedented emergence of a large class (or class fraction) of salaried employees who were clearly not capitalists but who were also not wage-laborers in anything like the traditional sense: the "professional-managerial class," as they have been called in one vocabulary, or the "new petty bourgeoisie," in another. For Marx himself, however, the petty bourgeois appeared primarily as what we today regard as only its most classical instance: the small shopkeeper. In this understanding, the petty bourgeois is indeed a bourgeois, an entrepreneur who consumes the labor-power of others (though often only that of his—or, much more rarely, her—immediate family) and who attempts to make profits in what is very roughly the same commercial space as that occupied by the big, or "real," bourgeoisie. But the shopkeeper operates on a scale so much smaller than that of the real capitalist that the difference in degree becomes a difference in kind. Marx identifies *insecurity* as one of the primary characteristics of the petty bourgeois, who is constantly threatened by bankruptcy and subsequent proletarianization—a process abundantly illustrated in America today, as personal bankruptcies soar and small businesses, especially on the retail level, are increasingly squeezed out by vast chains and conglomerates. But the same basic process was well underway in Marx's own time, and, later, in Nixon's.

Nixon's own immediate background was precisely in the classical petty bourgeoisie. His parents Frank and Hannah Nixon owned a little grocery store that, as a sideline, also sold gasoline. The Nixon family business of Whittier, California, was fairly successful as small businesses go, and the family managed to avoid proletarianization. Nixon's claims throughout his political career to have personally experienced poverty—claims that became especially frequent during his 1960 race against the wealthy, Harvard-educated John Kennedy—were thus lies, like so many of his public statements. Indeed, they were lies that seemed to bespeak rather gross ingratitude toward his parents, who had both worked hard and successfully to *shield* their sons from poverty. Furthermore, Nixon, who did much of his growing up during the Great Depression—he was sixteen when the Wall Street crash of 1929 arrived—had ample opportunity to know what genuine poverty was like. During his high school and college years, the country abounded with homeless tramps and hobos, and more than a few of them turned up on Nixon's own doorstep (mainly because the saintly Hannah Nixon was widely known as a soft touch, usually good for a meal and a handout). From the viewpoint of the millions of actually poor Depression-era Americans, who often did not know—literally—where their next meal was coming from, the financial situation in which Richard Nixon grew to manhood would have seemed very enviable indeed.

If, however, the Nixons were far from being poor, they were at least equally far from being rich. All the members of the family had to work long hours in and for the grocery store in order to make it a success. The young Richard, for example, often made pre-dawn trips with his father to purchase fruits and vegetables from a wholesaler in Los Angeles. Money was always at least barely adequate, but rarely abundant. Luxuries were not necessarily out of reach, but they had to be carefully budgeted for; and in some instances they *were* out of reach. One such instance occurred in 1930 as Nixon prepared to enter college. By his academic excellence he had won a full scholarship to Harvard, and in a normal year his parents could probably have afforded the travel expenses to Cambridge and the living expenses after he arrived. Nixon would then have earned the most prestigious undergraduate diploma in the country, and his college career at Harvard might have slightly overlapped with John Kennedy's. In fact, however, the family was at that moment burdened with huge medical bills resulting from the expensive private care they were providing for Nixon's tubercular older brother, Harold; and so Richard had to remain at home and attend local Whittier College. At that time higher education of any sort was generally regarded as a considerable luxury, and in later years Nixon claimed that he was so excited at the prospect of going to college that he didn't really care if he went to Harvard or Whittier. Many Nixon commentators have assumed that this is a lie too—how could any smart, hard-working, ambitious young man *not* care?—but of course it is a lie impossible to prove and perhaps one that Nixon himself came to believe.

The Marxist tradition has long recognized that the social ideologies generated by and within the economic situation of the petty bourgeoisie can be various. Marx himself defined the petty bourgeoisie as a *transitional* class because of its inherent instability. A tiny handful of shopkeepers may, through "luck and pluck" (in a phrase of Horatio Alger's), ascend to the upper bourgeoisie; but far more will see their businesses go under and be forced down to the working class of wage-laborers. This condition of being squeezed between two different classes—one of which represents an ardently desired but improbable goal, the other of which represents absolute horror—can produce feelings of hostility directed in *both* directions; and such was the case with Nixon. True enough, and as we will discuss in the fifth chapter, the actual economic policies of the Nixon Administration were in many ways more liberal than those of any subsequent presidency of the twentieth century (though in many ways this says more about subsequent presidencies than about Nixon's). But there is no question that Nixon's personal—and quite public—feelings towards the poor were ones of intense hatred. For instance, he pursued no presidential goal more gleefully than the dismantling of Lyndon Johnson's War on Poverty. It is hardly accidental that he selected the single most reactionary member of his administration—Howard Phillips—to lead this "war" (officially designated the Office of Economic Opportunity) with the more-or-less open design of sabotaging it. Less politically consequential, but perhaps even more personally and culturally revealing, was the appearance of the singer Johnny Cash in the Nixon White House in April 1970. Nixon publicly requested that Cash sing "Welfare Cadillac," a nasty little ditty based on the right-wing fantasy that the welfare system enabled the inner-city poor to enjoy extravagant luxuries. When Cash demurred (also publicly) on the grounds that he did not want to sing a song that degraded others, the difference in common decency between a country musician and the president of the United States was widely appreciated to be spectacular.

Yet Nixon's hatred for the poor was by no means accompanied by any particular love for the rich. Like any American president, especially any Republican president, he of course looked after the interests of the wealthy, though less extravagantly than nearly all presidents (of both parties) have done since the Reagan "Revolution" (or Counter-Revolution) of the 1980s. It is also true that, perhaps in response to the (never realized) threat of poverty in his youth, Nixon throughout his political career doggedly pursued private wealth by means legal and illegal—though, at least prior to his White House years, he managed to conceal this aspect of his career from public view so skillfully that he fooled nearly all observers (even Garry Wills, the most acute of all the Nixon scholars). It was not until Anthony Summers's pathbreaking research in the 1990s that the extraordinary scope of Nixon's personal avarice finally came to light. Nonetheless, despite his willingness to represent the interests of the wealthy and his intense eagerness to become wealthy himself, Nixon's own attitudes toward the rich were always ambivalent at best. He affected a furiously petty-bourgeois work ethic—often, especially in the White House, pretending to work much longer hours than he actually did—and, with a few carefully hidden exceptions (like his knowledgeable enthusiasm for expensive French wine), he never developed much taste for the extreme luxuries so integral to the lifestyles of the rich and famous. It seems significant that, though he appointed a number of wealthy men to high office, few appeared native to the culture of wealth, and almost none was actually born with big money. When he named his original cabinet in 1969, for example, its members were all, like himself, from middle-class or lower-middle-class backgrounds.

It is also suggestive that, in an era when it was comparatively rare for the rich, and especially the hereditary rich, to enter electoral politics (the two presidential Roosevelts had been striking exceptions), an astonishing number of them turned up as Nixon's opponents. Jerry Voorhis, Helen Gahagan Douglas, and Adlai Stevenson were all independently wealthy, while John Kennedy and Nelson Rockefeller came from two of the richest and most powerful families in America; and, especially in the cases of Stevenson and Kennedy, Nixon tried to make the well-born status of his rivals into a campaign issue. Though this tactic fit well with a certain sort of long-standing American populism, no journalist observing Nixon doubted that he was also motivated by quite sincere feelings of envy and bitterness. In a famous (and brilliant) bit of phrasemaking, Murray Kempton summarized what many felt about the campaign against Kennedy: "Nixon ended the 1960 campaign wandering limply and wetly about the American heartland begging votes on the excuse that he had been too poor to have a pony when he was a boy." Contrariwise, of all Nixon's opponents the one toward whom he displayed the *least* evidence of personal rancor was undoubtedly Hubert Humphrey in 1968; and Humphrey came from a petty-bourgeois background almost precisely similar to Nixon's own. The Humphrey family had owned a small drugstore just as the Nixon family had owned a small grocery store—something that Nixon himself pointed out during his speech (delivered in Humphrey's presence) at the 1968 Al Smith Dinner in New York.

The distance that the petty bourgeois typically feels from both the common people, especially the outright poor, and the ruling elite is not the only ideological effect of the position of the petty bourgeoisie as a transitional class. Marx emphasizes (most notably in *The Eighteenth Brumaire of Louis Bonaparte,* his astonishingly prescient and wide-ranging study of French politics between 1848 and 1851) that one of the most politically consequential of petty-bourgeois attitudes is the notion of standing "above" or "beyond" class entirely. The fact that the petty bourgeois cannot be identified with either the exploited masses or the wealthy exploiters—and, indeed, often feels decisively alienated from *both* of the primary classes of capitalism—can lead to the illusion that the petty-bourgeois viewpoint is uncontaminated by class interests altogether. The petty-bourgeois viewpoint is thus taken—by the petty bourgeois—to represent the "universal" viewpoint of either humanity as a whole or, perhaps more frequently, of some non-class fraction of humanity, like a nation. Of course, to affect such universalism is generally a shrewd tactical move in any sort of electoral politics. Since a candidate necessarily wishes to garner as many votes as possible from all sectors of the electorate, why should he, or she, risk offending some voters by openly identifying with one specific class? What is more, this tactic is particularly coherent with the ideological contours of politics in America, where, at least since the Russian Revolution of 1917, explicit mention of economic class has been a semi-taboo when not an absolute one. One might thus say of Nixon's own petty-bourgeois universalism what his dwindling band of defenders said of his high crimes and misdemeanors during Watergate: "everybody does it." But, as so often, the special fascination of Richard Nixon is that, as we will see, he "did it" with a thoroughness and intensity that few have matched.

The advice of Nixon in old age to young, aspiring Republican politicians is often cited: Run as far to the right as you need to in order to secure the Republican nomination, and then run as fast as you can back to the center in order to win the general election. This advice is not, in fact, quite so widely applicable as it is often taken to be. For example, Ronald Reagan, probably the most brilliantly successful of all Republican politicians in the history of the party, did not run with any conspicuous speed to the "center" after winning the 1980 Republican presidential nomination. But Nixon's avuncular wisdom does distill, in rather crude, pragmatic form, one of the defining impulses of his own political career: the impulse, I mean, to evade substantive political "labels" (class or other), the determination to stand for nothing less than the most morally pristine universalism.

At the very beginning of his Congressional career, for example, Nixon quite deliberately avoided identification *either* with the liberal-to-moderate (and mainly East Coast) Republicans, who supported, or at least accepted, many of the essential economic reforms of the New Deal, *or* with the Republican Old Guard led by Robert Taft, whose Bourbon economics were inherited by Barry Goldwater, and, later, by the Reaganites. Nixon remained on generally good terms with both factions. In 1952, he was selected as Eisenhower's running mate partly because he was far enough right to provide some ideological (as well as geographic and age) balance to the more liberal Eisenhower: and yet not *so* far right as to make the Eisenhower-Nixon pairing seem intrinsically implausible. In the race for the 1964 Republican presidential nomination, he stood almost alone among nationally prominent Republicans in managing to remain aloof from both the Goldwater movement and its opponents (Ike maintained formal neutrality but was widely believed to sympathize with the anti-Goldwater camp—an entirely plausible belief, since a deep contempt for the Eisenhower presidency was universal among the hard-core Goldwaterites). During the 1968 general election campaign, Nixon skillfully presented himself as the "moderate" alternative to both the too liberal Humphrey and the openly reactionary George Wallace. The slogans he offered to the electorate that year (and again four years later) were universalistic to the point of nearly lacking content altogether: "Nixon's the One," "Nixon Now," and (in 1972) "Four More Years!".

It would be a mistake to see these moves as dictated *merely* by immediate tactical contingencies, though each of them was indeed tactically shrewd and effective; and it would be somewhat reductive simply to "read off" the Nixonian universalism from the classically petty-bourgeois home in which Nixon was raised, though one can hardly doubt that his socio-economic origins left a deep and permanent imprint on everything he did. Even more consequentially at issue here are some of the most important sources of Nixonian cultural power, and some of the strongest affinities between Nixon and the country he rose to govern.

For America in toto might almost be considered a petty-bourgeois country. It is, after all, a country with no feudal past and hence no genuinely aristocratic conventions; and it is also the major country, of all those in the industrialized world, that (with the possible exception of Japan) possesses the weakest traditions of working-class socialist solidarity. "Shopkeeper" has frequently been a term of abuse in Europe—as when Napoleon derided Britain as "a nation of shopkeepers"—but "small businessman," in hegemonic US ideology, is generally synonymous with the salt of the earth, with the most profoundly and virtuously American of all the American types. Not coincidentally, America has always been a universalistic nation as well. Founded, for most ideological purposes, less by the genteel slavemasters of Virginia than by the middle-class Puritans who landed on Plymouth Rock, America at its most characteristic has always regarded itself as morally exceptional—as the last, best hope of mankind, in Lincoln's resonant words. Indeed, to distinguish, in a Nixonian or any other American context, between a petty-bourgeois universalism that is *genuinely* universal, that addresses itself to humanity as a whole, and one that is bounded by the limits of nationality and nationalism, is to pose the question in a potentially misleading way. For the whole point of American exceptionalism is to *erase* any distinction between the interests of the US and those of the entire human race. Woodrow Wilson remains perhaps the most historically prominent ideologue of this view. At the end of the First World War, he inspired or appalled people everywhere by insisting that his country had no national interests in the sense that the European nations frankly claimed to have, but only wanted what was best for everyone. And it would be difficult to name any other major American political leader quite untouched by such moralistic universalism. President George W. Bush was being as American as apple pie—and thoroughly Nixonian—when, after the al-Qaeda organization murderously attacked his country, he responded by declaring war *not* on al-Qaeda itself but on "terror" in the abstract, and by identifying America's position with that of humanity.

It is deeply revealing—as Garry Wills was, I think, the first to notice—that Wilson, despite having been a Democrat, was the twentieth-century president that Nixon revered above all others. For in no way was Nixon more deeply at one with his country than in his petty-bourgeois moral universalism. This quality is illustrated by his skillful avoidance of defining political "labels," his expert navigation around opposed political factions, and also by his more specifically Wilsonian design to do "great things" on the world stage—ending American involvement in the Vietnam War, for instance, and shattering forever the Sino-Soviet alliance by establishing American détente with both China and the USSR. But the Nixonian moralism can perhaps be savored even better—in purer form, as it were—in the perusal of his literary remains. He wrote eight books, all of them subsequent to the collapse of his presidency except for *Six Crises*, which was written in the wake of his defeat in 1960. These volumes—composed with extensive literary assistance, to be sure, but all conveying the vintage Nixon tone—provide one of the most remarkable expressions of petty-bourgeois American moralism since Benjamin Franklin's *Autobiography*. This is most amply true of *RN: The Memoirs of Richard Nixon*, by far his longest and most interesting book, which was written immediately after his White House years came to an abrupt close. In this volume and the others, Nixon paints a consistent portrait of himself as always driven by motives that are not only legitimate or even admirable but invariably heroic, even to the point of saintly self-sacrifice.

Unsurprisingly, the theme of heroic moral universalism is especially prominent in discussions of his central obsession, the 1960 campaign against Kennedy. Take, for instance, the religious issue, one of the most talked-about of that election year, in which Kennedy successfully strove to become the first Roman Catholic president. Nixon did in fact subtly exploit anti-Catholic bigotry during the campaign, not only through surrogates like the best-selling author and Protestant clergyman Norman Vincent Peale, a close family friend of the Nixons, but also in more direct ways: chiefly by reminding audiences time and again that Kennedy was Catholic and then piously adding that this fact ought not to be a political issue. But Nixon was wise not to identify himself more robustly with anti-Catholicism. Such a move would have been offensive to many normally Republican liberal Protestants and, even more consequentially, would likely have produced a huge backlash among Catholic voters—who, in the actual event, gave Kennedy only a modestly higher vote total than a Protestant Democrat would have been expected to win from them that year.

When, however, one turns to Nixon's own account of this matter (mainly in *Six Crises*), one finds not just the flat denial of anti-Catholicism that any politician would issue, but the extraordinary claim that a high-minded crusade *against* anti-Catholic prejudice was, in effect, Nixon's chief concern in 1960, even more important to him than winning the White House. "I felt a responsibility to keep the lid on the boiling cauldron of embittered anti-Catholicism," he solemnly claims. Nixon insists that this lofty purpose led him to refuse personal political advantages, as when he turned down a potentially valuable public endorsement by his friend Billy Graham—not, *of course,* because Graham harbored any bias against Catholics himself, but, because, as Nixon explains, some people would nonetheless have assumed that an endorsement by a Protestant clergyman of a Protestant candidate against a Catholic one must be religiously motivated. Nixon gives us to understand the saint-like patience that such noble self-denial must have required, especially in view of the fact that—as he claims—the Kennedy forces were *themselves* exploiting the issue, both by appealing on sectarian grounds to the senator's co-religionists and also by challenging Protestant voters to "prove" their tolerance by supporting a Catholic candidate. But Nixon refused to retaliate, even though, he assures us, his many Catholic friends and supporters urged him to do so.

Nixon as universalistic moral exemplar? Even before Watergate, Nixon was often portrayed by his opponents as a man of shabby morality—the thuggish, badly shaven, shifty-eyed used-car salesman and sewer-dweller of the Herblock editorial cartoons—and after Watergate this view of him became a prominent and indelible part of his public reputation. We therefore often forget that by his own lights Nixon was nothing less than a moral hero: and not *only* by his own lights. Nixon's petty-bourgeois self-righteousness struck a tremendously significant chord in petty-bourgeois, moralistic America, always the country of Cotton Mather and Jonathan Edwards more than the country of Mark Twain and H. L. Mencken. But having traced, in Marxist fashion, some of the filiations between the socio-economic and the moral, we should now explore the latter category more extensively. Here the necessary intellectual tools are supplied less by Marx than by the greatest and most extreme of all critics of morality (and Mencken's chief intellectual hero), Friedrich Nietzsche.

2

One of the chief philosophical tasks that Nietzsche set himself was the dismantling of the moral basis of ethical monotheism: of the morality, that is, whose roots can be traced to the Mosaic law of the Hebrews and to the ethic of the Platonic Socrates, but whose most influential and disastrous flowering is to be found in

Christianity, always for Nietzsche the most hated and hateful of all belief systems. Such morality is "slave morality" in Nietzsche's vocabulary, because it is based on the self-sacrifice and self-denial sociologically appropriate to the members of a slave class. But it is, for Nietzsche, intrinsically contemptible, and all the more so when freely chosen: for such choosing is the "free" choice of unfreedom. A *genuinely* free, heroic morality—the morality worthy of a superman, that is, a man of exemplary spiritual and intellectual stature—would take as its supreme value the unfettered development of one's own powers, the evolution towards the maximum in strength, brilliance, beauty, health, pleasure, and joy. The Christian ascetic not only turns away from all such affirmative qualities, but declares war upon them in the name of moral goodness. The Christian, in Nietzsche's argument, can conceive of the good only negatively, as the repression of instinctual and intellectual fulfillment, and as the actual choice of ugliness and frustration over beauty and gratification—and all for the sake of self-privation and self-denial. This is *ressentiment*. The French term that Nietzsche employs is (unlike any of the approximate German equivalents) cognate with the English "resentment," but, at least in Nietzsche's own usage, has a wider and more systematic application. *Ressentiment* is not merely a contingent personal feeling but a whole system of (depraved) values that bases ethical goodness on the consistent denigration of all that is truly good—almost, in a sense, *biologically* good—for the human organism (hence the prominence that the "mortification" of the flesh—literally, the doing to death of the flesh—assumes in Christian practice). "Perhaps," writes Nietzsche in his notebook, "there has never before been a more dangerous ideology, a greater mischief *in psychologicis*, than this will to good: one has reared the most repellent type, the unfree man, the bigot; one has taught that only as a bigot is one on the right path to godhood, only the bigot's way is God's way."

This comment on the bigotry intrinsic to the will to good points to one of the most important features of *ressentiment*, namely, its overweening arrogance. Ostensibly, of course, the moralist, and most emphatically the Christian moralist, maintains a position of humility: and the unworthiness that he or she attributes to the self is congruent with the punishments and deprivations to which the moralist's self is typically subjected in ascetic practices. But Nietzsche insists that such humility is entirely fraudulent. For it is based on nothing more, nor less, nor other, than pure *hatred*: hatred of all that is really free and noble—brilliance, strength, beauty, and so forth—and, by extension, hatred of those that honestly and joyfully pursue such positive values. The arrogant bigotry of *ressentiment* inheres precisely in this slandering and besmirching of those qualities and persons that are authentically good in order to erect an alternative, and pernicious, conception of the good on the basis of just such negations. In this way, *ressentiment* is not only the quintessence of weakness, but it is a *dishonest* weakness as well, a weakness that systematically falsifies its nature as such. For *ressentiment* leads to an obsession with the strength that it denies and to a groveling, hypocritical insistence that one has found a superior form of strength through the negative way of self-denial. The man (or woman) of *ressentiment* abases his or her own self, to be sure, but only to be exalted, in the despicable manner of the Christian saint, as a self-abaser.

The almost unparalleled brilliance of Nietzsche's writing has nonetheless persuaded relatively few to accept his theory of *ressentiment* in toto and without qualification. Certainly no one of left political tendency can do so, for Nietzsche, however "radical" in the etymological sense of pursuing phenomena to what he regarded as their root causes, is perhaps the most thoroughly and unflinchingly *reactionary* of all major thinkers. He viewed the major progressive political currents of his time and place—most notably the labor and feminist movements—as themselves mere flowerings of *ressentiment* based on the envy and slander of what lay beyond the reach of workers or women (not, however, that he displayed the slightest admiration for the capitalists or patriarchs of his day either). To Nietzsche, the critique of society mounted by political radicals was but an imitation of the Christian hatred of all worldly value, and very nearly as contemptible as any ascetic moralism. But it may be possible to detach Nietzsche's philosophical and psychological insights from the specific political conclusions that he himself drew from them. Despite Nietzsche's own emphatic opposition to the socialist and democratic values upheld by Marx, I suggest that our essentially Marxist analysis of Nixon's petty-bourgeois moralism can be deepened by a Nietzschean moral critique. To that end, I now return (as promised in the first chapter) to the Checkers speech, a masterpiece of *ressentiment*.

Although, as we have seen, much—indeed most—of the speech was not dominated by the sentimental vein in which Nixon famously referred to his wife's coat and his children's dog, it is not inappropriate that these references should be the best remembered parts of the address, or that the cocker spaniel Checkers should have become the most famous pet in American political history. For it was with such flourishes that Nixon most memorably constructed the central moral dynamic of the speech as one of self-abasement.

Near the beginning of the speech, Nixon began to establish his credentials as a self-sacrificing moral exemplar, for instance by noting the extraordinary moral virtue displayed by the fact that his wife, unlike many other political wives (including, he was careful to point out, the wife of Senator John Sparkman, the Democratic candidate for vice-president) was not on his office payroll. "I have found," he explained, "that there are so many deserving stenographers and secretaries in Washington that needed the work, that I just didn't feel it was right to put my wife on the payroll"—as though, setting up his office, his first thoughts were not of his household's finances or even of his office's efficiency (for he noted in passing that Pat Nixon was "a wonderful stenographer"), but instead of his responsibilities as a kind of one-man employment agency for the worthy clerical workers of the nation's capital. Warming to his theme, he went on to strip himself naked for the cameras by offering (unprecedentedly, he claimed, for an American politician) a financial history of his life: "everything I've earned; everything I've spent; everything I owe." "I'll have to start early," he said; and he indeed began with his work in the Nixon grocery store, going on to narrate his income and expenses in what felt like excruciating detail (though professional accountants noticed that the speech actually revealed somewhat less than it seemed to), and consistently stressing the modesty of his circumstances and how little money he had ever had in his life. "It isn't very much," he admitted, or rather bragged.

Watching the speech on television, the intensely private Hannah Nixon—a woman so private, indeed, that, though prayer was the central activity of her life, she never prayed even in front of other members of her own family—felt deeply pained as she watched her son again and again violate his own privacy. But, after some brief initial nervousness, Richard Nixon (by all appearances and also by his own later account) was having a wonderful time—and all the more so as the speech continued. Lest any particular of his humble and even deprived material situation should go unmentioned, he included this detail of his assets: "I should say this, that Pat doesn't have a mink coat. But she does have a respectable cloth coat. And I always tell her that she'd look good in anything." He evidently considered this such a satisfying rhetorical turn that he soon returned to his wife and her coat, this time describing the latter as "a respectable *Republican* cloth coat." The partisan adjective made no logical sense at all, because, of course, the vast majority of mink coats in America, then as now, were undoubtedly worn by Republicans.

But it was consonant with the tenor of the whole address that Nixon should stress his distinction as a willingly and even *gladly* deprived victim by spreading the victimhood of cloth-coat wearing beyond his immediate family to his entire party (and never mind that rarely in Washington, and almost never in southern California, is a fur coat appropriate to the weather anyhow).

It was in the same vein that he then spoke the most famous words of the speech:

> One other thing I probably should tell you, because if I don't they'll probably be saying this about me too. We did get something—a gift—after the election. A man down in Texas heard Pat on the radio mention the fact that our two youngsters would like to have a dog. And, believe it or not, the day before we left on this campaign trip we got a message from Union Station in Baltimore saying they had a package for us. We went down to get it. You know what it was? It was a little cocker spaniel dog in a crate that he sent all the way from Texas. Black-and-white spotted. And our little girl—Tricia, the six-year-old—named it Checkers. And, you know, the kids, like all kids, love the dog, and I just want to say this right now, that regardless of what they say about it, we're going to keep it.

Many of the details here are false (for instance, the dog was picked up in Washington, not Baltimore, and not by the Nixons personally), and the final sentence is completely illogical. Nixon was under fire, after all, because wealthy friends and supporters had secretly given him significant amounts of cash, not because a total stranger had openly given his daughters a pet of almost zero market value. But it is the image of Checkers that anchors the *ressentiment* expressed by nearly every syllable of the Checkers speech. So poor that a spotted puppy counts as a gift worthy of mention in his financial autobiography, Nixon emerges as a man willing to fight *not* for himself but for the helpless, innocent canine and on behalf of his equally helpless, innocent girls. At the same time, he implies that victory in this fight is far from certain. He is armed, after all, only with his own self-denying moral purity, and faces the ominous (but conveniently vague) third-person plural of the paranoiac ("*they'll* probably be saying this about me," "regardless of what *they* say about it"): so that his rhetoric suggests the dark possibility that "they" may actually succeed in rudely tearing the little pooch from the tender embraces of Tricia and Julie.

Of course, the ascetic, masochistic Nixonian humility is inseparable—in precisely the way diagnosed by Nietzsche—from moralistic arrogance and belligerence. After establishing himself as the moral champion of dogs and children, he went on to attack his opponents, unctuously referring to Adlai Stevenson's patrician status ("I believe it's fine that a man like Governor Stevenson, who inherited a fortune from his father, can run for president") and suggesting that his own financial strip-tease should serve as a model for the Democrats' behavior. Stevenson had recently admitted to having a slush fund of his own, though Sparkman's finances had never been accused of irregularity (unless one counts Nixon's own reference to Mrs. Sparkman's being employed in her husband's office). But Nixon proclaimed that both of them were "under attack" and therefore needed to emulate his own purifying ritual of self-revelation. If they should refuse to, "it will be an admission that they have something to hide." This was partisan gut-fighting of the classic Nixon sort, of course. But his target was not only the Democrats but also the transcendent Republican hero, Eisenhower. Though Nixon prudently avoided overt mention of the man who still had the power to derail his political career with a single phone call, the unstated implication of his remarks was clear enough. If three of the four national candidates were morally obliged to reveal their finances, why not the fourth one too? Furthermore, and as Nixon well knew, Ike had good reason to be reticent about his money matters. Not only had business interests given Ike substantial sums for political purposes, but he had benefited from a special tax break, created for him personally, whereby the huge royalties on his memoirs were considered not income but capital gains, and thus taxed at a much lower rate. Eisenhower's dealings were not technically illegal, but then neither was Nixon's (or Stevenson's) fund; and full disclosure on Ike's part was unlikely to make him look as "clean as a hound's tooth," in the phrase he himself had used to suggest the standard Nixon had to meet in order to remain on the ticket. Eisenhower understood at once what Nixon was up to. When Nixon said that a refusal by Stevenson and Sparkman to emulate his own financial revelations would mean that they had "something to hide," Ike jabbed a pencil against a pad of paper so violently that the sound startled the people in the room with him.

Even with more than half a century of perspective, it is not "perfectly clear," as Nixon might put it, just what Nixon thought he had to gain by baiting Eisenhower in this way. Conceivably, he might have been trying to work a subtle blackmail against Ike. Perhaps the intended implication was that, if Nixon were dumped from the ticket, then the issue of financial accountability would only grow more burning, and that he would personally (if discreetly) help to see to it that *all* the remaining candidates, Eisenhower not excepted, were thoroughly grilled on just what they had to hide. But this is, admittedly, speculation. What *is* clear is the inexorable Nietzschean logic of the Nixonian *ressentiment*. Upholding his own ascetic moral goodness, his own self-sacrificing universalistic purity, Nixon is inevitably led—even in the possible absence of any strategic political motive, and even at the cost of forever alienating, at least to some degree, his most valuable political patron—to a hate-driven negativity. He *must* besmirch others, including that particular other—Eisenhower—

who, for most Americans of the time, most convincingly stood for all that was best and most decent in the American character. Called upon by Eisenhower to defend himself, Nixon—who surely felt in his heart that he required a moral defense less than almost anyone else he knew (his mother doubtless excepted)—will teach Eisenhower that it can be risky to force the man of *ressentiment* into such a position.

What the Checkers speech, along with the entire career of which it is so beautifully emblematic, also makes clear, I think, is the way in which the theory of *ressentiment* can indeed be freed from the aristocratic (or pseudo-aristocratic) values that Nietzsche himself expounded and used to extend the Marxist theory of petty-bourgeois ideology. Marx stresses the *faux*-classlessness of the petty bourgeois, the illusion of moral universalism generated by the "middle" position of the shopkeeper between capitalist and worker. What Nietzsche helps us to see is that this position—because based not only on distance from but also resentment of the other two classes—must tend to be a negative and destructive one ideologically. In the twentieth century the most prominent political role played by the petty bourgeoisie was to form the mass partisan base of Italian and German fascism; and it may be recalled that the analysis Marx offers, in *The Eighteenth Brumaire*, of the Bonapartist coup of 1851, and of the role of the French petty bourgeoisie in helping to make it possible, has often, and convincingly, been taken as providing an anticipatory account of that later and incomparably destructive political system invented by Mussolini and perfected by Hitler. Is it mere co-incidence that the most consequential (though not invariable) ideology of fascism has been one and the same with the destructive prejudice which Nietzsche despised more completely than any other and which he considered the very apex of *ressentiment*—namely, anti-Semitism? The pertinence of this topic in the Nixonian context is of course notorious; but our detailed consideration of Nixon and anti-Semitism must wait until the next chapter.

Whatever else the Checkers speech may have been, it was certainly a roaring success. Or was it? Nixon ended the address—which had been watched by sixty million Americans, the largest television audience ever assembled until that time, and a record that would not be broken until Nixon's own first debate with Kennedy eight years later—by asking viewers and listeners to express their opinions on whether he should remain the Republican vice-presidential candidate. Jonathan Aitken, the most emphatically pro-Nixon of all the serious biographers (and whose book was produced with the active co-operation of Nixon himself), has claimed that 160,000 telegrams and 250,000 letters were sent in response, and that these communications supported Nixon by the astonishing ratio of 350 to one. Since these figures most likely derive, ultimately, from Nixon himself, they might well be suspected of exaggeration. Even so, there is no doubt that the public response was both overwhelming and overwhelmingly favorable to Nixon, who had created exactly the effect he intended to. Sympathy for Nixon was especially intense among the core Republican faithful, who had always regarded the questions about Nixon's finances as partisan smears, and some of whom, moreover, were still rather dubious about Eisenhower's own nonpartisan history. So Ike had no feasible alternative but to concede that Nixon had made his point. Whatever his personal feelings toward the young senator may have been, Ike was no man of *ressentiment* himself, but a practical old soldier who knew when to cut his losses and make the best of a less-than-ideal situation. With his famously radiant smile and a general show of enthusiasm, Eisenhower publicly told Nixon, "You're my boy!", and welcomed him to remain on the ticket as his running-mate. The Checkers speech had done its work, and a new model for how politicians might make direct, emotional appeals to the American public had been established.

In immediate impact, then, and even, to some extent, in

historical importance, the Checkers speech ranks as one of the great addresses of American political history: on a level with Daniel Webster's Second Reply to Hayne in 1830, with Lincoln's Gettysburg Address and his Second Inaugural Address, with William Jennings Bryan's Cross of Gold speech at the Democratic Convention of 1896, with Franklin Roosevelt's First Inaugural Address, and with Martin Luther King's "I Have a Dream" speech at the March on Washington in 1963. Yet it looks odd in that company, and mention of the Checkers speech is more likely to elicit snickers or groans than the awe and reverence which those other storied orations command. Stephen Ambrose, the most voluminous of the Nixon biographers, has argued that the speech was actually more a failure than a success, that its sentimentalism created more new enemies than new friends for Nixon; and he points out that (though Nixon himself celebrated the anniversary of the speech every year thereafter) the Checkers speech eventually became a favorite topic among Democrats and anti-Nixon satirists while vanishing from the historical record in the Republicans' own propaganda. On the other hand, in 1968, a Nixon aide asked Garry Wills, who was covering the presidential campaign as a journalist, what he thought of Nixon's acceptance speech at the Miami convention. When Wills replied that it reminded him of the Checkers speech, the aide looked horrified, and another of Nixon's subordinates rushed to say that people had forgotten what a stroke of political genius the Checkers speech had been. Wills explained that he had not forgotten at all—that that was exactly his point.

This curious doubleness—the nature of the Checkers speech both as overwhelming pragmatic success in saving Nixon's career in 1952 and as object thereafter of ridicule, embarrassment, and derision—reflects some of the deepest and most paradoxical truths about Nixonian cultural power. The petty-bourgeois *ressentiment* of the Checkers speech resonated so deeply with the American electorate that it not only solved at a stroke Nixon's immediate political problems but—like so many of Nixon's campaign innovations—helped to set a new pattern for American politics. Franklin Roosevelt had been the last great innovator before Nixon in American political communication, and the informality of his fireside chats was one of his most valuable rhetorical tools. But imagining FDR publicly indulging in confessional, masochistic moralism is as impossible as imagining him giving a press conference while standing on his head. But after Checkers it has all been quite different. Indeed, American politicians now sometimes go even further in the Nixonian direction than Nixon himself ever did. The Checkers speech almost looks like a restrained, dignified discussion of public policy compared to—let us say—the climactic section of Al Gore's speech accepting the vice-presidential nomination at the 1992 Democratic Convention. In this astonishing oration on the most public evening of his life to that point, Gore picked his son to be his own spotted puppy. He described, in immense, painful detail, his personal feelings on the occasion of the young Gore's near-fatal car accident: and the moral purity that this incident was meant to display in the Tennessee senator supplied the affective and ethical heft behind his thundering but politically vague attacks on the Republicans (identified by a Nixonian *they*) who had controlled the White House during the twelve years of the Reagan-Bush and Bush-Quayle administrations. Yet Gore, like Nixon almost exactly four decades earlier, was generally considered to have done an excellent job. Had he been capable of honest self-analysis on that evening, Gore could only have agreed that Nixon was indeed, as Tom Wicker put it, "one of us."

But "we" have never been unambiguously happy about the association. Perhaps the most acute moment in the entirety of Oliver Stone's long and brilliant film about Nixon comes towards the end. Wandering the halls of the White House during his last night as its occupant, Nixon gazes up at a portrait of John

Kennedy and addresses his dead predecessor and rival thus: "When they look at you, they see what they want to be. When they look at me, they see what they are." While one may doubt whether Nixon ever actually had the insight to speak such words, Stone represents what Nixon *ought* to have said with superb exactness. Nixon was a hero of our politics, but not a hero in the mode of Roosevelt or Kennedy or Reagan. We are, in one of our aspects, a nation of resentful shopkeepers, striving for some universalistic standpoint "beyond" class, deeply convinced of our own moral righteousness, and determined to bury our nagging insecurities with emphatic demonstrations of absolute superiority. So naturally we respond vibrantly to the paradigmatic resentful shopkeeper of our politics, Richard Nixon. But the image of the resentful shopkeeper is not a particularly attractive one even from the resentful shopkeeper's own viewpoint. For self-loathing is of course fundamental to the self-denying quality of *ressentiment,* as the Nixonian masochism abundantly illustrates. Furthermore, there are of course other aspects of America as well, aspects associated with such names as Twain and Mencken, both of them Nietzscheans in fact and one of them in name too (and the late Twain, though never Mencken, came within touching distance of Marxism as well). So, even as we respond to Nixon, we can never escape the feeling that there is something deeply wrong in our response. We *loved* the Checkers speech. The historical record proves so. But we have never really liked the fact that we loved it.

3

It remains to co-ordinate Nixonian cultural power with Freud's concept of anal eroticism. At the outset of this part of our discussion, however, it is necessary to distinguish between two related but separable dimensions of Freud's thought on the matter. On one level, Freud proposes an essentially descriptive—and culturally contextualizable—account of the anal-erotic character: something that we will consider shortly. But, on a somewhat different level—the level of his clinical theory of human psycho-sexual development—Freud also links this character type to certain factors in the sexual make-up of the infant. Freud maintains that human libido (that is, sexual desire in its general form) goes through a predominantly oral phase, in which the mouth functions as the body's chief erotogenic zone, and then a predominantly anal phase, in which the anus succeeds to this position, before ultimately being organized in properly "adult" form under the primacy of the genitalia. But, Freud argues, we humans do not pass through these sexual phases as a train passes through stations. We always remain, to some degree, what we have ever been. Oral and anal components persist in the sexual constitution of the fully genital adult; and Freud believes that it is possible to link the adult character type that he identifies as anal-erotic to an abnormally strong persistence of anal libido left over, and sublimated, from childhood. It is, of course, the investigation of early sexual vicissitudes that forms one of the chief aims of psychoanalysis as a clinical, therapeutic practice.

But therapeutic practice requires extended, intimate personal contact between analyst and patient. Indeed, even *with* the benefit of such contact the analyst can seldom attain more than tentative glimpses into the repressed psycho-sexual history of the patient on the consulting-room sofa. To attempt such investigations into a figure that one knows only from books, newspapers, television, and other such public records seems to me imprudent. To be sure, many have attempted this sort of second-hand (or third-, or fourth-hand) analysis, including Freud himself, who, interestingly, collaborated in a long-distance psychoanalysis of Nixon's own political hero, Woodrow Wilson. But I decline to follow his example, and the reader may be relieved to hear that speculations into the early sexual development of Richard Nixon will play almost no role in what follows (though such speculations, used to hilarious and brilliant effect, may be found in Mark Maxwell's remarkable novel *NixonCarver*). We shall not attempt to guess just how the young Nixonian rectum may have ultimately exercised a historic impact on the political culture of the United States of America.

Even as we abjure engagement with the clinical aspect of psychoanalysis, we can, however, nonetheless recognize that Freud's theory of anal eroticism provides an acute description of a certain character type, one that remains valid and recognizable no matter what its ultimate connections to the sexuality of the anus may be. The three personality characteristics Freud stresses as associated with anal eroticism are *orderliness*, *parsimony*, and *obstinacy*. None of these traits, in strict logic, necessarily implies either of the others, and there is doubtless considerable empirical evidence to indicate that the combination of the three qualities is not invariable. Most of us have known slobs who can be very stubborn in intellectual argument, misers willing to be reasonably flexible in matters not involving money, people of real generosity for whom no job of house-cleaning is ever quite adequate, and so forth. Nonetheless, orderliness, parsimony, and obstinacy do all have much in common, and the three qualities do seem, logically and observably, to cluster together often. All involve a certain rigidity, a fixity in one's habits or views. Each is the opposite of being relaxed or laid back. All encompass an emotional restrictedness, a kind of unfreedom that paradoxically appears to be freely chosen. Nixon's curious antipathy to *sleep*—surely the most relaxed of all human activities—seems, for instance, to exemplify his anal eroticism with particular force and clarity. Not only was Nixon a lifelong insomniac, but he was, so to speak, a "principled" insomniac, who frequently bragged about how little he slept, and who regarded a fondness for sleep as a mark of contemptible weakness. Or, to take another example: Garry Wills, contrasting Nixon with the youth counterculture of the 1960s that Nixon so bitterly opposed, suggested that "the kids," as Wills called them, stood for "a literally unbuttoned and unbra'd openness, a celebration of hair and nudity," whereas Nixon, on the other hand, was "the most doggedly *dressed* man imaginable" (emphasis in the original). Wills is no Freudian, but this phrase he coined to describe Nixon—"the most doggedly *dressed* man imaginable"—hits off very well what Freud meant by the anal-erotic personality.

Each of the three psychological components that Freud identified in anal eroticism correlates well with the petty-bourgeois moralism that we have seen to be fundamental to Nixonian, and American, culture. The first, orderliness, is the most important, for, if there was one value that Nixon stood for throughout his political career, it was order. "Law and order" was the most prominent substantive slogan of his 1968 presidential campaign (and of many other right-wing campaigns that year). On one level it is, of course, deeply ironic that that slogan helped to usher in an administration that, to a considerable degree, functioned as a sort of organized-crime syndicate. But the irony involves something much more complex and important than simple, transparent hypocrisy. The two components of the term "law and order" exist, though not in strict logical contradiction to one another, at least in a state of considerable tension. The essence of law is the restraint of brute power, and not only the power of the criminal but, at least equally important, the power of the state itself. Law necessarily involves due process: and scrupulous respect for the law must thus include toleration of some possibility of disorder—as in Sir William Blackstone's famous maxim, generally considered foundational to the Anglo-American legal and judicial system, that it is better for ten guilty defendants to go free than for one innocent defendant to be punished. Conversely, if order is to be the prime value then there will be times when the repressive illegalities of the crooked cop or the vigilante must be overlooked, excused, or even encouraged. The ideological reality behind the rhetoric of "law and order" is often the insistence that one must choose law *or* order.

There was no question in anyone's mind as to which half of "law and order" Nixon, during the 1968 campaign, actually chose. Indeed, one of the most prominent themes in Nixon's speeches that year was the one sounded in his frequent and bitter attacks on the United State Supreme Court (led by Chief Justice Earl Warren, Nixon's old rival from the early days in California) and on the incumbent Attorney General, Ramsey Clark, for their supposed hypersensitivity to the legal rights of criminal defendants and their correlative squeamishness about doing whatever needed to be done in order to preserve order. Basic points of law were derided as "technicalities," and actual legal rights needed, so Nixon claimed, to be "balanced" by other "rights" that were in fact not rights in the classic sense at all but positive social goals like "the right to walk the streets in safety." No outright fascist—something that Nixon never, quite, was—has ever engaged in more robust demagoguery on behalf of anal-erotic yearnings for order, stability, security, and predictability.

For this was, it will be remembered, the campaign against the niggers—and against the "niggers." Despite the heavy and politically crucial racialization of the law-and-order issue in 1968, African-Americans in general and exponents of Black Power in particular were, as we have seen, not the only agents of disorder that Nixon meant to stigmatize. Other "niggers," of various skin colors, included militant opponents of the Vietnam War, young flower children who openly and proudly flouted taboos against illegal drugs and premarital sex, and the earliest cohorts of second-wave feminism—all of whom seemed deeply threatening to the sense of order cherished by that instinctively conservative bloc of Americans that Nixon came to call the "Silent Majority" (a phrase that, interestingly, appears to derive from the Homeric Greek *sigoi polloi,* which refers to the dead—who are surely the most orderly of all people). To exploit the desire for order was, of course, nothing new for Nixon. The brilliantly successful Red-baiting that had launched his career and helped to sustain it in the early days was, at least in psychological terms, extremely similar to the demagoguery of 1968. For—though it is considerably more difficult now to reconstruct, imaginatively, the public mood of the late 1940s and early 1950s than that of the late 1960s—there is no question but that orderly Americans during the Truman-Eisenhower era really did feel as personally threatened by the spectre of domestic Communist subversion as they later would by mass-produced images of unpatriotic draft resisters, bra-burning lesbians, dope-smoking fornicators, and, above all, angry and vengeful young black men.

Yet the pragmatic skill with which Nixon sensed and exploited the American fear of disorder in its varying forms was never merely a cynical campaign trick unrooted in his own political and class personality. The historic connection that we have already noted between fascism and the petty bourgeoisie finds at least part of its psychological cement in the fact that the petty bourgeois lives in constant danger of so horrendously disorderly a fate as proletarianization, and is thus especially attracted to the ordered security that fascist movements promise. But Nixon's own rage for order, especially during the last phase of his career, seems to have been extreme even by the standards of his socio-economic background. The available evidence, particularly in the Haldeman diaries and the White House tapes, suggests that the perceived disorders of the late 1960s and early 1970s disturbed Nixon as deeply as they disturbed his rank-and-file supporters, and that he seriously feared the possibility of electoral defeat in 1972. The result, of course, was that he attempted to order the American political process through the series of crimes and dirty tricks known today as "Watergate," which aimed to manipulate the Democratic nominating process and to weaken, mortally, the eventual Democratic nominee, but which ultimately also destroyed Nixon's own presidency. By the end, Nixon's craving for order and personal political security was so desperate that not only was he willing to sacrifice law itself, but, in addition, he also deliberately blinded himself to the fact—which should have been obvious to one who had for so long been such a shrewd master of the practice and theory of American politics—that his 1972 re-election was overwhelmingly probable, and that he had far more to lose than to gain by sanctioning burglaries and wiretaps.

As always, however, the fact that Nixon in the end destroyed his own career should not cause us to forget how successful he was for so long; and few aspects of his appeal resonated more strongly with the country whose political heights he rose to conquer than the anal-erotic drive for orderliness. This is a point generally repressed in liberal discourse. But American liberals deceive themselves much more than they do anyone else when they pretend that the essence of their country is typified solely by such things as the Declaration of Independence, the Bill of Rights, and the popular Jeffersonian tradition (something that is by no means entirely at one with the historical record of the sometimes repressive Jefferson Administration). Though it would be cynical and unjust to deny that free speech and due process have a real place in American culture, it is delusional to think that they are the whole story. America is, after all, also a country of lynch law and vigilantism: an aspect of his culture that Nixon seemed clearly to embrace when, as president, he pronounced Charles Manson to be guilty of murder while the trial was still taking place and, during the same week, praised the John Wayne film *Chisum*, in which those who Nixon identified as "the good guys" take the law into their own hands. America is a country with a long history of the illegal repression of labor unions, racial minorities, and other marginalized groups. America is a country where censorship has always flourished; it flourished even as the First Amendment was being ratified. It is a country with a long history of criminalizing victimless activities from prostitution to pornography to the sale of whiskey. And it is a country where many people have always displayed a strong moralistic drive to order other people's lives for them—to regulate by force what they may read or say or wear or believe, what they may do with their own bodies or with the bodies of other consenting adults. It is a country where the American Civil Liberties Union counts, for most political purposes, as a "special interest." An anal-erotic nation, America, as the Stone film has it, long saw what it was—a country in love with orderliness—when it looked at Richard Nixon.

Parsimony, or miserliness, the second of the anal-erotic character traits listed by Freud, does not loom anything like as large in American culture. But it is certainly not without cultural and political significance. On the personal level, to be sure, it has never been considered attractive. Whereas the orderly personality possesses genuine appeal for many—though usually not appeal of the most glamorous or exciting sort—hardly anyone has ever been liked or admired for being stingy with money and other material possessions. In the folklore and mores of the world, the miser is almost universally a figure to be mocked and disdained, and open-handed generosity (like that displayed by Hannah Nixon toward the homeless poor) is almost universally applauded. We need to remember, however, that the fundamental ethical principle of any capitalist civilization is, necessarily, the assumption that the socio-economic system is somehow capable of transforming private vices (like avarice) into public virtues (like "prosperity"). And nowhere is belief in this weird alchemy more emphatic than in the American political culture that produced Richard Nixon and in which he flourished so stunningly.

The private vice of parsimony was abundantly Nixon's own. As we have noted, he managed throughout his career to amass large sums of money, far larger than anyone except his few most intimate business associates (like Bebe Rebozo) knew until after his death. Since, apart from expensive French wine, his taste for luxurious consumption was always modest, and since he was never much of a philanthropist either, it seems clear that his interest in money was mainly in just piling it up to be hoarded, like the mountains of cash in Uncle Scrooge's money bin in the Donald Duck comic books. Perhaps such private miserliness was the understandable result of a youth spent during the Great Depression.

A more complex instance of Nixon's parsimony concerns the White House tapes. Since it was Nixon's own recorded words that finally shattered his presidency, and since Nixon must have known how damaging the evidence of the tapes could be, many people have long wondered why he didn't simply destroy the tapes while he still had the opportunity to do so. The wholesale elimination of such potential evidence would doubtless have created a political firestorm in itself, but one that Nixon could have probably survived. For his opponents would have been forever deprived of the "smoking gun" generally thought to be necessary for so unprecedented a step as the removal of a sitting president. Part of the answer may lie in simple miscalculation: Nixon really did believe he could maintain control of the tapes until the Supreme Court (four of whose members he had placed there) unanimously ordered him to hand them over. Still, the question remains: Why did he take the chance?

His attachment to the tapes can be interpreted in a pretty deeply Freudian way. Freud argues that the small child tends to develop an attachment to his own excrement, an attachment empirically familiar to many parents during toilet-training. The child becomes reluctant to see *his* faeces, the product of his own body, vanish down the toilet. Since Freud also posits a profound psychic and cultural link between excrement and money (most obviously illustrated in such common expressions as "filthy lucre"), he maintains that parsimony during one's adult years can generally be connected to an abnormally high investment in the product of one's bowel movements much earlier in life. In this way, it easy enough to see the tapes—Nixon's own leavings, as it were, the product of his own daily business, and full of scatological epithets to boot—as symbolically excremental, and thus to interpret his determination to hang onto them as anal-erotic in something like the strict clinical sense. But a more mediated, and more financial, sense is easily to hand as well. As J. Anthony Lukas (whose early book on Watergate, *Nightmare*, remains the best journalistic account of the matter) was the first to point out, Nixon, had he been able to retain possession of the tapes, could quite possibly have used them to avoid paying any income taxes for the rest of his life. He would only have had to donate them (after careful editing and sanitizing, of course) to the federal government, at a pace sufficient to secure an annual deduction that would wipe out all tax liability year after year. Though no direct evidence has come to light that Nixon had precisely such a plan in mind, Lukas's hypothesis is entirely plausible. Like many misers, Nixon had a special aversion to paying the federal income tax; and we know that Nixon thought in terms of such schemes as Lukas suggests, because, earlier in his presidency, he had gone so far as to violate the law by backdating a document in order to obtain the best possible tax break for the donation of his vice-presidential papers. The White House tapes were not only Nixon's leavings but leavings that could have been worth millions of dollars to him.

Of course, Nixon's secret bank accounts and his personal feelings toward the White House tapes were not matters that he publicly advertised. But his private parsimony was displayed to the world in the form of apparent governmental *frugality*, of that very well advertised determination to be sparing with the public purse that constitutes the acceptable, virtuous, public version of the private vice of stinginess. A man who might be suspected of ugly miserliness with his own funds is often thought, especially among the American petty bourgeoisie, to be especially reassuring when it comes to looking after the public's money. Logically, the ideology at work here is completely irrational. After all, almost 100% of the government's money comes from American taxpayers, and almost 100% is returned to American taxpayers in one way or another (with that small percentage not so returned—like the funds spent on foreign aid or the rental of overseas military bases—being spent, at least in principle, on the American public's best interests). It is nearly impossible, mathematically, for "the taxpayer," in the abstract, to be a net loser.

Nonetheless, middle-class and especially lower-middle-class Americans have long been haunted by the gnawing fear that high rates of government taxation and expenditures must somehow mean that *their* money is being taken from them and given to others. The moralistic resentment this fear generates is especially acute when it is suspected—as it usually is—that the others include the hated undeserving poor, and especially the doubly hated undeserving black poor. This is the current in American political culture that responds so warmly to anal-erotic parsimony, to "frugality" with the public treasury; and few presidents have exploited such feelings more ably than Nixon. There is, of course, considerable irony in the fact that Nixon was, in actual budgetary terms, quite the "big spender" on domestic programs (especially as compared to nearly all his successors, Republican and Democratic alike). Yet he mastered the *rhetoric* of public frugality so well that this fact went largely unnoticed during his administration by nearly all save a handful of right-wing intellectuals. One doubts that Nixon was especially troubled when Johnny Cash rebuked him by refusing to sing "Welfare Cadillac" at the White House. For those who considered that a country singer had given the president of the United States a much-needed lesson in basic human decency were, for the most part, those who were unlikely to vote for Nixon in any case. To his core constituency, to the voters he *had* to hold in order to win re-election, Nixon had delivered exactly the message he intended to convey: that he hated "welfare cheats" just as much as they did, and that he intended to be just as tight-fisted with the public's money as they would want him to be.

Finally, we come to obstinacy, the third of Freud's anal-erotic characteristics. Compared to orderliness and parsimony, which have a specifically Nixonian pertinence, the political function of obstinacy is more generic. To be fixed in one's views is a rather standard professional virtue in the politician, like compassion in the physician, piety in the clergyman, or erudition in the scholar. Not, of course, that politicians (or others) typically brag about being stubborn. But it is useful, in this context, to recall Bertrand Russell's famous "conjugation": "I am firm. You are stubborn. He is a pig-headed fool." The empirical evidence seems to suggest that "firmness" in an American politician—the refusal to admit that one has ever made a mistake and the insistence on the total consistency of all the words and actions of one's public career—is a quality the electorate demands. True enough, people do sometimes say that it would be refreshing to hear a presidential candidate admit past error or confess uncertainty on a particular issue—just as people quite often say that they dislike "negative campaigning" that aims at the moral and political destruction of an opponent. But, when the actual votes are counted, those who have practiced negative campaigning with maximum emphasis and skill—Nixon himself remains the pre-eminent example—are usually the winners. As for "firmness," i.e., anal-erotic obstinacy, an especially clear example of how this virtue—or the lack of it—actually functions is provided by the fate of George Romney in 1968. Romney, while still considered by many (though probably unrealistically) to be the front-runner for the Republican presidential nomination, admitted—very publicly and very honorably—that his pro-war position on the Vietnam War had been wrong (and that he had been "brainwashed" by US officials during a trip to Vietnam in 1965). His reward for this unusual candor was to be almost universally ridiculed in the press and to sink so low in the polls that he withdrew from the New Hampshire primary before balloting had even begun—thus ending his presidential hopes forever and leaving Nixon to win New Hampshire with nearly 80% of the vote.

The American fondness for obstinacy in politics would appear to rest, logically, on a premise that few would defend in the abstract: namely, that those forever certain of their own rightness are in fact more likely to *be* right than those who admit to doubts and an evolution of views. In cultural practice, however, we need to recall again that, ideologically, modern America is far more the outgrowth of Puritan Massachusetts than of Enlightenment Virginia (leaving aside here the interesting irony that today Massachusetts is more enlightened, Virginia more puritanical). A certain stubbornness in belief is, almost by definition, a necessity for any religious system—that is, any system based on the evidence of things not seen but taken on faith instead—and it has always been especially strong in the tradition of puritanical religiosity so integral to the petty-bourgeois moralism of Nixonian, and American, culture. In this light, an anal-erotic obstinacy becomes almost a necessary sign of morality itself.

Yet, if such fixity is therefore more widely shared among American politicians than parsimony or even orderliness—if, so to speak, "everybody does it"—then, as usual, Nixon did it more and better than most. As with his miserliness and his craving for order, the political effectiveness of Nixon's fixity of belief was in no small part dependent on the extent to which the quality was "sincerely" grounded in his own psyche. The proof is perhaps less convincingly to be found in his active political career—where, it might be argued, he did little but what any politician not given to Romney-like self-immolation would do—than in his post-presidential literary remains. Here one reads for hundreds of pages at a time without coming across any admission of honest error or even honest doubt. Probably the only real exception—the only occasion on which Nixon clearly confesses to having been wrong on a significant matter of policy—concerns the wage and price controls he imposed in August 1971, much to the shock and surprise of those who had believed his consistent professions of belief in orthodox neoclassical economic principles. In *RN*, he notes that the results of the controls were politically useful to him but probably did not constitute sound economic policy. Even here, though, the student of Nixonian anal eroticism should note that Nixon briefly relaxes his habit of obstinacy only to reiterate his faith in neoclassical economic orthodoxy, itself closely related to his habit of parsimony with government money.

The anal-erotic character; *ressentiment;* the petty bourgeoisie—if these concepts are crucial to the understanding of Nixonian cultural power, it is neither mere contingency, nor, of course, due to any unconscious and anticipatory collective intellectual analysis by Marx, Nietzsche, and Freud of Richard Nixon. But Marx, Nietzsche, and Freud remain the pre-eminent analysts of *modernity* (and, if you like, of "postmodernity" as well). Since American culture is in many ways the current paradigm of the modern, it is hardly surprising to find an especially close fit between Marxist, Nietzschean, and Freudian concepts and Nixon, our dark hero of modern America.

IV. Nixon and the Other: Elements of Anti-Semitism and of Racism

> It was my philosophy professor, a native of the Antilles, who recalled the fact to me one day: "Whenever you hear anyone abuse the Jews, pay attention, because he is talking about you." And I found that he was universally right.
> —Frantz Fanon

1

Even during the heights (or depths) of Watergate, with all its various sensations, a particular sensation was created by the revelation that the president was in the habit of making anti-Semitic remarks. This news was generated by some of the first of Nixon's White House tapes to be released to the public; and, since his resignation in 1974, and especially since his death twenty years later, a substantial percentage of Nixon's headlines have concerned more of his comments about the Jews, disclosed in further releases of the White House tapes and also in the Haldeman diaries (the latter being a daily record of Nixon's presidency by his chief of staff so voluminous—nearly three quarters of a million words—that to this day it has not been fully published except in CD-ROM form). It is worthwhile to recall just a few of the rhetorical *fleurs du mal* in which Nixon privately indulged.

He issued a grave warning about people involved with the arts on the grounds that "they're Jews, they're left-wing—in other words, stay away." He used the term "cheap kike" to refer to the businessman Robert Vesco, his own supporter, who was criminally indicted and eventually fled the country because of a secret $200,000 contribution he made to Nixon's 1972 campaign. He enthusiastically agreed with Billy Graham's contention that a Jewish "stranglehold" on the American media threatened the very survival of the nation, and approvingly told Haldeman that Graham believed a conspiracy of "Satanic Jews" to be at work in the land. He bragged that his White House was "trying to run this town [i.e., Washington] by avoiding the Jews in the government." He mused to Haldeman about why "all the Jews seem to be the ones that are for liberalizing the regulations on marijuana." He insisted that the businessman Robert Abplanalp, a friend of Bebe Rebozo's and, to a lesser degree, of Nixon's own, was being persecuted by "some Jews in New York"—evidently business competitors of Abplanalp's—with the support of "a Jewish Congressman." He flatly averred, "Most Jews are disloyal," and, after making exceptions for several of his own Jewish aides, insisted to Haldeman, "But, Bob, generally speaking, you can't trust the bastards. They turn on you." He astonishingly identified Alger Hiss and Whittaker Chambers as the "only two non-Jews in the Communist conspiracy." Referring to his difficulties gaining support from Jewish American voters, he complained, "If anybody who's been in this chair ever had reason to be anti-Semitic, I did."

And so on and so forth. The remarks quoted above are but a fraction of Nixon's anti-Semitic comments that have come to light, and it is reasonable to suppose that many more lie hidden in the White House tapes yet to be made publicly available. We might note in passing just one more of Nixon's comments, this one concerning his attitude toward Israel. Logically, of course, anti-Semitism is a matter entirely separate from support for or opposition to the policies of the Israeli government. Since, however, Nixon's appallingly numerous Jewish defenders continue to cite his resupplying of the Israeli military during the war of October 1973 to prove that he could not have been "really" anti-Semitic, it should be pointed out that—even on the view that falsely conflates support for Israel with the absence of anti-Semitism—the actual evidence proves nothing of the sort. Unlike later Republican presidents such as Reagan and George

W. Bush, Nixon harbored no fondness for Israel. In 1973 he *refused* frantic Israeli pleas for military aid until the last minute, when the resupply was dictated by larger questions of *Realpolitik*: specifically, by the exigencies of the vast geopolitical chess game that he and Henry Kissinger were playing with the Soviets, who backed the Arab countries at war with Israel. As Nixon himself privately put it, "I'm not pro-Israel; I'm not going to let Israel's tail wag the dog."

We should consider several factors that may somewhat moderate the sensationalism that surrounded the publication of Nixon's Jew-hating rants and allow us to set the remarks themselves in some sort of historical context. First, we should remember that Nixon was, after all, a small-town, lower-middle-class Republican Protestant, born in 1913 and hence well into his thirties by the time the details of the Holocaust became widely known (an important point, since the Holocaust, for Americans, eventually gave anti-Semitism a connotation of ultimate evil that it had not possessed before). Though there were doubtless many—or at least some—people of similar background genuinely free of such bigotry, still, to reveal that a person of such demographic profile harbored anti-Semitic feelings is not much more astonishing than to report that a goose was seen walking barefoot. Though this consideration may sound like a version of the classic Watergate defense of Nixon that we have encountered before—"everybody does it"—it is nonetheless true that the political and ideological valences of an individual's bigotry may vary depending upon how common or how exceptional that particular bigotry is within the individual's social cohort.

Second, and relatedly, we ought also to remember that the unique circumstances that produced and disseminated the Haldeman diaries and the White House tapes have made public an immense number of Nixon's private comments in a way and to a degree true of no other American president and perhaps no other important public figure in world history. The nineteenth-century *mot* defined a kike as "a Jewish gentleman who has just left the room"—a rather pertinent saying in this context, since, as we will see, a fair number of Jewish gentlemen were commonly entering and leaving Nixon's Oval Office—and it is true that many people sometimes talk among their most trusted associates in ways that they would not like to become part of the public record. What, one may wonder, were the innermost thoughts expressed by Herbert Hoover about Catholics, or by Dwight Eisenhower about blacks, or by John Kennedy about homosexuals? Nixon, of course, had mainly himself to blame for the unique access we enjoy to his private conversations. The tapes are the product of his own bugging, and the Haldeman diaries are the generally admiring but extraordinarily detailed notes of his closest White House aide. Even so, and without falling into the "everybody does it" defense, we should consider that, were comparable historical sources available for other presidents, then Nixon's anti-Semitic ravings might not stand out in quite the way they actually do. There is a certain ring of truth to the scene in the Oliver Stone film in which Nixon, chiding his aides who are preparing written versions of some of the tapes, bitterly complains that one transcript "makes me sound like an anti-Semite."

Finally, the fact that our evidence of the Nixonian anti-Semitism derives almost entirely from his private musings points toward an important distinction: namely, that Nixon's anti-Semitism was personal and not, for the most part, political. With the exception of several Jewish civil servants who may have been demoted as a result of Nixon's paranoia about an anti-Nixon "Jewish cabal" at the Bureau of Labor Statistics, it would be hard to prove that any individual Jew, as such, directly suffered from the Nixonian anti-Semitism.

By European standards, of course, political anti-Semitism has always been fairly minor in the United States. American history contains no major national movements, like the anti-Dreyfusards in France or the Nazi Party in Germany, whose primary ideological cement was provided by anti-Semitism. Probably the nearest thing to an exception was the Ku Klux Klan of the 1920s, which briefly became an influential faction of the national Democratic Party—though in Klan ideology anti-Catholicism and anti-black racism were both as important as anti-Semitism. The most prominent appearance of political anti-Semitism in Nixon's own career occurred, as we have seen, during the 1950 Senate race, when he ran perhaps the nastiest of all his campaigns against Helen Gahagan Douglas, whose husband Melvyn was Jewish. Douglas was frequently attacked in specifically anti-Semitic ways, most notably by the Protestant clergyman Gerald L. K. Smith, the most prominent purveyor (since Henry Ford) of anti-Semitic ideology in modern American history (and one of the wildest: at different times he claimed that Franklin Roosevelt, Harry Truman, Dwight Eisenhower, and the Nazi war criminal Adolf Eichmann were all Jews). In 1950 Smith urged California voters to "help Richard Nixon get rid of the Jew Communists" and to "do one thing very soon to further the ideals of Christian Nationalism," namely, "not to send to the Senate the wife of a Jew." Nixon, of course, avoided such language and publicly repudiated Smith's support, even insisting that, as a Quaker, he belonged to a minority religion himself. Perhaps Nixon could have gotten Smith to shut up if he had really (privately) tried, and perhaps he was quietly grateful to Smith for helping to nail down the hard-right vote, which at that time was almost unanimously anti-Semitic. It is certainly true that during the campaign Nixon occasionally referred to his opponent as "Helen Hesselberg," thus making her Jewish connection clear by using Melvyn Douglas's original surname, which neither he nor his wife ever used themselves. But, even in 1950, Nixon cannot really be accused of much more than a hint of programmatically political anti-Semitism; and it is worth recalling that his campaign manager that year was the Jewish Murray Chotiner.

The mention of Chotiner—the only political mentor that the mightily self-driven and self-taught Nixon ever took—suggests a further perspective important for understanding Nixon's anti-Semitism. "Some of my best friends are Jewish"—this is the classic defense spoken by the anti-Semite whose bigotry has not risen to the delusional heights of a Gerald L. K. Smith. One cannot understand anti-Semitism without realizing that, as we will see, the sentence often contains a certain kind of truth. It is noteworthy that, in an era when, unlike today, few Jews were to be found in conservative Republican circles, a surprising number of Nixon's close associates, including some of the very closest, happened to be Jewish. In addition to Chotiner, there was Arthur Burns, the Columbia economics professor who served as chairman of the Council of Economic Advisers under Eisenhower, and who was one of the few of Ike's senior people who actually liked Nixon. The professorial Burns gave informal tutorials in economics to the eager-to-learn vice-president and later, when Nixon was in the White House, was rewarded by being named chairman of the Federal Reserve, the most economically influential position in the national government. There was Leonard Garment, a partner in Nixon's New York law firm, who, as not only a Jew but also a serious amateur musician and a self-described liberal Democrat, seemed to conform to Nixon's stereotype about people in the arts. Nonetheless, Nixon did not "stay away" from Garment, as his own advice would have had him do, but instead brought Garment into the White House, where, if he never became one of the most powerful aides, he did seem to have one of the closer personal relationships with the president. There was Herb Stein, who was never particularly close, in strictly personal terms, to Nixon, but who did become his top White House economic adviser. There was William Safire, Nixon's most talented White House speechwriter, who left Nixon's service just in time to miss most of Watergate, and who went on to become one of the country's most prominent journalists and the (barely) unofficial American spokesman for the Israeli right. Most prominent of all, of course, there was Henry Kissinger, who arrived in the United States as a persecuted refugee from Nazi Germany and who became, thanks to Nixon, the single most influential shaper of US foreign policy and the international order during the second half of the twentieth century.

Were these men Nixon's Jewish best friends? It has often been pointed out that the Jewish "friends" of whom the anti-Semite boasts typically turn out to be, upon inspection, not exactly friends in the intimate personal sense but something more like associates or colleagues. They tend to be people with whom the anti-Semite has professional or business dealings and with whom he may sometimes eat meals in restaurants, but not, usually, people who are frequently invited into his home or whose children are encouraged to socialize with or marry his own. Though this pattern seems to fit Nixon fairly well, it is somewhat complicated by the fact that it remains very much an open question as to whether Nixon had *any* truly close friends at all, Jewish or otherwise. Kissinger has maintained in print that Nixon did not, and Eisenhower told his secretary that he did not understand how a man could go through life as friendless as Nixon. And the evidence does seem to indicate that a talent for friendship was not among Nixon's many abilities.

Bob Haldeman, for example, was Nixon's associate for 17 years, and during Nixon's presidency the two men spent several hours together nearly every day, with much of that time spent *tête-à-tête*. No president has ever relied more heavily on a chief of staff than Nixon did on Haldeman. But, at the end, Haldeman realized that Nixon did not even know how many children he, Haldeman, had, or what their names were. He also realized that Nixon had never once offered to shake his hand—until the handshake Nixon extended on the occasion of firing his top aide when Haldeman became enveloped in the Watergate scandal.

John Ehrlichman, who became second in power only to Haldeman among the Nixon White House staffers, was fired on the same day and, except for a single phone call the following Christmas, never heard from his old boss again. Nixon did send Ehrlichman an inscribed copy of *RN*, but, when Ehrlichman opened the volume, he found that the president he served so loyally had managed to misspell his name—"the ultimate insult," he said.

Of course, a politician's political helpers are not necessarily his intimate pals. John Kennedy's speechwriter Theodore Sorenson was one of his closest White House colleagues, perhaps his very closest; but the president usually preferred to relax with Red Fay, his politically insignificant Navy buddy. But the same kind of almost pathological distance that marked Nixon's dealings with Haldeman and Ehrlichman seems to have been a characteristic of his relations with nearly everyone else too. He was often observed to treat even his wife Pat frostily, the two frequently sleeping in different rooms or (in their vacation compound in Key Biscayne, Florida) even different buildings. In the speech he made to the White House staff on his last morning as president, in which he praised his dead parents, especially his mother, at some length, he never thought even to mention the woman who, despite her own intense distaste for the political life, had faithfully stood by his side throughout his entire public career, nearly three decades from the race against Voorhis in 1946 until the forced presidential resignation of 1974. Even Bebe Rebozo, who formally filled the role of "best friend," is an ambiguous exception. Many observers did believe that Rebozo was the one person with whom Nixon could be informal and spontaneous. For instance, the two men sometimes cavorted together in the White House pool, taking turns in a game in which each tried to knock the other off an inflated rubber raft. Yet one reason that Nixon became fond of Rebozo's company was that Rebozo (who, even before meeting Nixon, had always had a powerful taste for hanging out with politicians) was willing to spend hours together in complete silence. A Nixon aide quipped that Nixon liked to be alone and that with Rebozo he was. As Nixon himself put it to a journalist: "I never wanted to be buddy-buddy. . . .Even with close friends. I don't believe in letting your hair down, confiding this and that and the other thing."

Nixon's disinclination from personal intimacy helps to explain how his anti-Semitism could co-exist with his choosing to surround himself with Jewish associates to a greater degree than any American president before him (or, perhaps, *since* him too, for that matter). He may well have felt as close to Garment or to Kissinger as to almost anyone else, but, since genuine human closeness was not on his agenda in any event, it was easy enough to dislike the Jews in general while dealing on an everyday basis with individuals who happened to be Jewish.

2

But the matter is also a good deal more complicated than that. For what is at stake here is not just Nixon's "toleration" of individual Jews but the whole complex relation between anti-Semitism and philo-Semitism, and, indeed, the defining overall structure of ethnic or racial bigotry in general. In nearly every concrete variety of bigotry, the object of hatred is constructed in such a way as to include some features that, in and of themselves, could be regarded as favorable. They become *un*favorable only in the total context of the bigot's paranoia. In the case of anti-Semitism the ascribed Jewish feature most pertinent in this regard is nearly always intelligence. The stereotypes of anti-Semitism are wildly various and often self-contradictory—Jews have been represented as almost everything from tight-fisted misers to sexual predators, and they have been condemned with equal vigor for a clannish avoidance of Gentiles and for obnoxiously attempting to push their way, uninvited, into Gentile company—but, unlike such parallel cases as the Pole, the Irishman, or the

African-American, the Jew has almost never (during Nixon's lifetime or since) been constructed as stupid. To be sure, Jewish intelligence is not, for the anti-Semite, necessarily a redeeming trait. On the contrary, it may, especially in the more extreme versions of anti-Semitism, become part of the indictment itself. For it is typically understood as intelligence of an uncreative and hypercritical sort, an intelligence divorced from larger qualities of "character," and an intelligence that is ultimately destructive in its aims. But the mythical intelligence of the Jew (like the equally mythical earthy vitality of the black or warm-hearted generosity of the Irishman) does function as a kind of switching-point that allows anti-Semitism and philo-Semitism to function not as simple opposites but in complex, dialectical collusion with one another. The notion that Jews are smart is an ideological stereotype just as much as the notion that Jews are miserly or disloyal; and individuals who harbor many sorts of anti-Semitic attitudes may nonetheless deliberately seek out Jews when, say, the expert skill of a surgeon, an attorney, or a stockbroker is wanted. In other words, anti-Semitism and philo-Semitism are not opposed answers to a particular logical question—as though we were rationally debating a political issue like whether to raise or lower the marginal income tax rates—but somewhat discordant components of the *same*, and ultimately anti-Semitic, ideology. "There is no anti-Semite who does not basically want to imitate his mental image of a Jew," as the German (and Jewish) philosophers Max Horkheimer and Theodor Adorno put it in their ground-breaking essay, "Elements of Anti-Semitism."

Did Nixon see himself as in some sense Jewish, as at least "a bit of a Jew," in Sylvia Plath's resonant phrase? Not long after he resigned the presidency, he offered the following analysis of his own career and character to his aide Kenneth Clawson:

> What starts the process, really, are the laughs and snubs and slights you get when you are a kid. Sometimes it's

> because you're poor or Irish or Jewish or ugly or simply that you are skinny. But if you are reasonably intelligent and if your anger is deep enough and strong enough, you learn that you can change those attitudes by excellence, personal gut performance, while those who have everything are sitting on their fat butts...So you are lean and mean and resourceful and you continue to walk on the edge of the precipice...

It is worthwhile to pause over the list of personal characteristics that Nixon finds relevant to his own situation. Nixon had some Irish ancestry, though he did not stress it as part of his political identity. He was, as we have seen, never actually poor, but he often pretended to have been, and very likely he did *feel* poor, especially in his earlier years, compared to the rich men with whom he came into contact and, sometimes, into conflict. His relative skinniness in youth was probably one reason that he never excelled on the football gridiron as he passionately yearned to do. Finally, though his looks were in fact no worse than about average, he was frequently made to feel physically ugly, especially by political opponents (as in the Herblock cartoons he so hated) and especially when he came into direct competition with the stunningly handsome John Kennedy. Jewishness, then, is the only trait on Nixon's list that has no direct, obvious relevance to his own history. Why did he include it?

It is reasonable to speculate that, just as Nixon often seemed to feel considerably less prosperous and less good-looking than he really was, so he also felt himself to be, in some complex and counter-factual sense, Jewish. Or, more precisely, perhaps we should say that, as Horkheimer and Adorno would lead us to expect, Nixon identified to a significant degree with his own anti-Semitic (yet also philo-Semitic) image of the Jew. It is noteworthy that, in the remarks quoted by Clawson, intelligence and anger are the two main qualities he names that enabled him to resist his own social marginalization and to fight back against the "laughs and snubs and slights." In an ideological space largely defined by anti-Semitism, there is something recognizably "Jewish" in the profile of Richard Nixon that he himself tended to favor. For one thing, Nixon, like the Jews, was accused of many bad things but never of stupidity. Indeed, even despite the fact that, generally speaking, liberal Democrats like to think that their side has a monopoly on intelligence and frequently characterize their political opponents as mentally inferior, Nixon's intellectual capability was simply too obvious for the insult to work in his case. Yet the Nixonian intelligence was of a recognizably "Jewish" variety: cold, penetrating, analytical, based on sheer studiousness (his "iron butt") and on intrinsic intellectual firepower, but utterly detached from the "well-roundedness" that athletic prowess and an engaging, honest, outgoing personality would supply. Richard Nixon, as understood *by* Richard Nixon, was a man born with the world against him, a "lean and mean" man forever full of angry grievances. He was also one who, through sheer power of brains and will, used his anger to *force* the world to reward him in ways it never really wanted to—while all the time necessarily walking the edge of the precipice that overlooked disaster (in the actual event, of course, it turned out to be the *unique* disaster of forced presidential resignation in August 1974).

Is this anything other than the mythic image of the Jew in traditionally dominant ideology? In its connotations of monomaniacal intellectual coldness and at least potentially destructive intent, it is, of course, an anti-Semitic image, but one that, depending, so to speak, upon the lighting, may look philo-Semitic as well. For the Jew, in this understanding, is something of a Jack the Giant-Killer or (a more obvious comparison) a David against Goliath: i.e., a smart poor boy who succeeds in the teeth of all the odds and against all the normal expectations. This is precisely the favorite self-representation of Nixon himself, who, in his writings, claims to have done hardly anything of importance that was not exceedingly difficult, often to the point of seeming to be all but impossible before it was actually accomplished by him.

It is, then, possible to appreciate why, as the Haldeman diaries and the White House tapes make clear, Nixon was so haunted by the figure of the Jew, why he saw Jews everywhere, especially throughout his own government, hindering and plotting against him—and yet also why indeed Jews *were* everywhere in his own government, in the sense of having been chosen by him in unprecedented numbers to serve as his own top aides. All bigotry is based on the definition of an Other whose stigmatization allows the bigot to define his own identity in a reassuring way. The anti-Semite, like Nixon, is pleased to consider himself as, at least, not Jewish, not one of *them*. But this operation turns out to be a good deal more complex, slippery, and dialectical than it first appears. In the way classically analyzed by Hegel in his philosophy of the master-slave dialectic, the fact that the authentic bigot has chosen to stake his own identity on the identity of the hated Other means that he is bound for life *to* the Other—and even that the boundaries that are meant to separate Self from Other will inevitably grow blurry. The anti-Semite wishes to overmaster the Jew but thereby becomes enslaved by his own mental image of the Jew. In the end, the look of anti-Semitic hatred directed at the Jew becomes difficult to keep entirely separate from the look in the mirror, since the mirror—like the Jew for the anti-Semite—is after all the place where identity is confirmed. It is impossible to loathe others for no particular reason, and especially to base one's life project on such loathing, as the consistent bigot does, without committing oneself to a good deal of *self*-loathing. Was Nixon "a bit of a Jew"? *Every* anti-Semite, as Horkheimer and Adorno understood, is on one level a bit of a Jew, so long as this "bit" is understood as the anti-Semite's own ideological construction. This, indeed, is the dirty little secret of anti-Semitism (and of such parallel ideologies as anti-black racism) that neither anti-Semite nor Jew is typically eager to discuss.

But Nixon fulfills this general pattern with a special thoroughness, partly because he was, so to speak, "really" a bit of a Jew to begin with. That Nixon largely conformed to the anti-Semitic stereotype of the Jew, and on some level was well aware and even proud of the fact, meant that in his case the borders between Self and Other became *especially* unclear. The collusion between anti-Semitism and philo-Semitism became especially complex and thoroughgoing; and the apparent (but only apparent) contradiction between his obsessive loathing for the Jews and his insistence on surrounding himself with Jews became especially glaring. Accordingly, the ironies of Nixon's anti-Semitism are particularly intense. Jews are disloyal, he told Haldeman: you can't trust the bastards. But, if Murray Chotiner had been disloyal, he could have sabotaged Nixon's political career when it was just beginning. If Arthur Burns had been disloyal, he could have tried to wreck the American economy and impaired Nixon's chances of re-election in 1972. If Henry Kissinger had been disloyal, he could have unraveled the intricate geopolitical schemes that were Nixon's chief professional pride and joy. In fact, all the men whom Nixon might have cited to prove that some of his best friends were Jewish remained loyal, most of them grotesquely so. Even after Nixon's death, some continued to publish apologias for their late boss. There is richly dark humor—it is nearly a sort of cosmic Jewish joke—that the one important Nixon aide who really *was* disloyal was no Jew but rather the almost stereotypical WASP, John Wesley Dean. It was Dean's testimony before the Senate Watergate Committee in the summer of 1973 that set in motion the chain of events and disclosures that led to Nixon's being forced to resign the presidency in disgrace.

It should be evident, then, that anti-Semitism is a special form of the *ressentiment* that we discussed in the preceding chapter—as, indeed, Nietzsche himself was acutely aware (hence Nietzsche's special loathing for the anti-Semite, and the importance that Richard Wagner's anti-Semitism assumed in Nietzsche's withering polemics against the composer). The anti-Semite attaches himself to the Jew just as the man of "classical" *ressentiment* attaches himself to the hero. The fact that the attachment is an entirely negative, reactive one, an attachment based on hatred and besmirching, does not render it any the less intense or compelling—quite the contrary. As we have seen, anti-Semitism, like *ressentiment* in general, can be so compelling as to be crucial to the anti-Semite's own sense of self. For Nietzsche, of course, Christianity is the privileged matrix of *ressentiment*, the most important tradition in which selfhood is based on reactive bigotry. And it is hardly a co-incidence that the roots of anti-Semitic movements and ideologies are overwhelmingly Christian: both in the sense that historic Christendom has been the geographic homeland of anti-Semitism (the relative tolerance traditionally—though not recently—extended toward Jews by Islamic culture is the main point of contrast), and in the sense that anti-Semitism has generally been most virulent in those sectors of Christian Europe where the churches have exercised the greatest ideological and temporal influence.

In this context, it is worth mentioning that Nixon's own Christianity was not nearly as superficial as many have assumed from the politically opportunistic uses to which he put it. He was raised in a strictly religious household, though he seems to have responded somewhat less consequentially to the particular doctrines of his mother's Quakerism, with its special opposition to war and racism, than to his father's more generically Protestant-fundamentalist heritage. Although he did not spend his life as a missionary (Hannah Nixon's hope for her son), he did establish the unprecedented institution of the White House prayer breakfast. He also maintained important long-term connections with such prominent religious figures as Norman Vincent Peale and Billy Graham—the latter, as we have seen, himself a vicious anti-Semite (though, like Nixon, a *private* anti-Semite, who, on the White House tapes, is heard musing about how shocked his Jewish friends would be to learn his true feelings).

The Nixonian anti-Semitism fits as well with his petty-bourgeois background as with his Christian *ressentiment*. Jean-Paul Sartre, in his important book *Anti-Semite and Jew*, maintains, indeed, that anti-Semitism in general is essentially a petty-bourgeois phenomenon. The working class, says Sartre, tends to be largely immune to such bigotry, whereas the rich, though they may cynically exploit anti-Semitic ideologies for their own political purposes, rarely abandon themselves wholeheartedly to anti-Semitic passion—"they have better things to do," as Sartre puts it. Sartre writes within a French and European context, of course; and it is surely more from the Old World than from the New that one would take historical examples to support his thesis. Sartre is doubtless thinking not only of the overwhelmingly petty-bourgeois character of the anti-Dreyfusards in that controversy which constituted such a watershed in modern French political and cultural history, but also—writing, as he was, in a Paris only recently liberated from German occupation—of the fact that the German petty bourgeoisie was the only social stratum from which the Nazi Party managed to mobilize a mass base prior to Hitler's seizure of state power in 1933 (their considerable attempts to recruit from the German proletariat having proved generally unsuccessful).

It would be difficult to cite similar instances from American history, partly because, as we have noted, political anti-Semitism in America has never been anywhere near as important as in Europe—and also partly because, for reasons discussed in the second chapter, the cultural and ideological divisions between socio-economic classes in America have always been less sharp anyway. Still, even in America, there does seem to be something intrinsic to the economic situation of the lower middle class that is especially congruent with anti-Semitic feeling. What anti-Semitism offers above everything else, after all, is *identity*, a sense of selfhood based on stigmatization of the Jew; and identity is precisely what is likely to be most wanted by the petty bourgeois, with his ambiguous and insecure social place as neither worker nor "real" bourgeois. Unable to enjoy the luxury of looking down on people in the manner of the big bourgeoisie, the petty-bourgeois anti-Semite can at least look down on the Jew—who, indeed, can be regarded as both quasi-proletarian (as society's oppressed outsider) *and* as quasi-bourgeois, thanks to the remarkably persistent anti-Semitic myth of Jewish control of finance capital. It is in this way that Sartre describes anti-Semitism as "a poor man's snobbery." We might add that Nixon's upbringing took place not only within the lower middle class, but in the especially rootless, transient, and identity-poor environment of southern California. Beyond even that, his hunger for a sense of self could only have been aggravated by the almost absurd gap between the national and even global ambitions he harbored from an early age and his evident prospects as the son of a Whittier shopkeeper. It is not difficult to understand why Nixon, like so many lower-middle-class Christians before him, should have clung strongly to the identity granted by anti-Semitism: so strongly, indeed, that, on the evidence of the White House tapes, he sometimes almost seemed incapable of privately discussing any public issue without giving vent to his hostility toward the Jews—except, of course, when he was conferring with one or more of his numerous Jewish associates.

As a special and especially petty-bourgeois form of *ressentiment*, anti-Semitism is, then, crucial to Nixon's political and cultural identity. But, because of its private nature in the

Nixonian case—because there were no anti-Semitic public roads to supreme power in Nixon's America—it was only *indirectly* crucial to Nixon's political and cultural impact. In order to move beyond the fascinating but ultimately limited universe of the Haldeman diaries and the White House tapes, and into the greater public world of overt cultural power, it is necessary to "translate," so to speak—as Nixon himself did—anti-Semitism into another form of bigotry, one that has historically played a role in the US roughly equivalent to that played by anti-Semitism in Europe: anti-black racism. Whereas Nixon's anti-Semitism was a mainly private matter, racism was the issue that contributed more than any other to Nixon's capture of the absolute summit of American politics.

3

It will be useful to begin with a review of certain historical facts: facts that, owing to the remarkable transformation of the Republican Party for which Nixon himself was more responsible than any other single individual, have become difficult to grasp today. Indeed, re-acquaintance with the racial character of the party's pre-Nixonian past may involve a certain shock of defamiliarization. Of course, everyone knows that the GOP began its electoral success as the Party of Lincoln. The Great Emancipator was, in 1860, only the second Republican presidential nominee ever. But it is in the period just after Lincoln's assassination that the Republicans, under the leadership of such Radicals as Senator Charles Sumner and Congressman Thaddeus Stevens, made a truly decisive commitment to freedom for blacks. The Civil Rights Act of 1866 and the Fourteenth Amendment to the US Constitution (proposed in 1866 and ratified two years later) retroactively established the principle that the Civil War had been fought not only to preserve the Union or even to free the slaves but also to establish racial equality in America—a point on which Lincoln himself had always been somewhat ambiguous. The project of Radical Reconstruction, promoted by the Republican Party and guaranteed by federal troops stationed in the South, ushered in the only period of political democracy that the South ever enjoyed until about 1970. The administration of the Republican President Ulysses Grant (1869-1877), traditionally so maligned by white historians, provided a golden age for black aspirations. To this day, the major Radical Republicans—most especially Stevens—have never been matched among nationally powerful Republican (or Democratic) leaders as passionate and effective advocates for racial justice.

The Radicals' hey-day was brief. Even at the height of their influence, in 1868, they suffered a major setback when they impeached the ferociously racist President Andrew Johnson but narrowly failed to remove him from office. In 1877 their defeat was decisive. That was the year of the Hayes-Tilden Compromise, in which, in effect, the Democrats agreed to let the Republicans steal the hotly disputed presidential election of 1876, and the Republicans, in return, agreed to withdraw federal troops from the South and to abandon their commitment to civil rights for blacks. Thus marginalized within their own party, the Radicals passed from the center stage of American history.

But—and this is the point that has been almost totally forgotten today—the influence of the Radicals, even if, often, in very attenuated form, persisted within the GOP for most of a century after Hayes-Tilden. Though the Republicans never again stood forthrightly for black freedom, the Democrats, with their dependence upon the Solid South, *did,* for many decades, stand pretty forthrightly for white racism. Partly by default, then, as well as partly due to the Radical heritage (and also to the luster of the increasingly iconic figure of Lincoln), the Republicans continued, long after 1877, to be the natural home, insofar as the major parties were concerned, for African-Americans (and also for whites concerned with racial justice).

It is, for instance, quite typical that, early in the twentieth century, it was the Republican President Theodore Roosevelt who deeply outraged Southern whites by inviting an African-American guest (Booker T. Washington) to the White House. It is equally typical that, a few years later, it was the Democratic President Woodrow Wilson (born in Virginia) who instituted racial segregation in the federal civil service. Even as late as 1964, when the Civil Rights Act of that year was proposed and passed—by far the most important move toward racial justice taken by the national government in nearly a century—the partisan line-up on civil rights looks totally bizarre according to the normal assumptions of today. Everett McKinley Dirksen, the deeply conservative leader of the Senate Republicans, was instrumental in passing the act, playing a far more prominent role than the Democratic leader, Mike Mansfield. Furthermore, Dirksen's pro-civil-rights position was supported by all but six of his 32 Republican colleagues, including such legendary right-wingers as Karl Mundt of South Dakota and Roman Hruska of Nebraska—both of whom were, on nearly every other issue, as crustily reactionary as anyone the Senate could boast. On the other side of the aisle, nearly a third of the 67 Democrats adopted the Ku Klux position and voted against the bill. Among the nay-sayers were such relatively "moderate" Southerners as Albert Gore of Tennessee (father of the future vice-president) and William Fulbright of Arkansas—both soon to become liberal heroes because of their opposition to the Vietnam War.

Still, by the 1930s the partisan dimension of racial politics in America had gotten complicated. Franklin Roosevelt's New Deal, after all, represented the greatest flowering of social democracy in the entirety of American history. Despite the Democratic Party's evil racial history, and despite its continuing institutional commitments to the racist white oligarchies of the South, New Deal liberalism included a measure of racial liberalism. To be sure, the attraction of the New Deal for blacks may well have had more to do with Eleanor Roosevelt's outspoken views on civil rights than with any racially specific policies that her husband actually implemented. FDR even refused to support a federal anti-lynching law, for fear of offending influential Southern Democrats in Congress. Still, the fact that African-Americans were overwhelmingly poor and working-class did mean that they benefited tremendously from racially nonspecific New Deal programs designed to alleviate the Great Depression. With the Republicans, then, usually stuck somewhere between being unable and being unwilling to do much for them, and with the New Deal appearing to offer something better, black voters flocked increasingly to the Rooseveltian and post-Rooseveltian Democratic Party. Unfortunately for the Republicans, this party shift was taking place just as blacks, though prevented from voting in the South by bureaucratic obstructions and by open physical terror, were becoming an important electoral force because of their increasing concentration in the big states of the Northeast and the northern Midwest. The Democrats, amazingly, became the party of *both* the black civil-rights advocate in Harlem *and* the white Ku Klux lyncher in Mississippi: an extraordinary balancing act, the underlying instability of which FDR himself was well aware. But, for the time being, the Democrats were having their cake and eating it too.

This was the basic situation confronting Richard Nixon when, in the 1950s, he was busily fashioning himself to be the future Republican nominee for president. The Republicans continued to be close to nonexistent in the South and yet, despite the heritage of Lincoln and Stevens, had lost much of their traditional pro-civil-rights constituency as well. It was no wonder that, except when they had the extraordinarily popular (and relatively nonpartisan) war hero Eisenhower as their nominee, they had failed to win any presidential election since 1928. How to improve this discouraging situation? Nixon reckoned that the South would in any case remain solidly Democratic for the indefinite future, but that the Republicans might be able to win back many black voters by making a bolder commitment to civil rights than they were generally in the habit of doing. The GOP could afford to continue writing off the South if they measurably improved their ability to win states like New York, Pennsylvania, and Michigan.

Though Nixon never did seem *totally* convinced of his own strategy, he took a number of significant steps toward implementing it. The historian Stephen Ambrose's description of Vice-President Nixon as "foursquare for civil rights" is an exaggeration, but an exaggeration of a solid truth. Most prominently, Nixon was a leading champion of the Civil Rights Act of 1957. This was the first civil-rights bill to become law since Reconstruction. Substantively weak, it was nonetheless considered of major symbolic value by many (though not all) civil-rights leaders, including, most notably, Martin Luther King, Jr. King worked closely with Nixon on the bill, and praised the vice-president's leadership as "an expression of your devotion to the highest mandates of the moral law." Though King, on principle, never endorsed candidates for political office, Nixon began the 1960 presidential campaign with the public support of King's father, the Rev. Martin Luther King, Sr. Admittedly, this endorsement was based partly on John Kennedy's Catholicism as well as on Nixon's civil-rights record. Even so, at that time there was nothing odd or surprising in the fact that a leading figure of the black church and the civil-rights community—which is what the elder King had been since long before his son attained even greater fame—should want Nixon for president.

These political factors and calculations ought to be remembered whenever one reads the moist-eyed tributes to Vice-President Nixon's anti-racism that a number of his admirers have penned. Even so, the fact that Nixon expected to gain electoral advantage by his work for civil rights does not necessarily mean that his convictions on the issue were counterfeit. There is even some reason to suppose that his distaste for segregation was largely sincere. Emphatic opposition to white racism was, after all, one of the fundamental tenets of the Quaker morality in which Hannah Nixon had raised her son. American Quakers had traditionally regarded black slavery, along with its aftermath in racial segregation, to be one of the supreme moral abominations of the world. Nixon's overwhelmingly Quaker home town was named after the New England poet John Greenleaf Whittier, a hero to the town's founders much less for his modest poetic skills than for his ardently Abolitionist stance against slavery. Even though Nixon was in some ways more his father's than his mother's son on moral and spiritual matters, that hardly means he was unaffected by the Quaker ethics of his mother and of his other relatives and most of his neighbors. Indeed, he emphatically considered himself a Quaker his entire life (though much to the horror of many other Quakers during the Vietnam War). Furthermore, Whittier, though small, was in some ways surprisingly cosmopolitan, and Nixon grew up in company with a number of Asian-American and African-American children and teenagers. Later, his Southern classmates at the Duke Law School in Durham, North Carolina, were shocked to hear that Nixon had actually eaten meals at the same table with blacks. No evidence that I have seen establishes that he was ever actually called a "nigger-lover"—the most insulting epithet that could at that time be hurled at a white person in the South—but his general views on race seem to have had just such connotations for his Southern acquaintances. Nixon's support for civil rights when vice-president seemed, then, to follow more-or-less predictably from his past.

But racial politics began to change dramatically—for Nixon and for the Republican Party overall—during the 1960 presidential campaign. In October, Martin Luther King was arrested in Georgia and, on a technicality involving a traffic infraction, was sentenced to four months in prison. His family was terrified (with good reason) that the authorities intended to murder King while they had him in custody; and the King family hoped that the situation might be saved if a nationally prominent political leader could be persuaded to intervene. Given the established relationship between Nixon and the Kings, they naturally contacted him first. When the Nixon campaign refused to help, they turned, essentially as an afterthought, to the opposing Kennedy camp. Senator Kennedy made a soon-to-be-famous phone call to King's wife, expressing sympathy and support, while Robert Kennedy, the campaign's manager, called the judge handling the case. King was soon released, and the response among African-Americans was overwhelming. John Kennedy, who, unlike Nixon, had never before displayed any particular interest in black freedom, remained forever after a hero to black America. King himself expressed gratitude to Kennedy, though he continued his policy of official electoral neutrality. But King's father (always, in many ways, a more outspoken figure than the younger Rev. King) called a highly publicized press conference to announce that he was withdrawing his endorsement of Nixon and now considered himself an enthusiastic supporter of Kennedy for president (despite the Massachusetts senator's unfortunate religious affiliation).

The rest, as they say, is history. The incident of October 1960 proved a watershed in that area where racial and party politics in America converge. The movement of black voters toward the Democratic Party that had begun under Roosevelt accelerated and led to the situation we know today, when African-Americans constitute the most reliably solid Democratic voting bloc in the country. Even more important, the Republicans began to understand that it was time for them to abandon the heritage of Lincoln—and, even more, of the Radicals—once and for all. They grasped that the way to build a nationally stable Republican majority (something that had not existed since the 1920s) was to win the loyalty of racist white Southerners who felt increasingly alienated by the anti-segregationist stands being taken by the national leaders of their own Democratic Party.

Of course, this transformation in Republican politics did not happen overnight. As we have seen, Republican support for the Civil Rights Act of 1964 was crucial to getting the bill through the Senate. But that same year, in the presidential election, Senator Barry Goldwater (who had broken from most of his Republican colleagues to vote against the Civil Rights Act) performed the historically extraordinary feat of carrying five Deep South states against the incumbent Texas Democrat, Lyndon Johnson. A few earlier Republican nominees had chipped away a little at the Solid South: Herbert Hoover in 1928 because of the Catholicism of his opponent, Al Smith, and Eisenhower in 1952 and 1956 because of his immense popularity as a war hero throughout the land. But Goldwater shattered the Solid South forever. At the time, the significance of Goldwater's achievement was obscure to most. His five Southern states were, aside from his native Arizona, the *only* states he won. The big story of the evening was naturally Johnson's precedent-breaking landslide. But the Johnson victory turned out to be the last hurrah for robust New Deal liberalism. It was Goldwater's Southern success that contained the promise—or threat—of the future.

No one, in the 1960s, understood this better than Richard Nixon. Even before the general-election campaign of 1968 began to unfold, Nixon formed a special relationship with the white South in order to help secure the Republican nomination. To some extent, this move was dictated by his unusual lack of a natural geographic base within the party. New York, where he was currently living and practicing law, was firmly controlled by his arch-rival Nelson Rockefeller, while his native California was now dominated by Ronald Reagan, who, despite his coyness on the matter, clearly had White House ambitions of his own. So Nixon, as we have seen, formed a crucial alliance with Senator

Strom Thurmond of South Carolina, who, upon his switch from the Democratic Party four years earlier, had instantly become the most influential of all Southern Republicans. Thurmond was also, as we saw in the first chapter, second only to George Wallace as a hero to white racists. Thurmond was thus the ideal ally to keep Southern Republicans (most of them former Democrats like himself) in line for Nixon; and he managed to do so even late in the pre-convention campaign, when many Southern Republicans began to cast yearning looks at Reagan.

But the Nixon-Thurmond axis and all it represented were even more important for the general election. This campaign was the one we designated, in the first chapter, as "the campaign against the niggers"; and it is remarkable how successful Nixon was in competing for white racist votes in an election where Wallace was on the ballot in all fifty states. "Law and order" was the dominant code phrase that year for hatred and fear of blacks, in large part because the cycle of inner-city riots over the past several years had revitalized the venerable American image of blacks as a mad, violent horde, and had sent much of white America into frenzies of racial paranoia. Nixon obliged prevailing sentiment with repeated thunderous denunciations of "lawbreakers" and of the federal courts, which were bitterly hated by racist whites for their crucial role in attacking school segregation as well as for their increasing sensitivity to the rights of criminal defendants. He also launched an especially nasty campaign of vilification against Attorney General Ramsey Clark, who had become a monster in racist eyes because of his position that black rioters ought to be arrested and prosecuted rather than shot on sight. In addition, Nixon went out of his way to express sympathy for whites being forced to endure some measure of school desegregation (even though, ironically, his own administration would go on to enforce such desegregation much more vigorously than any other had done). Indeed, the substance of Nixon's message in 1968 was virtually identical to Wallace's (who, it should be remembered, also talked in code, never explicitly denouncing blacks as such). At the same time, Nixon managed to speak in a sufficiently bland, suave tone that he distanced himself, rhetorically, from the popular stereotype of white racism defined by Wallace's fiery enthusiasm. Theodore White, whose then-popular "Making of the President" books specialized in gossip flattering to politicians, went so far as to write, in his volume on the 1968 campaign, "In 1968, Nixon conspicuously, conscientiously, calculatedly denied himself all racist votes, yielding them to Wallace." But it is questionable whether even White believed this bizarre falsehood, and certainly no one else did. The chief effect of the sentence was to make White a laughingstock.

Nixon's strategy was brilliantly successful. Though Wallace carried five Deep South states—almost, though not quite, the same five Goldwater had carried in 1964—Nixon took *every* other state of the Old Confederacy, excepting only Texas, where Lyndon Johnson's political muscle was still strong enough to carry the state one (almost) last time for the Democrats. Indeed, though the 1968 election has gone down in the schoolbooks as a close election, this is true only in a technical sense. Admittedly, Nixon only narrowly edged out Humphrey in the popular vote: "I know what it's like to lose a close one," he quipped in sympathetic response to Humphrey's concession statement the morning after (still apparently consumed, even in the moment of his greatest triumph to date, with resentment and humiliation over 1960). But, if one adds together the votes garnered by the two racist candidates, the election looks like an ideological landslide. While Goldwater had shattered the Solid South four years earlier, Nixon and Wallace had, between them, very nearly *re-solidified* it, but with a reversed electoral orientation, that is, *against* the national Democratic Party. Although, as we have seen, numerous specific factors relating to Nixon's strengths and George McGovern's weaknesses contributed to the immense

Nixon landslide of 1972 (and not least important, of course, was the fact that the Nixon campaign employed all manner of crimes and dirty tricks), the basic lineaments of 1972 were already implicit in 1968. One might say that, in a long-term perspective, Wallace had "borrowed" the votes he won in 1968 from Nixon and the Republicans. In 1972 Nixon was able to reclaim his rightful property—unshared ownership of the race issue—owing to the convenient co-incidence that Wallace was shot and paralyzed before he could launch another third-party effort.

4

How did he do it? How did the Whittier Quaker, with his at least moderately pro-civil-rights record, manage so quickly and so decisively to become a campaigner who could first compete with George Wallace on the race issue and then outstrip him—and who, in so doing, succeeded (by building on the Goldwater run of 1964) in recasting American electoral politics into a racial pattern that endures to this day? To be sure, Thurmond's imprimatur, as we have seen, was of considerable importance here. The South Carolina senator had been the most durable national hero of white racism ever since 1948, when (anticipating Wallace by two decades) he made a third-party presidential run based on the white South's savage attachment to segregation. Still, Thurmond in 1968 was an important ally and helper of Nixon's, but not a kingmaker—a political animal that had pretty much ceased to exist in America by Nixon's time anyhow. Fundamentally, nobody ever *gave* Richard Nixon anything, as he would have been the first to insist. He became the dominant, if relatively "moderate," political face of American racism—in a way that confused a few naïve journalists like White but was instantly clear to white racists and African-Americans alike—primarily by his own qualities and efforts. Furthermore, with regard to the Thurmond connection, one should after all consider just how Nixon managed to win the loyalty of the South

Carolina senator in the first place. For no serious student of Thurmond's career ever doubted that his hatred of black aspirations was as deeply felt as it was politically useful ("Look at ol' Strom up there—he really *believes* all that stuff," as one Southern senator is said to have murmured to another while they watched Thurmond filibuster against a civil-rights bill). Winning over Thurmond was not necessarily easier than winning over the millions of racist voters who revered him.

The answer is implicit in Nixon's entire character and career up until 1968. Though anti-black racism happened not to be a significant component of his earlier personal make-up or political tool-kit, it fit with fearful ease into his general public and private personality. As the politician of petty-bourgeois *ressentiment* and anal-erotic rectitude, and as one who indulged in anti-Semitism as a kind of deadly serious hobby, Nixon operated from within an ideological formation whose gravitational field attracted nothing so "naturally," in America, as anti-black racism. Nixon was a past master at moralistic and demagogic scapegoating, at stigmatizing the threatening Other or outsider in order to play on the darkest fears and loathings of those who ardently craved "normalcy" (President Harding's coinage) and a secure sense of identity. It was precisely in this way that he had become one of the two supreme Red-baiters of the 1950s, and even more skillful, in the long run, than Joe McCarthy, though lacking McCarthy's histrionic genius. Furthermore, Nixon's own gnawing, obsessive anti-Semitism must have made him aware of how the fire of ethnic hate burns hotter than even the most extreme political antipathies. In retrospect, Nixon's very un-Quaker adoption of racism looks nearly inevitable.

We might say that Nixon and American racism were a marriage just waiting to happen, if a marriage made quite a few miles lower than Heaven. For, as we have noted, it has always been racism, rather than anti-Semitism, that has served as the privileged expression of lower-middle-class resentment and hatred in the US. The savage, rapacious black has served roughly the same mythic function in this country that the wily, treacherous Jew has in Europe. To pick two examples, nearly at random, from widely separated points in history and from vastly different places on the aesthetic scale: The representation of blacks as a mad, murderous horde in Herman Melville's powerful novella *Benito Cereno* (1855) amounted to (implicit) propaganda for the racist Democratic Party (for racial issues would be crucial in the presidential contest of 1856, when the passionately anti-slavery John Fremont became the first Republican presidential nominee), just as the image of the crazed black killer Willie Horton in the television commercials that Roger Ailes made for the elder George Bush in 1988 were (explicit) propaganda for the racist Republican Party. A very crooked but unbroken line connects Melville to Ailes (who got his start in politics as a Nixon staffer); and this line often leads to the White House, as the victories of James Buchanan over Fremont and of Bush over Michael Dukakis illustrate. Though a racist campaign does not, of course, *invariably* produce victory (Goldwater's Deep South appeal could not save him from landslide defeat, and in 2008 an extraordinary combination of circumstances made Barack Obama the first African-American president), race has been, at least since the 1840s, the most durably successful issue in American politics.

Indeed, since racism fit so well with Nixon's political identity as the pre-eminent spokesman for petty-bourgeois *ressentiment* as well as with his own practical goal—winning the presidency—the real question is perhaps not how and why he became such an effective racist campaigner in 1968 but how and why he had generally *avoided*, and sometimes even opposed, racism earlier in his career. Doubtless some of the credit should go to Hannah Nixon and to Whittier Quakerism in general, and some, also, to his mistaken calculations in the 1950s as to how the Republican Party might be strengthened nationally. What is more important to stress, however, is that the racist solution Nixon found in 1968 not only won for him two terms in the White House (and what would have been two *full* terms had Nixon not destroyed his own presidency during Watergate) but also helped to restructure American electoral politics permanently. In the very short run, admittedly, it may have superficially appeared that Nixon's (and Goldwater's) party-building work had gone for naught. For in 1976, in the first post-Watergate presidential contest, Jimmy Carter rebuilt the Solid South for the Democrats. But this achievement turned out to be a one-time fluke, based largely on an apolitical regional pride at the prospect of the first unambiguously Southern president since the Civil War (Lyndon Johnson always stressed that he was a Southwesterner, not a Southerner, while Woodrow Wilson's Virginia birth was much less prominent in his public profile than his New Jersey political base). Furthermore, even in 1976 a majority of the *white* Southern vote went not to Carter but to the incumbent Republican Gerald Ford, an affable Michigan conservative who did not play the race card with anything like Nixonian flourish. Already the Republican Party had become, thanks mainly to Nixon, the "default" choice, so to speak, of the racist voter.

This pattern has only grown clearer and stronger in the years since. In 1980 Carter himself lost the entire South save only his native Georgia. On the basis of the same issue—white racism—the region has become very nearly as solid for the Republicans in presidential elections as it once was for the Democrats. And the identical story is plain on the Congressional level. When the Democrats were the preferred party of racism, their House and Senate leadership was dominated by Southern whites. The same is true today of the Republican leadership in those bodies, with a special prominence having at times attached to such virulently overt racists as Tom DeLay of Texas in the House and Trent Lott of Mississippi in the Senate. Kevin Phillips, who in his youth was Nixon's most brilliant political aide, and who today writes as an acute journalistic observer of the US political scene, once said, during Nixon's 1968 campaign, that "the whole secret of politics" lay in "knowing who hates who." Nixon understood that secret even better than Phillips himself, and, owing mainly to Nixon, Nixon's party has never forgotten it.

Of course, more than simple hatred is at work here. As we have discussed, the immense power of an ideology like racism lies not only in the (quite real) pleasures of hatred as such but, as thinkers from Hegel and Nietzsche to Adorno and Sartre have analyzed, in the larger sense of identity and order that such hatred supplies. "Hate," indeed, becomes a somewhat ambiguous term here. There are plenty of people who "hate," in a perfectly cool, straightforward way, Sylvester Stallone movies, or fast food, or televised golf tournaments, or what-have-you. But nobody builds a life on such aversions; one simply avoids those things and moves on. But white racism, like anti-Semitism, is precisely about building a life—a self—and no modern politician has ever seen more clearly than Nixon just how many millions of Americans, especially though by no means entirely in the South, construct selfhood largely through stigmatization of the black. Needless to say, there are many parallel operations in many other places. We have already mentioned the role of anti-Semitism in Europe, and Nixon's private "training," as it were, in anti-Semitism doubtless played an indispensable role in helping him to master the emotional valences of racism. There is certainly no shortage of other examples of such stigmatization: the significance of the Irish Roman Catholic for many Ulster Protestants, or of the Kurd for many Turks and Arabs, or of the Arab Palestinian for many Jewish Israelis, to give a few instances. Furthermore, anti-black racism is itself found nearly everywhere on the globe that white people are found. The cultural power of ethnic hatred is not uniquely American.

What *is* unique about America (or nearly unique: the exceptions are white-ruled Rhodesia and apartheid South Africa) is the degree to which racism has always been of not contingent but *systemic* importance for this country, economically, politically, and culturally. What the poet Langston Hughes called "The great mistake/That Jamestown made/Long ago"—that is, the importation, in 1619, of kidnapped Africans to serve as slaves in the first permanent English-speaking colony in the New World—set in motion the structuration of Anglophone America as a country *defined* by the opposition of white and black.

Originally, to be sure, this construction of "race," as it later came to signify in the US, was logically accidental. The slave-traders set sail for Africa not out of any disinterested desire to do harm to the dark-skinned people who lived there, but for purely economic motives. Chattel slavery began as important and soon became indispensable to the profitability of Southern agriculture. But the crime of the slavers was one of almost unthinkable proportions—certainly one of the most immense in the history of the planet. It is not "only" that the Africans were ripped from their homes, subjected to the frequently lethal horrors of the Middle Passage, and then, if they reached the New World alive, forced to work in conditions so painful and degrading that not even the poorest free laborers could be persuaded to endure them. On top of all that, they were also (and mainly in order to discourage insurrection) deliberately separated from others of their family or language groups, and, for at least the first few generations in the New World, were raised and bred in pens without benefit of coherent families at all—thus devastating the development of African-American culture. As the justification of this gargantuan crime became a psychological and ideological necessity, doctrines of black inferiority and white supremacy became fundamental to a viable sense of white American identity—particularly in the South, where alone slavery proved economically feasible in the long run, but also throughout the whole land. (At the dawn of American slavery, the project could be justified by arguing that it was actually an act of beneficence to expose the African heathens to the true Christian faith; but, since the slaves *were* soon Christianized, this argument became obsolete.) Racism became, necessarily, as American as apple pie: indeed, a great deal more so.

The overthrow of chattel slavery in the Civil War did not end or even measurably diminish the importance of white racism as the real bedrock of cultural power in America. Indeed, as the US became a more multi-ethnic and multi-cultural nation, racism took on a new kind of importance as one of the principal sources of the heat beneath the famous American "melting pot." For not the least attraction of America for European immigrants was the way that they could, upon touching US soil, instantly become "white" in the special American sense. Irish peasants condemned to forced starvation by their British economic and political rulers, or Jewish village-dwellers wont to being harassed and murdered by Cossack pogroms throughout the Russian Empire, might still face significant discrimination in the New World. But they belonged—incontestably, and, considering their history, astonishingly—to the New World's master race. Nor has the recent prominence of other "races" in the US polity fundamentally altered the basic white/black polarity of American culture. For instance, it is true that, for complex reasons, Hispanics (with the partial exception of Cuban-Americans) have generally been denied the opportunity to become white in quite the same way that the Irish, Jews, Italians, Poles, and other earlier immigrant groups were able to do. But what this means in ideological practice is that, especially in certain regions of the country, Hispanics are considered almost—*but never quite*—as bad, as stigmatized, as the blacks themselves. On the other hand, many groups of Asian-Americans seem now to be approaching the status officially granted by the apartheid government of South Africa to Japanese visitors, namely, that of "honorary whites." However complex the ethnic and "racial" make-up of US society may become—and leaving aside the extraordinarily complicated and important but numerically marginal situation of the Native Americans (who generally prefer to be called American Indians)—the original white/black opposition remains the central organizing principle of the culture.

Of course, the civil-rights efforts of the past half century or so have constituted a major ideological war on racism in America, with achievements that ought not to be underestimated. The opportunities available to many individual African-Americans today—extending even to the Oval Office—and the extent to which overtly racist discourse is now a semi-official taboo, are hardly even imaginable by the standards of 1950. But the success of anti-racism ought not to be exaggerated either. The civil-rights movement succeeded in diminishing white racism in some instances, and in navigating paths *around* white racism in others. But the desire of many white Americans to feel a sense of identity and distinction through superiority to the black remains powerful, even if it is often, today, forced beneath the surface of public discourse—where, perhaps, it may in some ways even be all the more virulent and dangerous for that. No American politician during the second half of the twentieth century—Robert Dole's "Age of Nixon"—understood and exploited American racism more consequentially than Nixon did. Though the point provides little raw material for Fourth of July speeches, white racism has always been one of the supreme forms of American cultural power. In this as in so many other ways, Richard Nixon, as Dole put it, indeed "embodied the deepest feelings of the people he led." By so doing, he reconfigured American politics more radically than any other politician since Franklin Roosevelt.

V. Nixon as Liberal?

1

Nixon as the quintessential petty-bourgeois, as a man of *ressentiment*, as an example of the anal-erotic character, as anti-Semite, as racist—all of these descriptions may be controversial to one degree or another, but none is likely to seem radically counter-intuitive. Or, to put it another way, anyone who belongs to the still considerable number of Nixon's admirers might find these notions objectionable, but I doubt that any admirer would be surprised that a writer on the left has proposed them. But Nixon as *liberal*? For many readers, the chapter title must seem a deliberate paradox or provocation. They will suspect that some weird joke is intended, or that "liberal" is being used in some highly specialized and counter-intuitive sense, or that reference is being made to some obscure, marginal aspect of Nixon's career. For did not those who are normally called American liberals detest Richard Nixon with a passionate hatred they felt for no other American politician of the twentieth century? Did not the Jew-hating Nixon, in his Red-baiting, in his public distaste for the poor, in his highly successful exploitation of resentment and fear of blacks, appeal to all that was *least* liberal in the American electorate?

And yet the idea of Nixonian liberalism is by no means a new one in Nixon studies. Even during the Nixon Administration, right-wing intellectuals often complained that the actual policies of the White House were a great deal less conservative than presidential rhetoric was meant to suggest. More recently George Will, perhaps the weightiest intellectual eminence on the US journalistic right, has written that the liberalism of Nixon's presidency, was, among all administrations since the Second World War, second only, and barely, to Lyndon Johnson's (though it should be noted that Will wrote prior to the election of

Barack Obama). On the other side of the political spectrum, *The Nation*, which is effectively the flagship periodical of radical left-liberalism in America, has editorialized (also before the Obama presidency) that Nixon's presidency was, at least, "not illiberal by the standards of his successors."

These journalistic generalities are supported by a good deal of concrete evidence, as professional historians of the Nixon era are increasingly coming to appreciate. During the Nixon Administration federal spending on domestic social programs exceeded military spending for the first time. The former accounted for 28% of the federal budget under Lyndon Johnson (who had expanded social programs more dramatically than any president since Franklin Roosevelt), but climbed to 40% by the time that Nixon left office. One lavishly funded new program was the so-called "war on cancer"—a huge infusion of cash into medical research on the disease—that Nixon himself, in later years, sometimes mentioned (for instance, in the David Frost interviews) as the most important achievement of his presidency, even more consequential than the opening to China. Hardly less momentous were the Clean Air Act of 1970—easily one of the two or three most important pieces of environmental legislation in US history—and the concomitant creation of the Environmental Protection Agency. The automatic cost-of-living adjustments to Social Security that Nixon supported were probably the most important expansion of the Social Security system since its creation in the New Deal. Despite Nixon's personal wariness of artists as left-wing Jews, federal support for the arts *quadrupled* during his administration.

Even on the race issue, Nixon's presidential record does not, at first sight, look like what one would expect from the racist nature of the 1968 campaign. Not only did Nixon become the first president seriously to enforce the 1954 Supreme Court decision that mandated school desegregation, but affirmative action—today the signature issue of racial liberalism in America—was effectively invented in Nixon's Justice Department under Attorney-General John Mitchell, who produced the "Philadelphia Plan" for the integration of certain labor unions. Nixon himself sometimes referred with pride to his liberalism. One of his all-time political heroes was Benjamin Disraeli, the Tory (and ethnically Jewish) British prime minister who was primarily responsible for (among other liberal measures) the Reform Act of 1867, which greatly expanded the franchise in the United Kingdom. It was with Disraeli in mind that Nixon commented to Daniel Patrick Moynihan, a fellow admirer of Disraeli's and, for a short time early in the Nixon presidency, Nixon's most important liberal aide, "Of course you know perfectly well that it has always been Tory men with liberal principles who have enlarged democracy."

Before, however, we become too enraptured with the image of Richard Nixon as Franklin Roosevelt *redivivus*, it should be admitted that, in many of its particular instances, there was somewhat less to the Nixonian liberalism than met the eye. Many of Nixon's most important liberal achievements, like the environmental measures and the Social Security COLAs, originated in the Democratically controlled Congress and were hugely popular with the public at large. Nixon, despite being unenthusiastic about or, sometimes, even initially opposed to such measures, in the end simply decided to go along with prevailing trends rather than to cast politically damaging vetoes. It should be remembered that, on economic issues, American political culture in the late 1960s and early 1970s was still, by post-1980 standards, overwhelmingly progressive.

Something much more sinister was at work in his support for affirmative action and school desegregation. For these moves were not a departure from his successfully racist 1968 campaign but, paradoxically, a continuation of it. Nixon reckoned that to force school integration on Southern whites who had fiercely resisted it for a decade and a half, and to give blacks an advantage in some hiring situations, would help to provoke an intense "white backlash"—especially in the electorally all-important South but also throughout large sections of the white Northern petty bourgeoisie and better-paid proletariat. Moreover, it would be a backlash, as Nixon accurately calculated, directed *not* at him or at his own party, but instead at imprecise ideological constructions of "the federal government" and "the liberal establishment," both entities strongly identified in voters' minds with the Democratic Party. The nature of the 1968 campaign would by itself have probably insulated him from white racist anger (except at the extreme, and politically negligible, fringes of Ku Kluxery). But, just to make sure, Nixon continued to augment his racist credentials by such decisions as his nomination to the Supreme Court of Harold Carswell—an unknown, undistinguished Florida judge whose only real qualification for the nation's highest bench was a record of clear hatred of African-Americans.

It may seem incredible that a sitting president could make himself the beneficiary of racist sentiment often euphemistically described as "anti-government" feeling. But the concrete link between racism and "anti-government" ideology was the fact that the federal government under Kennedy and Johnson had become the most powerful force supporting, to a significant degree, civil rights for blacks. Nixon's strategy was extremely successful, as was most abundantly confirmed by the huge margins he rolled up in the Southern states, and among white voters generally, in the 1972 election. He was particularly successful in his special aim of splitting the black from the white working class, becoming, as we have seen, the first Republican ever to win a majority of votes cast by members of labor-union households. Indeed, Mitchell's Philadelphia Plan was specifically designed to inflame racism among white trade unionists.

Nonetheless, even after all such allowances have been made for the characteristically Nixonian double purposes and hidden agendas, it is still true that the amount of liberal policy produced by the Nixon White House is striking in view of Nixon's fairly consistent electoral profile as a conservative Republican. Furthermore, it can be argued that the Nixonian liberalism is a matter not merely of this piece of legislation or that new government agency, but involves some of the fundamental components of his overall political character. Such, indeed, is the argument of Garry Wills's *Nixon Agonistes: The Crisis of the Self-Made Man* (1969), which remains, I think, the most important single work in Nixon studies. Though occasionally flawed by empirical errors—mainly as a result of being composed when professional historical scholarship of Nixon's career had not really yet begun—Wills's book is still the only major (nonfictional) treatment of Nixon that offers not only well-researched detail and engaging narrative but genuine conceptual brilliance too.

Wills's central conceptual category—constructed by means of an unusual combination of G. K. Chesterton's Distributism with certain elements of the then-contemporary New Left—is the (often capitalized) Market, which he sees as the fundamental value of all liberalism. The Market is understood as a radically individualistic site (or process) of unfettered competition, which its adherents hold to be both automatically self-regulating and productive of the best results attainable in any sphere of life in which it is allowed to operate. With particular reference to American history and culture, Wills identifies four varieties of the Market: the economic market, that is, traditional laissez-faire capitalism or "free enterprise"; the political market, that is, the system of American-style elections upheld as a sacred universal by Woodrow Wilson; the intellectual market, or, as it is more commonly called, the "marketplace of ideas," in which truth is held to be most likely to emerge from the widest and least fettered possible exchange of views; and, perhaps most complex, the moral market, a kind of Emersonian striving and self-reliance, an endless ethical compulsion to be constantly making and remaking oneself with as little assistance from outside oneself as possible. Wills argues that Nixon's largest significance is as the exemplar and exponent of market liberalism in all its forms, and that Nixon's chief ambition in the 1968 campaign (the book grew out of Wills's assignments as a reporter covering that election) was to re-affirm and even revitalize the Market at a time—the late 1960s—when skepticism of the Market and outright hostility to it were growing.

Wills's own attitudes toward Nixon and the Market are somewhat ambivalent. He displays genuine respect for the achievements of liberalism and for Nixon's struggle to continue upholding the primacy of the Market—an *agon* or struggle, he says, that is "loftier than men give him credit for." Yet Wills is, in his idiosyncratic way, basically hostile to liberalism from *both* the left (1960s radicalism) and the right (Chesterton—though Chesterton is, admittedly, on the right in a very complex and unusual way). His book probably does more intellectual damage to Nixon than anything else ever written about him. The rebukes of Nixon begin on the page after the title page, in the dedication to (evidently) a relative of the author's, who is said to have "lived for others": in implicit but sharp contrast to the furiously individualist Nixon.

Wills's intellectual anatomy of market liberalism, though fruitful and illuminating, is not without its limitations. It is never clear in *Nixon Agonistes* whether the four markets have a merely metaphoric relationship to one another, on the one hand, or whether, on the other, the Market is meant as an indwelling Hegelian essence that expresses itself in different forms without ever ceasing to be itself (or Itself). In other words: is the Market one essential thing, or are there four different markets that display certain structural similarities? It is even less clear whether the four markets stand in any hierarchy of importance with regard to each other, and, if so, of what kind. Wills notes that those popularly called liberals in American politics tend to have an almost religious attachment to the intellectual market while being quite skeptical of the untrammeled economic market. With those popularly called conservatives, he adds, the situation is exactly reversed. But can we finally *have* one without the other? Wills does not say. Then too, the rather home-made conceptual structure of the book sometimes leaves Wills stranded out of his philosophic depths: as, for instance, when he attempts to discuss the Marxist humanism of Herbert Marcuse with hardly any evident knowledge of the whole Central European intellectual tradition in which Marcuse's thought is rooted.

A critique of *Nixon Agonistes* should also note the extent to which Wills often exaggerates Nixon's devotion to the liberalism of the Market. Admittedly, many of the most prominent counter-examples to Wills's generalizations come from the Nixon presidency, nearly all of which took place after Wills's book was completed. Still, Nixon's record of (for example) employing all sorts of lies and dirty tricks in electoral contests goes back, as we have seen, to the race against Jerry Voorhis in 1946, and simply found its highest and most spectacular expression in Watergate. This record can hardly be squared with a pristine Wilsonian worship of free elections. You would not say that a boxer was fanatically devoted to the Marquis of Queensberry rules if he habitually kicked and bit his opponents. Then too, during his presidency Nixon showed, by imposing wage and price controls in 1971, that he was even willing to violate, to some degree, the economic market, in a way that deeply outraged those (like most of Wills's old colleagues at *National Review*) who considered themselves the true apostles of laissez-faire. Though Wills could hardly have foreseen this turn to a measure of state planning of the economy (a move that surprised nearly all Nixon watchers and that, as we have seen, Nixon himself ultimately repudiated), it was only a couple of years *before* Wills's book was composed—

when Nixon was campaigning in 1966 for Republicans throughout the land—that Nixon demonstrated his contempt for academic freedom and the intellectual market by loudly and repeatedly demanding that a young Rutgers University history professor be fired for the views he had expressed about the Vietnam War.

Nonetheless, with all its imperfections—and some imperfections are inevitable in a book of such scope and ambition—*Nixon Agonistes* stands as perhaps the most compelling analysis we possess of the cultural power of the market, of the American liberal tradition. And it remains unmatched as an attempt to provide not just an empirical account of Nixon's career but a genuinely conceptual understanding of his overall significance. Wills's is the one book that no later attempt at serious conceptual analysis of Nixon—like the one undertaken in this volume—should fail to engage in some depth.

2

How should Wills's portrait of Nixon as "the last liberal" be understood in connection with the view of our thirty-seventh president that has been developed in the preceding pages? We should begin by agreeing that modern liberalism is indeed the philosophy of the market in Wills's sense; and we should note that this commitment to ceaseless individualistic competition renders liberalism's own self-identification as a philosophy of freedom deeply ambiguous. For liberalism, of its very nature, abhors all dogma, all fixed convictions, all first principles, all absolutes. In an overwhelmingly liberal intellectual atmosphere, the absolute becomes what a current Marxist philosopher has called "the fragile absolute." To the liberal, the only constant is perpetual change. In the economic market, capitalism must be allowed to proceed with its getting and spending in as unfettered a way as possible, regardless of the devastation to human beings and to their natural and cultural environment; and we should add that the limited degree of state intervention into the economy (such as Nixon's wage and price controls) proposed by the "liberalism" of social-democratic and New Deal Keynesianism can be understood not, ultimately, as an assault on the economic market but, on the contrary, as a tactical adjustment designed to save it from collapse. In the intellectual market, liberalism demands that everything must be questioned but that no definite conclusions can ever be drawn from this questioning process. Liberal intellectuals are fond of portraying themselves as embarked on a "search for truth," and yet (as Wills notes) they are also certain—*dogmatically* certain—that truth is the one thing that can never actually be found.

But how, after all, can any rational person expend effort on a search that is known in advance to lead nowhere? You can consider truth worth seeking even if you know the process to be arduous and uncertain of success, and the quarry never to be caught except in fragmentary, and perhaps ultimately statistical, form. But without the possibility of arriving at *some* kind of definable conclusion the whole attempt becomes preposterous. The extreme skepticism to which the intellectual market logically leads produces a kind of intellectual nihilism, which is incapable of affirming any positive value—including freedom itself, in whose name the liberal claims to be acting all along. Perhaps no thinker has ever formulated the paradoxes at work here more pointedly than Wills's theoretical mentor, Chesterton. In his most important conceptual work, *Orthodoxy*, Chesterton observes:

> At any street corner we may meet a man who utters the frantic and blasphemous statement that he may be wrong. Every day one comes across somebody who says that of course his view may not be the right one. Of course his view must be the right one, or it is not his view.

Chesterton goes on to make clear that the paralysis he thus

identifies is not only intellectual but entirely practical too. For you are not likely to act effectively on your beliefs unless you think that they are, in fact, correct. It is not easy to display the courage of your convictions if you *have* no convictions in the first place—or, to express the liberal's dilemma more precisely, if you have no convictions save the conviction that all convictions are to be viewed with unappeasable suspicion. As Chesterton puts it, "A strict rule is not only necessary for ruling; it is also necessary for rebelling. This fixed and familiar ideal is necessary to any sort of revolution." Or again: "There must at any given moment be an abstract right and wrong if any blow is to be struck."

It is important to understand that Chesterton's attack on liberalism is in no way a defense of conservatism, which he takes apart just as devastatingly:

> [A]ll conservatism is based upon the idea that if you leave things alone you leave them as they are. But you do not. If you leave a thing alone you leave it to a torrent of change. If you leave a white post alone it will soon be a black post. If you particularly want it to be white you must be always painting it again; that is, you must be always having a revolution. Briefly, if you want the old white post you must have a new white post.

Extrapolating a bit from this metaphor, we might add that the new white post will never be exactly the same as the old white post. The chemistry of paint-making changes, as do the most effective technologies of painting (entirely practical questions of just this sort do, in fact, often crop up during the "restoration" of old works of visual art). The one thing that is thus absolutely certain about the original white post is that it will inevitably *change*—and the choice Chesterton presents is between the destructive and wholly unplanned "torrent of change" to which conservatism will lead and the constructive, at least partly restorative change that he himself advocates. Chesterton is today most vividly remembered as a defender of tradition, which indeed he was. But what he shows is that tradition (the white post) and conservatism are in some ways antithetical. The conservative places himself in the strictly impossible position of being against change, like King Canute trying to block the tide. The traditionalist, by contrast, attempts to synthesize a certain continuity with the kind of change judged necessary to concretize the most desirable values of the past: and some of the measures that Chesterton himself thought necessary in his own time and place were actually pretty radical. They included, for instance, the abolition of capitalism. At this point, Chesterton's thought shows an interesting convergence with that of the Marxist critic and philosopher Walter Benjamin, who maintained that conservatives could never be true traditionalists and that it was socialist revolutionaries who needed and should care for tradition more than anyone else.

Furthermore, what Chesterton can also help us to see—though he himself never, I think, puts the matter in quite this way—is that there is a certain extremely consequential congruence between conservatism and liberalism. In philosophical terms, both are varieties of formalism. Both liberalism and conservatism represent themselves as social philosophies, yet both are remarkably reticent when it comes to specifying any positive *content* that would define the sort of social formation they regard as desirable. The conservative opposition to change means that the preservation of any given set of social arrangements in its actually existing form must take precedence over practical judgments as to the wisdom or unwisdom of particular features of the society in question—matters that conservatism regards as distinctly secondary in importance at best and as wholly irrelevant at worst. The core intellectual assumption here is the Burkean notion that the status quo, having been produced over an extended period of time by a great many individuals mainly unconscious of their ultimate object, is *bound* to be superior to any hastily conceived conscious planning. But conservatism is, like any formalism masquerading as a social philosophy, self-contradictory: not only in principle, by what we may call the Chestertonian paradox of the white post, but also in practice, in the sense that the conservative is likely to be troubled by this or that instance of relatively recent innovation and thus to demand not just the preservation of the status quo but the restoration of a status quo *ante*. In practice, conservatism often shades into reaction.

Nonetheless, the fact that conservatism does involve, however self-contradictorily, an image of the status quo (or status quo ante) means that it is not quite so desperately formalist as liberalism. For liberalism does not pursue a distorted and impossible goal, but, as we have seen, specifically abjures, in its strict form, all goals whatever. It favors, instead, ceaselessly changing processes of individualistic competition: the intellectual search for a truth that can never be found, the economic expansion of capitalism to no definable social end in particular, the institution of free elections regardless of the actual policies of those elected. To be sure, the radically formalist character of liberalism has in certain strategic ways been a source of strength; and we should not underestimate (as Wills, perhaps, sometimes does) the genuine debt owed to liberalism for its role in resisting a great many tyrannies large and small. The famous remark attributed to Voltaire, "I disapprove of what you say, but I will defend to the death your right to say it," is on one level the most empty proceduralism; and it certainly can be (and has been) applied in grotesque ways. Still, there can be little doubt that the overall effective force of this *bon mot* has been on the side of real, substantive freedom. Over the longer term, however, and in more intellectually fundamental ways, the formalism of liberalism has been an often disabling weakness. That a putatively social philosophy should decline, as liberalism does, to construct any image or concept of the social good save in entirely procedural, non-substantive ways means that at its heart lies a vast emptiness. As we will see, it is in this emptiness, this lack of content—which on one level is the inevitable emptiness of all individualism—that the real character of the Nixonian liberalism lies: the liberalism of this most desperately individualist of all American politicians.

For one thing, the relative absence of positive convictions in liberalism means that (as Chesterton would remind us) the courage of those convictions tends to be in short supply—and hence that, under pressure, liberalism may find it difficult to maintain itself. Nature abhors a vacuum, including the conceptual vacuum central to liberalism. Perhaps the most prominent modern American example of this weakness is the great anti-Communist purge of the late 1940s and early 1950s that formed the matrix of Nixon's own rise to power. The "great fear" has been so often associated by liberal journalists and historians with Republicans like Nixon and McCarthy that we often tend to forget that the purge was initiated by Democrats of thoroughly liberal profile, up to and including President Truman. Even after the anti-Communist witch-hunts (or, in a more accurate metaphor, heresy-hunts) were well underway, many liberals and Democrats did their pathetic best to hang on to the issue. It was, for instance, liberal heroes like Senators Wayne Morse of Oregon and Hubert Humphrey of Minnesota who tried (against the opposition of certain right-wing Republicans, ironically enough) to pass a bill outlawing the Communist Party. "I disapprove of what you say, and I'd like to put you in prison, or at least get you fired from your job, for saying it"—this, more than the Voltairean original, would have been a widely accurate motto for American liberalism during this period.

As was noted in chapter 1, Nixon's own first triumph of Red-baiting was achieved against a liberal Democrat—Jerry

Voorhis—who possessed a considerable record of Red-baiting himself, but who was (like every other American politician of the period except McCarthy) less skilled at the art than the (then) young and little-known Nixon. Furthermore, Nixon himself, during this time when anti-Communism was the common political currency across the spectrum of "mainstream" American discourse, did not look quite so *il*liberal as might today be assumed: and not only because of his consistently liberal internationalism, which contrasted with the isolationism still prevalent in the most conservative sections of the Republican Party. It is often forgotten that, when Congressman Nixon arrived in Washington in 1947, fresh from his victory over Voorhis the previous November, Joe Martin, the Republican House Speaker, rewarded him with a seat on the Un-American Activities Committee mainly because Martin wanted to give the committee a more *liberal* appearance. The committee was weighted down by very obviously crusty and cretinous reactionaries, and Martin hoped that Nixon would improve its image by contributing keen intelligence, youthful vigor, and a lawyer's sense of due process.

But the tendency of liberalism to collapse under pressure, as American liberalism largely did in the face of postwar anti-Communism, is only a specific instance of the more general instability that the overwhelmingly formal and procedural emphasis of liberalism tends to entail. Lacking the intellectual moorings of any more rigorously positive and principled system of thought, the adherents of liberalism often find themselves being buffeted this way and that, left or right, by the prevailing winds of the moment. Liberalism is in this way very close to pragmatism—that is, the cynical acquiescence in whatever seems to "work," regardless of exactly *how* it works, or for whom, or for how long, or whether it can be squared with any pre-existing principle, like justice. It is significant that, though it logically amounts to nothing other than the emptiest opportunism, the very term "pragmatism" is frequently used in a eulogistic sense within American liberalism. Liberal politicians often take pride in describing themselves as pragmatists. In contrast, politicians of (for instance) the Christian right, who actually profess substantive beliefs, almost never do.

It is in this way that Nixon can be most fruitfully considered a liberal. Nixon's skill, for example, at positioning himself (especially in 1964) between the Rockefeller and Goldwater wings of the Republican Party—remaining acceptable to both while never exactly committing himself to either—can be admired in a purely technical and tactical way. But it necessarily invites the largely justified accusation—extremely common among Nixon's detractors—that Nixon was always a hollow man, ideologically: one who opportunistically adjusted his politics to the pragmatic requirements of the moment, and never displayed real attachment to any goal save the accumulation of greater and greater political power in his own hands. Nixon, after all, was the exponent of strict neoclassical economics who, as president, imposed Keynesian wage and price controls. He was the sentimental campaigner who (falsely) claimed to have experienced poverty in his youth and who, in the White House, expressed the most unabashed and tasteless contempt for the poor. He was the law-and-order candidate who could demand reverence for the rule of law while also, and virtually in the same breath, inciting defiance of the Supreme Court. He was the heir of Quaker abolitionism and the co-worker with Martin Luther King who helped, more than any other single individual, to restructure the Republican Party as the party of white racism. He was the devotee of that "peace at the center" beloved in the Quaker tradition who rained devastation and death on Vietnam and Cambodia. He was the Red-baiting anti-Communist who, in the White House, initiated not only an opening to China but even a *de facto* alliance with the Communist Chinese government that he had himself done so much to demonize—and who also established the closest relationship with Soviet leaders of any president during the entirety of the Cold War.

The Nixonian opportunism cannot be understood apart from its cultural context within American liberalism. If Nixon often seems to be a hollow man, a politician whose views lack any consistent positive content, this emptiness must be situated within the larger, allied conceptual vacuum—that is, the formalism and consequent intellectual instability—of his liberal cultural and national situation. Ultimately, too, we must understand Nixon as liberal in conjunction with the other aspects of his political personality discussed in preceding chapters. It is now time to examine in greater depth a case-study of Nixonian liberalism by returning, as promised in chapter 1, to Nixon's 1960 presidential campaign against John Kennedy.

3

As we have seen, the 1960 presidential race was really the central event in Nixon's political career, the culmination of everything that came before and the beginning of everything that came after. Not co-incidentally, it was also, in many ways, the central American election of the twentieth century, as its chronological position near the century's middle point tends to suggest. John Kennedy was the first US president born in the twentieth century, something to which he expressly called attention in his inaugural address. But a more meaningful way to make much the same point is to say that he was the first president to fight as a young man in the Second World War. This fact points to the real generational shift that the 1960 election marked. Eisenhower (born in 1890) had been in the war, of course, but he was a middle-aged career officer when the war began; and he served as the supreme commander of all US and Allied troops in Europe. His immediate predecessors (Truman, born in 1884, and Franklin Roosevelt, born in 1882) were just a few years older than himself. By contrast, Kennedy (born in 1917) was more than a full generation younger than Eisenhower, and he performed *his* military service as a lowly PT boat commander in the Pacific theater. He was therefore young enough for the war years—that is, the years of the dominant geopolitical event of the twentieth century—to shape his early adulthood. The same was true of the six presidents who succeeded him. Of these, the oldest (Lyndon Johnson, born in 1908) was only nine years older than Kennedy, while the two youngest (Jimmy Carter and George H. W. Bush, both born in 1924) were only seven years younger. Nixon himself, it will be recalled, was born in 1913 and so just four years older than Kennedy. Like Kennedy, all six successors served as junior officers in the war (except for Carter, who spent the war years training at the Naval Academy in Annapolis and graduated a year after World War II had ended). The 1960 election thus ushered in a cohort of seven "G.I. Generation" presidents, who collectively occupied the White House for more than three decades. There was not another such generational shift until 1992, when the election of Bill Clinton (born in 1946 and hence more than a generation younger than the first President Bush) ushered in the first "Baby Boomer" president.

But some generational transitions are more significant than others, and the one marked by the 1960 election was probably the most significant for America of any since the Civil War and its aftermath. The fundamental national and global changes set in motion by the Second World War itself and by its most direct immediate consequences—such as the development of the Cold War and the unparalleled postwar economic boom—produced an authentically new era: an era that was, to be sure, already well underway in the 1950s (for the Eisenhower period, contrary to certain once-popular images of it, was a time of furious social and technological change, not of dull somnolence) but that intensified mightily during the century's seventh decade. Economically, the extraordinary boom of capitalist prosperity that produced a self-image of the US as an "affluent society" (in the much quoted phrase that John Kenneth Galbraith coined as the title of his popular 1958 book) reached its zenith in the 1960s, and began to abate soon afterwards. Technologically, the social changes wrought by such innovations as mass air travel and television—which were directly related to advances sparked by military necessity during the Second World War—really took told in the 1960s, as the first generation raised with these things began to come of age. In addition, the automotive revolution begun early in the century accelerated considerably with the rise of suburban housing patterns. In military and foreign affairs, the build-up of the anti-Communist Cold War and the national-security state—developments that included the unprecedented institution in America of a large peacetime standing army and even a peacetime draft—not only accelerated in the 1960s but also achieved their greatest single disaster with the Vietnam War. At home, the most enduring of all American agonies—race—entered a new phase in the 1960s, as the civil-rights movement that had been launched a decade earlier attained new force and recognition, and also gave birth to the Black Power and Black Pride movements: as well as helping to inspire an entire new series of insurgent social movements, such as environmentalism, women's liberation, Hispanic militancy, and gay liberation.

Accordingly, the 1960 election was devoted to choosing America's first president of a genuinely new age; and there was some awareness of the fact even at the time. Probably the most widely displayed campaign poster offered by the Kennedy-Johnson ticket promised that the Democratic candidates would provide "leadership for the 60s." Though "the 60s" could not, of course, have had quite the same connotations in the fall of 1960 that the phrase does today, there was already a widespread sense—related to the youth of both Nixon and Kennedy in contrast to the relatively old Eisenhower—that new things were in the air.

The stakes thus appear to have been so great that it may seem paradoxical to record that, in strictly ideological terms, the 1960 presidential contest was one of the *least* contentious in living memory. Various factors have combined over the years to camouflage this truth, most importantly the tendency to canonize Kennedy and demonize Nixon: so that, in retrospect, the competition seems to have been between a shining Sir Galahad of progress and enlightenment, on the one hand, and, on the other, a Count Dracula of the darkest reaction. It was not so. In the first place, Kennedy's credentials as a progressive were shaky at best. He had spent eight years as a fairly lazy and (as Northeastern Democrats at that time went) fairly conservative senator who, as Richard Reeves has pointed out in perhaps the best biography to date, had never—aside from his anti-Communism—displayed any particularly firm convictions about anything. In 1960 Hubert Humphrey and Adlai Stevenson, not Kennedy, were the preferred candidates of the left wing of the Democratic Party, that is, of those Democrats who most enthusiastically and unabashedly traced their political heritage to the New Deal—and who tended to regard Kennedy with considerable suspicion. As the 1960 campaign began, Kennedy was so far from being the hero of civil rights he later became that, as we have seen, Martin Luther King's family thought first to ask Nixon, not Kennedy, for help when King was jailed. Kennedy's greatest campaign exertions were devoted to running to the *right* of Nixon on foreign and military policy, railing against the Castro government in Cuba and insisting that the Eisenhower-Nixon Administration, despite Ike's own military background, had let down the defenses of the country and produced an ominous "missile gap"—something that Kennedy himself later admitted, in private, to be wholly false.

As for Nixon's campaign, there were structural reasons that made, willy-nilly, for a certain blandness. Nixon was the first serving vice-president in the modern era to run for president. Like his successors in this regard—Hubert Humphrey in 1968, George H. W. Bush in 1988, and Al Gore in 2000—he was thus in a somewhat awkward position: obliged to defend the record of the incumbent administration without being able to take primary credit for any its popular achievements. The demagogic attack style he had developed against Voorhis in 1946, against Helen Gahagan Douglas in 1950, and against Adlai Stevenson in 1952 was inappropriate to the circumstances of 1960—which in this regard more closely resembled 1956, when Eisenhower had told his campaigning vice-president to "give 'em heaven." Nixon was largely irrelevant to the 1956 contest, in which the Republican effort was driven by Eisenhower's huge personal popularity. But Nixon could hardly be irrelevant to his *own* presidential campaign.

Furthermore, there was a considerable dearth of substantive ideological divisions between Nixon and Kennedy, who had come to Congress in the same year and who, as fellow war veterans of the Pacific theater with a shared special interest in anti-Communism, had once formed a certain bond. Nixon had no choice but to defend the military status quo against Kennedy's hawkish attacks, and sometimes his defenses made him sound very liberal indeed ("liberal," that is, especially in the later sense that would be applied to those who questioned Cold War bellicosity). When Kennedy demanded that the US support an armed attack on Cuba—something that the Eisenhower Administration, with Nixon's enthusiastic support, was secretly planning and that would bear rotten fruit during Kennedy's presidency as the failed Bay of Pigs invasion—Nixon chided him for irresponsibly advocating a dangerous course that would violate US treaty commitments. In *Six Crises* Nixon noted the irony that he had felt he "must go to the other extreme" from Kennedy's saber-rattling, though why he felt that this "extreme" (that is, advocating compliance with international law) was needed to protect the secrecy of the planned invasion remains unclear.

On one foreign-policy issue Nixon did regain something of his old Red-baiting fire. The tiny Chinese islands of Quemoy and Matsu—located very near the Chinese mainland and claimed by the Communist government in Beijing, but controlled by Nationalist Chinese forces from Taiwan—were in the news, and Kennedy, in an atypical moment of military sanity, pronounced them of no strategic importance to the US. Nixon replied that the islands were "in the area of freedom," and he found it "shocking for a candidate for the presidency to say that he is willing to hand over a part of the Free World to the Communist World." He pledged himself never to "hand over one square foot of the Free World to the Communists." This was good vintage Nixon, but it was not in essential contradiction to the liberalism of the Democratic Party at the time; and Kennedy's own general hawkishness was so pronounced that Nixon gained only limited traction from the issue.

Nor did domestic issues offer the sort of sharp contrast between the candidates that Kennedy idolaters like to believe they remember. Both contenders were generally liberal on civil rights, though without much visible enthusiasm or emphasis; and, prior to Kennedy's phone call to Mrs. Martin Luther King, Nixon had more credibility on the issue. On economic policies, the candidates reflected the long-term institutional commitments of their respective parties, but in somewhat muted form on both sides. All Democrats in those days professed fealty to the New Deal (Bill Clinton's explicit repudiation of "big government" was far in the future), but perhaps no prominent Northeastern Democrat displayed a more lukewarm attachment to Rooseveltian social democracy than Kennedy did. For his part, Nixon was necessarily associated with Eisenhower's "modern Republicanism," a term coined to distinguish Ike's qualified acceptance and consolidation of the New Deal (combined with opposition to further expansion of it) from the older Republican stance of flat opposition to all of Roosevelt's works. Between tepid New Dealism and "modern Republicanism" the distance was rather less than a million miles. For example, construction of public housing had stalled during the Eisenhower Administration, and Kennedy wanted to build two million new units per year. Nixon agreed that more federal money should be spent on housing than Ike had allowed, but declined to say how much more. Kennedy advocated direct federal aid to public education, with some money earmarked for teachers' salaries. Nixon proposed to limit federal aid to construction loans to the states. Kennedy wanted to expand the Social Security system to include health insurance for the elderly (the idea that, after Kennedy's death, became Medicare). Nixon argued that the same goal would be better attained through government support of private insurance. Such differences, though significant, were not sensational; and all these positions could be described as more-or-less liberal by the standards of the time.

The 1960 presidential election may be considered, then, as one of the great triumphant paradoxes of American liberalism: an election structurally crucial to the political history of the American century, an election that really did usher in a new generation of leaders (as Kennedy claimed in his inaugural address) and mark a generational shift perhaps more socially and culturally dramatic than any since the Civil War—and yet an election largely devoid of actual political *content*. In the core sense described by Chesterton and Wills, it was thus a remarkably liberal affair: an individual competition directed toward no very clear goal beyond the purely pragmatic one of electoral victory. It is significant that, though most people today feel sure that Kennedy was incomparably the superior candidate, when they are pressed to remember *exactly what*, at the time, made Kennedy so much better, the memories invoked (whether personal or historical) tend to concern not policy but style: Kennedy's movie-star physical glamour, as against Nixon's irredeemably ordinary looks; Kennedy's appearance of bouncy athletic vitality, as against the physically awkward and sometimes physically exhausted impression that Nixon gave (although, ironically, Nixon was actually in much better health than the seriously, but secretly, ill Kennedy); Kennedy's sparkling wit and good humor, with his jokes often aimed at himself or his family, as against Nixon's tendency to humorless whining and maudlin self-aggrandizement; Kennedy's oratory, which could genuinely inspire, as against Nixon's mode of public speaking, which could seldom do more than to instruct or to harangue. Kennedy was very obviously the more *attractive* of the two candidates. If one points out that that has little to do with substantive political principle, the latter is something to which, as we have seen, liberalism is pretty allergic in the first place.

But, of the two 1960 contenders, Nixon was the more deeply liberal: not in terms of sharply defined ideological divisions, which, as we have seen, were in short supply anyhow, but on the level of what Garry Wills calls the Emersonian "moral market," or what has been discussed in earlier chapters of this volume as Nixon's petty-bourgeois striving and relentless competitive individualism. Kennedy, though only a few generations removed from penniless Irish immigrants, managed to attain, at least in his public self-presentation, the effortless superiority of the historic aristocrat—the "natural" confidence of a rich man's son who had never known a time when he was not assumed by everyone around him to be a very important person. As Nixon was acutely and enviously aware, Kennedy's innate advantages were at the basis of much of Kennedy's magical "Superman" style, as Norman Mailer termed it; and Nixon himself was by no means entirely immune to the spell of this magic. If Kennedy, unlike Nixon, could publicly laugh at himself in a way that made voters love him all the more, it was surely because of his serene knowledge that, unlike Nixon, he was never likely to be the butt of other people's jokes. If he could, as he once did, address a Democratic Party fundraiser with a wicked parody of his own inaugural address, it was because he was pretty confident that the original was destined for the standard anthologies of great American speeches. If he could humorously disparage his own skills at golf or football, it was because he knew that he looked like a natural athlete and moved with the physical grace of one.

Nixon, of course, enjoyed no such advantages. In the pure way of liberal individualism, he had been forced to sweat and claw for everything he had. It is hardly surprising that the lower-middle-class *ressentiment* that, as we have discussed in the third chapter of this volume, characterized Nixon generally should have been especially intense when confronted with a rival whose own path to power and prominence had been so much easier than his own: and a rival who was, indeed, seen by much of the American electorate as, in effect, a kind of Nietzschean *Übermensch* or hero. Here is how Nixon—a decade and a half after 1960, and after he had won the presidency himself and then lost it in Watergate—remembered 1960 in his memoirs:

> Kennedy's organization approached campaign dirty tricks with a roguish relish and carried them off with an insouciance that captivated many politicians and overcame the critical faculties of many reporters. I should have anticipated what was coming as I observed some of what went on in Kennedy's brilliant but coldly mechanical destruction of Hubert Humphrey [Nixon's fellow petty-bourgeois, it should be recalled, and the political rival toward whom he always displayed *least* personal animus] in the primaries. . . .I was not prepared for the blatant and highly successful way the Kennedys repeatedly made religion an issue in the campaign even as they professed that it should not be one. Led by Robert Kennedy, they managed to turn the election partially into a referendum on tolerance versus bigotry. From this point on I had the wisdom and wariness of someone who had been burned by the power of the Kennedys and their money and by the

> license they were given by the media. I vowed that I would never again enter an election at a disadvantage by being vulnerable to them—or anyone—on the level of political tactics.

Before looking more closely at this remarkable passage—perhaps *the* quintessentially Nixonian view of the 1960 campaign, in some ways even more than the long account offered in *Six Crises*—we should acknowledge that Nixon's resentment of the Kennedys was, after all, to a certain degree justified. Nixon and John Kennedy both seem to have been gifted with first-rate intellects, but Kennedy (for all his expressed concern with "vigor") was as lazy in intellectual matters as in most other things outside of bedding attractive women in vast numbers. Nixon (as President De Gaulle of France, who knew them both, recognized) really *was* the much harder worker, the better read, the more widely informed, and certainly the keener student of history and geopolitics. Then too, Nixon had a perfectly valid point with respect to the Kennedy money. As even so close a Kennedy friend and ally as the late House Speaker Tip O'Neill (whose House seat had been John Kennedy's before he moved up to the Senate) has testified, a great deal of the Kennedy success (especially the early success) in politics was based on nothing more complex than throwing cash into the electoral process in literally unprecedented quantities. Nixon, by contrast, never could raise political funds simply by turning to his family's bank accounts.

Still, when all such allowances have been made, the voice heard in the above passage is definitively that of the liberal-individualist competitive ego—and swollen to the point of paranoia, with all the attendant psychological projection. Thus, for example, Nixon accuses the Kennedys of "dirty tricks," doubtless counting on the reader to remember how that phrase became associated with his own campaign in 1972. But what he is actually, though silently, referring to are just the practical jokes of the legendary Democratic operative Dick Tuck—who, for instance, once during the 1960 campaign donned a signalman's hat and waved a train out of the station just as Nixon, standing on the train's rear platform, was beginning a speech. (In 1968, Tuck hired a group of very obviously pregnant women to march outside the Republican Convention, carrying signs emblazoned with Nixon's chief slogan of the year—"Nixon's the one!") Though practical jokes seldom seem very funny to those on whom they are played—and least of all to anyone as humorless as Nixon—Tuck's antics hardly seem "dirty" when compared not only to the burglaries and other felonies that Nixon's men would perpetrate during Watergate, but also to the whispering campaign against Voorhis in 1946 and the tentative hint of anti-Semitism used against Helen Douglas in 1950.

A similar example of paranoid projection is Nixon's charge that "the Kennedys repeatedly made religion an issue in the campaign even as they professed that it should not be one." As we have seen, this clause very precisely describes Nixon's *own* strategy. Nixon seldom lost an opportunity to remind audiences that Senator Kennedy was a Catholic before adding, as though with an invisible wink, that a candidate's religion ought not to be a political issue: a perfect example of the familiar principle that the surest way to get people to think of something is to tell them not to think about it. In Willsian terms, what we see here is Nixon's competing as strenuously and furiously as possible in both the moral market of self-creation and the political market of the electoral contest. Determined to inflate, rhetorically, the odds against him and then to triumph in the end anyhow, Nixon in this passage displays the very core of his brand of liberalism. Again in Wills's terms, this is Nixon agonistes, Nixon the contender, stripped naked.

Indeed, we might say that what Nixon's view of the 1960 campaign, and his entire set of grievances against John Kennedy and the Kennedy family, boil down to is simply the complaint that the market of liberal-individualist competition doesn't *work* when one is in the arena against the Kennedys. The "playing field," as the popular American cliché has it, is not level. The Kennedys have so much money, so much glamour, so much ability to charm journalists and voters, that they don't even *have* to compete in the normal way. Thus, for instance, John Kennedy got his Harvard education simply by enrolling at his father's alma mater, where the tuition and fees added up to a negligible item in the Kennedy family budget. Nixon, by contrast, got his Harvard scholarship only through the talent, discipline, and long hours of hard work required to win a statewide scholastic competition—and then he was unable to accept the scholarship after all, when his brother's illness deprived the Nixon family of the ability to pay young Richard's travel and living expenses. How fair was that?

It began early, of course, as Nixon himself put it—well before he encountered or even, probably, had heard of the Kennedys. And Nixon's devotion to competitive liberal individualism can help to explain even some of his most decidedly *il*liberal actions, which, as we have seen, Garry Wills sometimes tends to gloss over. How fair, after all, was the contest against Jerry Voorhis? Voorhis was a wealthy and popular incumbent who held what was generally considered to be one of the safest Democratic Congressional seats in the US. Nixon, in 1946, was a young lawyer and Navy veteran almost unknown except to his immediate friends and neighbors. In the face of such odds, were a little Red-baiting and a few whispering campaigns anything but attempts to make the playing field a bit more nearly level? In Nixonian logic, the most savagely reactionary tactics may be necessary to establish the conditions under which *genuine* liberalism, true liberal competition, can operate.

But, as the passage quoted above from *RN* makes clear, it was, in Nixon's mind, only after what seemed to him the massive unfairness of 1960—when, as Nixon saw it, the Kennedys possessed every innate advantage and still had to steal votes at the very end—that he gained the true "wisdom and wariness" to know what kind of exertions might be necessary to level the playing field when he met them again; or, in the actual event, when he met the long-time Kennedy associate George McGovern in 1972. Only after 1960 and his unfortunate encounter with the false quasi-aristocratic liberalism of the Kennedys did Nixon fully realize how arduous the defense of *true* liberalism might be. And this was, of course, the path that led directly to Watergate and to ultimate political disaster.

4

If Nixon found in 1960 that ordinary liberal competition fails to work against the Kennedys, an obvious question is thereby raised: does it *ever* work? It does not. This is perhaps the ultimate self-contradiction of liberalism, which neither Nixon nor any other liberal has ever been able to face squarely. Liberalism begins by abjuring positive social policy in favor of a formal proceduralism, pragmatically trusting that the application of a certain set of rules will "work" in the sense of yielding the fairest attainable results. But such results are absolutely precluded by the initial liberal move of waiving the question of justice: for justice is a social goal with positive, determinate content, though the precise character of that content has of course been strenuously debated at least from Plato's *Republic* onwards. In the place of justice, liberalism substitutes the sort of content-free procedures that liberals try to designate by such metaphors as "a fair deal," "equal opportunity," or, especially, "a level playing field." A close examination of any of these metaphors will, in fact, reveal the essential falsity of the notion that liberal-individualist competition can ever be "fair." For what each of them assumes is that equality in only *one* social factor, or at least a limited number of them, will yield appropriate results. This assumption is false, based, as it is, on a drastically simplistic view of the social field. The playing field may be level enough, for instance, but how if one team is playing on dry, smooth ground while the other side of the field is muddy and broken?—or if one team has the sun in their eyes while the other doesn't? For that matter, how about the advantages of the individual players—in weight, height, "natural" athletic skill, early access to good nutrition and health care—that no amount of training and discipline may be able to overcome? Furthermore, while real athletic contests take place for finite periods with a specified number of players, the "game" of politics (or life) is continuous. One is born into it and dies while it is still ongoing, so that an uncountable number of "players" are entering and leaving the game all the time.

Plato and subsequent serious thinkers—outside the liberal tradition—have recognized that justice is never something that merely "happens" once a few simple rules are in place. On the contrary, justice is something that must be *attained,* and the mind-numbing complexity of society is such that this attainment will necessarily be an extraordinarily difficult task. One may, indeed, conclude that the task is not just hard but impossible, and that attempting it is likely to make things worse rather than better—thus arriving at a kind of Burkean conservatism. That position is not without its own problems, as we have seen. But, in strictly intellectual terms, those problems are less severe than the self-contradictions of liberalism—which repudiates the goal of attaining justice while nonetheless promising that comparable results can be attained through an empty, content-free proceduralism. The truth is that society is much too complicated and governed by forces far too powerful for any set of merely formal rules to be able to make things right. The "unfair" advantages that Nixon resented in the Kennedys were in part real enough. But they were the sort of advantages that inevitably crop up in any competitive, and especially capitalist, society. Nixon—as he naturally failed to acknowledge—enjoyed his own advantages too, and the largest of these was much more important than any of Kennedy's: namely, the simple fact that, as the Republican nominee, he was the preferred candidate of the American ruling class, of that small minority of citizens who owned and controlled most of the country's social wealth. At least once during the 1960 campaign, Kennedy himself came about as close to mentioning this fact as the taboo against the discussion of economic class in American electoral politics tends to allow. Kennedy noted that Nixon had recently been criticized on the editorial page of *The Wall Street Journal*, and quipped that this was "like *L'Osservatore Romano* criticizing the Pope." Himself born into his country's ruling class, Kennedy could, perhaps, see and speak about it more clearly than most "mainstream" politicians dared to do.

Here, again, Nixon was the more deeply liberal of the two. If Kennedy, from his quasi-aristocratic heights, could perceive that liberal competition never worked in quite the way that its devotees maintained—"Life is unfair," as he once famously said when president—Nixon remained determined, in his "wise and wary" way, that the market must be *made* fair, at least for him. In this as in so many other things, Nixon indeed, as Senator Dole said in his funeral oration, "always embodied the deepest feelings of the people he led." As was discussed in chapter 3, America has always been a quintessentially and congenitally petty-bourgeois country. With very weak traditions of aristocratic or quasi-aristocratic "natural" superiority, and even weaker ones of socialist solidarity, the US has adopted the validity of liberal-individualistic competition as something like a national creed. No idea is more deeply embedded in the national psyche than the notion that ability and application *must*, with sufficient perseverance and an ordinary amount of good luck, lead to success.

As the metaphor of the level playing field reminds us, America is also a sports-obsessed nation; and the two characteristics are probably related. Though sports are not wholly immune to the complicated vagaries and distortions of the market, it may well be that in this arena competitive success really is based on talent and hard work to a greater extent than in any other. The classic example is that Mickey Mantle's son ardently wished to be a major-league ballplayer but failed to attain this goal, even to a modest degree. His father's superstardom on the baseball diamond did not confer the sort of congenital advantages that John Kennedy possessed by virtue of *his* father's wealth and political connections. It does not seem accidental that Nixon himself was among the most zealous of sports fans. Hunter Thompson, the most relentlessly and imaginatively anti-Nixon journalist of all who covered him—and also a one-time sportswriter—once had an extended conversation with Nixon about football, and came away with the stunned admission that Nixon's passion for the game was not feigned or opportunistic (as Thompson had assumed) but authentic and deeply knowledgeable. Though Nixon himself had for the most part been a failure on Whittier College's football gridiron, perhaps he saw in the game a privileged instance of the free liberal competition to which he was so attached.

There is one final connection to be made between the core Nixonian liberalism and his most blatantly illiberal actions. On the face of it, nothing could be more illiberal than ideologies like racism and anti-Semitism. If liberalism upholds, above all, the primacy of the competitive individualistic market, then what could violate this principle more viciously than to exclude certain individuals from the contest because of factors of ethnic heritage over which they have not the slightest control? And, indeed, some of the people who most unabashedly describe themselves as liberals do have an honorable history of combating such bigotry. There is some truth to the familiar contrast between the way that conservatives normally tolerate bigotry—if not always as something intrinsically desirable, then at least as part of the traditional values of a given society, as an aspect of the status quo which it would be dangerous and potentially destructive to try to change radically—and the way that liberals sometimes fight against it. Yet the matter is also more complex than that.

What is at issue here is the essential *emptiness* that we have identified at the heart of liberalism: the substantive vacuity that results from abjuring the quest for any sort of positive social content and instead attempting to structure an idea of society through a procedural formalism. The consequent contradictions and instabilities that result are to be found on the affective as well as the intellectual and political levels. For what liberalism, with its relentless valorization of mere process—of ceaseless competition and change—necessarily fails to provide in its subjects is any sense of substantive personal identity. Or, to put it another way, the fundamental individualism of the liberal precludes radical self-definition through the sense of *collectivity* that seems to be a permanent psychic necessity in human beings. Genuine aristocracy, with its tranquil belief in the superiority of "blood," meets this need, and so, in a very different way, does the group solidarity that is integral to socialist and certain other radical movements (like feminism). But the prison-house of individuality that liberalism constructs has no space for such collective feeling, and thus must inevitably tempt its inmates to break free in any way that seems feasible—not excluding the ways of racism and anti-Semitism, which *do* offer collectivity, though in the latter's most vicious and regressive forms. It was with some awareness of this weird but not uncommon ideological mutation that the German Marxist writer and politician August Bebel described anti-Semitism, in a famous aphorism, as "the socialism of the stupid"—though the example of Nixon's anti-Semitism should make clear that such bigotry may become a substitute for more progressive and humane forms of collectivity even for individuals who are by no means stupid at all.

Thus it is that liberalism, in actual psychological practice, can with fearful ease become the opposite of itself. Is it really a coincidence that America has always been among the most liberal *and* the most racist of nations? Think of the Jeffersonian tradition—always claimed, and *accurately* claimed, by the most emancipatory currents in American liberalism, and also by John C. Calhoun, the Confederacy, and the Ku Klux Klan. In this terrible dialectic Richard Nixon—the co-worker with Martin Luther King, the most influential opponent of racism in the American twentieth century, and also the co-worker with Strom Thurmond, one of the most influential racists—clearly (to quote Dole yet again) "embodied the deepest feelings of the people he led."

VI. America's Nixon, Nixon's America

From petty-bourgeois resentment to procedural liberalism, from racism to an anal-erotic concern with order, the fundamental and interlocking components of Nixonian cultural power are, as the preceding chapters have been concerned to explore, deeply rooted in American history and tradition. It is in this sense that every age in America has been the Age of Nixon. But the profound emotional connections that Nixon forged with the American electorate—and hence the cultural power that he exercised—were also, of course, specific in form to his own era. As we have had occasion to notice in a variety of different contexts, the period defined by Nixon's active political career—that is, the years between 1946 and 1974—was a major watershed in US politics. Though the changes in our political system were, of course, determined by a wide variety of different factors, Nixon himself was an important, and sometimes a crucial, factor in many of them. In this concluding chapter I will examine four such sea changes that Nixon helped to implement and that in turn played a major role in establishing the years of his political prominence as the Age of Nixon: the progressive nationalizing of presidential campaigning and of American politics in general; the rise of television as the most effective vehicle of political communication and the concomitant refashioning of our politics as a branch of the modern advertising and "public relations" industry; the Republican assault on journalism and, to some degree, on the concept of objectivity itself; and the expansion of what Arthur Scheslinger famously termed (with specific reference to Nixon) "the imperial presidency". All of these developments are complexly interrelated, as we will see, but it will be convenient to consider them in turn.

1

The nationalization of American politics. Though the term *federal* is still with us to describe the national government in Washington, it is often forgotten just how radically federal was the American governmental system that the framers of the Constitution established in 1787. That system was, as the preamble to the Constitution says, a "union"—in many ways not unlike the European Union of today—in which a group of distinct and sovereign *states* agreed to pool their sovereignty for certain limited and carefully defined purposes. True, a national American identity existed even from the earliest days of the federal union; but for decades it was secondary to one's identity as a citizen of Massachusetts, or New York, or Virginia (precisely the distinction that, when it became a direct conflict, so agonized the conscience of Robert E. Lee). One reason that the Electoral College is such a cumbersome method of electing a federal president is that those who designed it tended to assume that (after George Washington, at that time the one undisputed national hero and the obvious first president, had passed from the scene) each state's electors would simply vote for some local favorite son, leaving the House of Representatives to make the final, actual choice. Early members of Congress, and especially of the Senate, saw themselves more like ambassadors from their respective states than as the genuinely national figures that their successors are today.

The main factor that prevented the emergence of a unitary national state in the 1780s and after was, of course, chattel slavery in the South. In 1860, as the Civil War loomed, there were elderly Americans who believed, reasonably enough, that they would live to see the end of the federal experiment whose beginning they could personally remember. In the event, however, the Civil War not only abolished slavery—and, to a limited degree, retroactively removed the implicit racial exception to Jefferson's assertion, in the Declaration of

Independence, that "all men are created equal"—but also re-established the USA as a far more unified country than anything of which Washington and his colleagues could have dreamed (or, perhaps, approved). Not the least important cause of this successful (re)building of the nation was the steely determination of Abraham Lincoln. Self-consciously and emphatically, Lincoln saw his task not merely as the preservation of the union established by the Constitution but as the radical *refashioning* of it—that is, giving it a "new birth of freedom," to invoke his own formulation at Gettysburg—in a more fully national way than ever before. With his characteristic way of using humor to address the gravest life-and-death issues, Lincoln once quipped that the Civil War was fought over a point of grammar: that is, over whether one should say "the United States are" (which had been a common usage in American English) or "the United States is." It is worth recalling again that, from his precocious boyhood studies of American history onwards, Richard Nixon admired Lincoln above all other heroes.

Despite the considerable nationalization of the American governmental system produced by the Civil War and by the subsequent adoption of the thirteenth, fourteenth, and fifteenth amendments to the US Constitution—and by the roaring postbellum successes of Northern capitalism, no longer fettered by a competing economic system south of the Mason-Dixon line—the country into which Nixon was born in 1913 remained, however, a federal union to a much greater extent than can easily be imagined now. States remained largely free to govern their citizens in ways that openly flouted what we think of today as fundamental Constitutional guarantees: for the Supreme Court had just barely begun its long-term project (essentially completed only in the 1960s) of using the due-process and equal-protection clauses of the fourteenth amendment to apply the protections of the Bill of Rights to state governments as well as to the federal Congress. And what was true in Constitutional principle was often even more true in everyday practice, especially, of course, with regard to the barbaric (and often terroristic) treatment of black citizens in the South.

Like law, electoral politics was also organized primarily on a state-by-state basis. The national Republican and Democratic parties were for the most part loose (and usually uneasy) confederations of the individual state parties. Those who emerged as national leaders tended to do so through prior leadership on the state level. To win a presidential nomination one did not launch a national campaign in the modern way, but instead assembled an *ad hoc* coalition of state and municipal political bosses who individually controlled important blocs of delegates. It is significant that, in the year of Nixon's birth, the two commanding American political figures were President Woodrow Wilson and former President Theodore Roosevelt, both of whom emerged on the national scene from major state posts (Wilson as governor of New Jersey, Roosevelt as governor of New York). It is also significant, however, that both presidents, who became particular heroes to Nixon, made important contributions to the concentration of power in Washington.

It is instructive to contrast the political genealogies of Wilson and TR with those of the men who occupied the White House during the years of Nixon's active career: Truman, Eisenhower, Kennedy, Johnson, Nixon himself, and Gerald Ford. None ever held an important state office. All came to national prominence in institutions that were themselves entirely national in character, namely the US Congress, the federal Vice-Presidency, and (in Eisenhower's case) the US Army. Even the state *identities* of these men look amazingly faint by the standards of an earlier America. Kennedy spoke with an often-parodied Massachusetts accent, but his actual connections with the Bay state were more familial and political than personal; he had mostly grown up elsewhere. Johnson posed as a proud Texas rancher, but spent the great majority of his adult life in the nation's capital. In other cases the connection with a state culture was even more tenuous. When Eisenhower won the White House in 1952, there was no significant sense in which he was a Kansas figure, and there was not much of a sense in which Nixon, by 1968, was a Californian.

Admittedly, since Nixon's time we have seen a resurgence of former governors in the White House: Carter, Reagan, Bill Clinton, and George W. Bush. But (with the partial exception of Carter) they are not really counter-examples to the growing nationalization of American politics. What they rather illustrate is that this nationalization had by the 1980s grown so thorough that even governors—especially of major states like California and Texas but also, at least for a campaigner so wily as Clinton, even of as small a state as Arkansas—could now function as national figures in ways that would have once been inconceivable.

The most powerful events that accelerated this centripetal tendency after the era of the Civil War took place when Nixon was a young man, just before his appearance as an active politician: namely, Franklin Roosevelt's establishment of the modern presidency in the New Deal—a centralizing movement enabled by the unprecedented economic crisis of the Great Depression—and then the Second World War, which not only gave more Americans a more unified national purpose than ever before, but also, in the usual way of military mobilization, helped to increase the nationalization of political power in Washington. "War is the health of the State," as Randolph Bourne famously put it. "It automatically sets in motion throughout society... irresistible forces for uniformity..."

Few better examples of how these forces for uniformity worked could be cited than the character of Nixon's first political campaign, the year after World War II ended. As we have seen, Nixon in 1946, though he had some reputation in the town of Whittier itself—largely because of the wide respect in which his mother was held—was basically unknown through most of the district whose Congressional representative he campaigned, successfully, to become. He had almost no local popularity on which to draw, nor did he take many pains to present himself as a champion of local values or interests. He did not, for the most part, ask to be sent to the US House of Representatives in order to build roads or bridges, or to bring home military bases that would invigorate the local economy. Instead, he defeated Jerry Voorhis—who *was* locally popular—by attaching himself to the triumphantly national movement of postwar anti-Communism and by trumpeting the cause of anti-Communist uniformity with a demagogic skill that quickly established him as the premier Red-baiting politician in the country. The all-American character of Nixon's anti-Communism was itself something of an innovation in US politics. As Richard Rovere pointed out in his widely read biography of Joseph McCarthy—who, as we have seen, became Nixon's only Red-baiting contemporary capable of playing in the same league—demagogic movements in American history had generally been based on local or at least regional protests against some larger national ideology. Though there were some traces of such sectionalism in the anti-Communism of the late 1940s and early 1950s—which always, for example, had more appeal in the traditionally Republican, isolationist precincts of the Midwest than in the "elite" and internationalist circles of the better educated Northeast—both Nixon and McCarthy operated as demagogues of fully, and successfully, national intent. From the very beginning of his career, then, and even before becoming well-known across the land, Nixon was, in a sense, already a national politician.

It is no accident, of course, that he attained national fame shortly thereafter, with the case of Alger Hiss—which transformed him from one unusually talented and successful follower of the nationwide anti-Communist crusade to its primary leader (a role he had to share with McCarthy after the latter's appearance on the anti-Communist scene in February 1950). It is important to recall just how national Nixonian (and McCarthyite) anti-Communism was—not only in the sense of being vitally current in all parts of the nation, but also in the sense of being constructed, and largely accepted, as integral to American national identity. Communism, in Nixonian terms, was increasingly understood not merely as a political philosophy or even a political movement, but as the antithesis of Americanness itself: hence the widespread use of the intrinsically vacuous term "Americanism" as a synonym for anti-Communism. Indeed, no small part of anti-Communism's appeal was precisely its promise that those who might earlier have felt excluded from full American identity on ethnic or religious grounds (like many of McCarthy's fellow Irish-American Catholics, or even some of Nixon's fellow Quakers) could by the adoption of an anti-Communist posture instantly become just as American as anyone else.

Nixon paid decreasing attention to anti-Communism as its popularity waned, but it helped to give him, from the start, a nationwide, all-American political orientation that proved invaluable throughout the remainder of his career. If, as we have seen, he captured the 1960 Republican presidential nomination more easily than any non-incumbent had ever done before, this was largely because he skillfully used his two terms as vice-president to establish himself as a more completely national Republican leader than anyone not actually occupying (or having recently occupied) the White House had ever been before. Even Eisenhower in 1952 had indirectly acquired a limited sectional coloration through the Northeastern roots of his most prominent and influential supporters; while Taft was clearly the candidate of Midwestern (and, what very little there was of it, Southern) Republicanism. But Nixon, after eight years of campaigning with and for Republicans everywhere, and of at least appearing to represent the US through his foreign trips to America's friends and adversaries, was, in 1960, Mr. Republican for the whole country—in an unambiguous way that Nelson Rockefeller and Barry Goldwater, despite their own (lesser) national followings, could only envy. Moreover, it is significant that Nixon's only important political mistake prior to Watergate—i.e., his campaign to become governor of California in 1962—represented a kind of retreat from his fully national status and an attempt to re-establish himself as a state leader in the older conventional way.

But Nixon recovered from his defeat by Pat Brown, and never again made this kind of slip. Indeed, his move from California to New York City in 1963 is best seen not merely as (what it was widely taken to be at the time) a peevish rejection of the state that had recently rejected him. It was also a shrewd strategic move to rebuild his career from the safety and prestige of a Wall Street law firm in a city that was, in all but the strictly governmental sense, the effective capital of the nation—and (much more so then than now) overwhelmingly more central than anyplace in California. In 1968, the national character of his race for the Republican presidential nomination was, to be sure, in part a matter of making a virtue of necessity. Since, as we have noted, his current home state of New York was firmly controlled, politically, by Rockefeller, and his former home state of California was now Ronald Reagan's turf, he had little choice but to play the all-American card. But he clearly recognized that it was now the best card in the political deck, whose value he had recently enhanced through his energetic campaigning in 1966 for Republicans throughout the nation. To the extent that he had any regional base in the 1968 Republican contest—and, with California and New York, the two largest states, both beyond his reach, he did, perhaps, have some need of one—it was the one he forged, with Strom Thurmond's help, in the South: a part of the country with which (aside from his law school years at Duke) he had no personal connection at all.

The "Southern strategy" of Nixon's fight for the 1968 nomination was only a dress rehearsal for the much more difficult and important general election campaign later that year. In the race against Hubert Humphrey and George Wallace, Nixon did not merely navigate and exploit, with peerless skill, the nationalizing, centripetal tendencies that had long been building in American politics. Now he began to make a major contribution to this centralizing movement, in ways that strongly resonate in American politics to this day. What was crucial here was—yet again—the issue of race. As we have seen, Nixon's use of white racism in 1968 was in one sense a reprise of his demagogic successes during the 1940s and 1950s. Once again he presented himself as the champion of middle-class resentment, of the virtually anal-erotic rage for order that so roiled the land, but this time with the black rather than the Red as the scapegoated object of anger and scorn. But, as the 1968 contest began, it was by no means obvious that racism could be made the basis of fully *national* political success to quite the degree that anti-Communism had once been. To do so was Nixon's particular contribution.

To be sure, the Wallace campaign proved what was already obvious enough: namely, that politically usable white racism in America was by no means confined to the Southern states. Wallace himself, indeed, was proud of the fact that his name was on the presidential ballot in all fifty states. He once claimed to have received more letters of support from New York than from anyplace else, and he often boasted, in one of the standard lines of his 1968 speeches, that the movement he led was not sectional but national. But this was not, quite, true. White racism itself may have been as all-American as apple pie, but Wallace, personally, was a fatally flawed contender for national leadership of the racist cause. His background, his history, his speaking style, his accent, perhaps even his facial features—all indelibly stamped him as a creature of what one analyst has termed the "Gothic" style of Deep South politics, a political tradition of cultural power that always defined itself, quite overtly and self-consciously, *against* the national mainstream. Despite his ambitions, Wallace could never truly overcome this regional orientation, and on election day he did not even come close to carrying a single non-Southern state.

Nixon's single most consequential achievement in 1968 was to *nationalize* the white racism that Wallace symbolized but was unable to make full use of. Nationalization was the ultimate logic of the gingerly way he handled Wallace during the campaign and the way he recycled Wallace's racist appeals in more suave, "moderate" tones. Nixon's strategy, after all, was necessarily twofold. He had to compete with Wallace for racist votes, while at the same time taking care not to alarm a great many Middle American voters (mostly, though not entirely, outside the South) who did not like to think of themselves as racist and who would not have voted for a crudely "Gothic" demagogue like Wallace—but who *did*, in many cases, tend to feel that, what with the Black Power movement and the cycle of about three hundred (mainly urban) race riots between 1964 and 1968, America's blacks were getting more than a little bit out of hand.

Nixon's "Southern strategy" was in this sense really a national strategy. For his restructuring of American, and especially Republican, politics on the issue of race—which we analyzed in some detail in chapter 4—was based not only on the incorporation of the South into the Republican coalition but also on making successful appeals throughout the land of a specifically, if subtly, racial sort that had previously found their main electoral use below the Mason-Dixon line. Nixon, one might say, nationalized Southern politics (or, perhaps, "Southernized" national politics). This remains, as we have seen, his most enduring legacy to the party that (before 1972) he served so faithfully and zealously. Of the three Republicans since Nixon who have won the White House—Reagan and the two

Bushes—only one, the younger Bush, has been an actual Southerner (and even *his* credentials as a Southerner, or a Texan, look a bit dubious when examined closely). But all have played the race card in the specifically Nixonian way. All have campaigned and governed on the Nixonian premise that—to borrow a venerable and witty African-American maxim—the *real* Mason-Dixon line is located somewhere around the Canadian border.

2

The selling of the president. So Nixon's part in the nationalization of American politics, especially racial politics, was an important contribution to the general centripetal movement in American history that existed independently of him and was well established long before his birth. Much the same thing can be said of his part in the rise of "public relations" in our political life that eventually led to the still growing dominance of the television presidency. But here Nixon's role was even more prominent and important. The two trends are, of course, intimately related. As the US became larger and more centralized, older political techniques based on voters' personal (if sometimes second- or third-hand) knowledge of politicians became increasingly obsolete; and the need for methods of communicating with thousands or millions of people at once became more and more urgent. Both trends, of course, long antedated Nixon. Popular journalism and photography—and even campaign songs—played an important role in reshaping American politics during the nineteenth century. Lincoln, after all, grew a beard for precisely the same sort of reasons that today lead politicians to heed the advice of television hair-and-makeup artists. But the greatest such innovation in Nixon's lifetime, prior to his own emergence onto the political stage, was undoubtedly represented by the fireside chats of Franklin D. Roosevelt.

It is worth noting that, with the exception of Stalin, all the leaders of the major nations that contended in the European theater of World War Two were distinguished by the quickness with which they recognized, and the skill with which they exploited, the political possibilities inherent in radio technology: not only Roosevelt, but also Churchill, de Gaulle, Hitler, and Mussolini. (Hitler seems to have had the keenest appreciation of the opportunities afforded by the parallel development of cinematic technology, though FDR was by no means blind to the political uses of Hollywood.) Within US politics, however, Roosevelt was in a class by himself. His crucial practical insight was that the technical apparatuses of radio broadcasting and receiving did not merely multiply the iterations of a speaker's voice, allowing him to reach many more listeners than could fit into the largest lecture hall or open-air arena. FDR saw that radio also, and just as importantly, called for a radical change in the form and content of political speech.

Before the era of the New Deal, political oratory in America was mostly a branch of the lofty, impersonal art of classical rhetoric—which held sway not only in the nation's legislatures and campaign trails but also in its courtrooms, universities, and (the only site where it is alive and well today) churches. Formal oratory was the means by which America's greatest political communicators—men like Daniel Webster and William Jennings Bryan—had distinguished themselves; and, in the nineteenth century, when people might devote a whole day's travel to hearing a few hours of campaign rhetoric, political orators also supplied much of the nation's popular entertainment. Roosevelt was trained as a classical political rhetorician, and could perform as such with considerable success: as witness his first inaugural address, or his speech to Congress requesting a declaration of war immediately after the Japanese bombing of Pearl Harbor. But FDR also recognized that the elaborate, impersonal periods of classical rhetoric—which had been designed for formal public occasions at which large numbers of people gathered together—

were inappropriate for the essentially domestic medium of radio. Though some radio listening was communal (in bars, for example), people generally listened at home, by themselves or with a few close friends and family members: so that, despite the unprecedented size of the audience, speaking on the radio was in some ways more like having a private chat than like making a public speech. Queen Victoria once famously complained that William Gladstone, her prime minister, addressed her as though she were a public meeting. Roosevelt sensed that Americans sitting at home next to their radio sets did not want to be spoken to in that way either. Public oratory was no longer a major form of entertainment anyway—there were too many competing alternatives by the 1930s—and Americans welcomed the intimate, informal approach that FDR perfected in his radio broadcasts. In his rich, re-assuring baritone he typically addressed the audience as "my friends". Though he of course never met more than a tiny fraction of his listeners, Americans, on the whole, responded as though the president really was a friend of theirs.

The connection, in this context, between Roosevelt and Nixon has been generally overlooked, no doubt partly because Roosevelt's most ardent fans have usually reviled Nixon and have thus found the idea of such a connection uncongenial. It is also true that, presumably because of his family's rigidly Republican orientation, Nixon in his teens and twenties displayed extraordinarily little political interest in FDR for an American born in 1913, in modest circumstances, and who, in addition, had a precocious interest in history and politics. (A pertinent contrast is with Ronald Reagan, who for many years considered himself a Roosevelt Democrat and never entirely ceased to admire the thirty-second president.) But Nixon himself was well aware that his pioneering role in political television was in direct succession to Roosevelt's role as the master, in America, of political radio. Like FDR with his medium, Nixon appreciated that a politician on TV was essentially a guest in people's homes, and would be most effective if he spoke in the low-key way that we normally expect of those we allow into our living rooms. Like Roosevelt, Nixon made himself into a publicly available *personality* in ways impossible for politicians before the age of electronic broadcasting. In the Checkers speech—the first great television performance by any US politician—Nixon decided to include mention of his daughters' cocker spaniel partly in self-conscious emulation of the effective political use that Roosevelt had made of *his* dog, the Scottish terrier Fala. Roosevelt often mentioned Fala in his talks and interviews, and the dog became part of FDR's warm, likeable, approachable public image. (Today a metal sculpture of Fala can be found alongside the larger one of his master in the FDR Memorial on the Mall in Washington.) Nixon's insistence that his family would keep Checkers despite any political consequences was, in part, a deliberate tribute to Roosevelt's mastery of political communication: though, with characteristic *ressentiment*, Nixon also enjoyed the thought of how much the most ardently partisan Democrats in the audience (whose votes had to be considered a lost cause for the Eisenhower-Nixon ticket in any case) would hate watching their *bête noire* steal a trick from their all-time hero.

This is not to say that Nixon was Roosevelt's equal. As we have seen, he never attained, or even much attempted, the folksy expansiveness that served FDR (and later Reagan) so well. But Nixon was the first important American politician to grasp and use the political possibilities of TV, and to appreciate the major role it was destined to play in the country's future. Of course, the full-scale barrage of television commercials for the Republican ticket in 1952—the first advertising campaign of its kind, prepared by some of the best talents on Madison Avenue—most prominently featured Eisenhower, not his running mate. But to watch those commercials today is to see that Ike was taking direction, like a good soldier, without much understanding of what was really going on. Nixon, by contrast, was always his own best media adviser. By the time of the Checkers speech he was already something of a veteran with the new medium—it will be recalled that the Congressional hearings in which he pursued Alger Hiss were the first ever to be televised—and, after Checkers had saved his political career and helped to put the Eisenhower-Nixon ticket back on the path to landslide victory, Nixon continued to use television with a skill then unmatched in US politics. It is no accident, that, in his 1959 debate with Nikita Khrushchev on the relative merits of the Soviet and American economic systems, Nixon cited color television as an instance of US superiority.

One can, indeed, imagine an alternative historical line in which Nixon sailed into and through the 1960s as the nation's supreme television politician, easily besting rivals like Lyndon Johnson (whose television performances during the worst days of the Vietnam War conveyed the impression of an exhausted, defeated man, determined to lie but unable to summon the energy required for any serious pretense of telling the truth) or Hubert Humphrey (who projected an over-the-top ebullience of the kind that can be inspiring on the campaign stump but which, when filtered through the "cool" domestic medium of TV, tended to make him seem like a hysterical fool). That things turned out otherwise is mainly due—with what Nixon himself would doubtless regard as sad, unfair appropriateness—to the fact that, as the 1960s began, he ran into John Kennedy.

The record of Nixon's general success on television has been largely eclipsed by the strong personal and historical memories of his loss to Kennedy in the first televised debate of the 1960 campaign. But certain important considerations have been generally forgotten. First, Nixon, who was recovering from the flu and appeared without makeup, *did* lose (that is, among television viewers, though not among radio listeners), but not in the overwhelming way that many Americans think they remember. Kennedy won on points, so to speak, not by a knockout. There were even many who scored the debate the other way—e.g., *The New York Times*, which, even though it backed Kennedy for president, opined that, in the first debate, "on sound points of argument, Nixon probably took most of the honors".

Second, it should be remembered that Kennedy won in large part because he benefited greatly from what political observers today call "lowered expectations." Nixon, after all, had had eight years of nationwide exposure as vice-president, which he skillfully (if deceptively) used to present himself as an experienced executive decision-maker. Kennedy was still little-known, and many of those who did know something about him regarded him as a rich, shallow playboy, without much intellectual or political substance. Merely to appear on formally equal terms with Nixon was in itself a coup for the Massachusetts senator. Of course, this raises the question of why Nixon agreed to the debates in the first place; many, including Eisenhower, urged him not to. But one can see the logic of Nixon's decision. He had been excelling in debate since his schooldays, and had reason to consider himself the most formidable television performer in American politics. Regarding Kennedy as a lightweight, Nixon might well have calculated—wrongly but not unreasonably—that he could use the first debate to deliver a crushing blow from which Kennedy would be unable to recover: thus effectively ending the 1960 campaign almost before it had really begun.

It was bad luck for Nixon that Kennedy, surprisingly, turned out to be a television politician of unprecedented gifts. The indolent playboy actually possessed first-class brains and political skills whenever he took the trouble to use them. On top of his telegenic good looks and physical poise, Kennedy displayed a smooth verbal fluency, an easy self-assurance, a dry low-key wit, and a generally "cool" self-possessed manner that were all exactly right for the small screen. Indeed, though the assassination cut Kennedy's career too short to be certain, he may well have been the most brilliant television politician that the US has ever produced. Only Reagan seems a plausible competitor for the title.

But—and this is my final point here about the Kennedy-Nixon match-up—the fact that Kennedy was even better than Nixon on TV does not mean that Nixon was less than very good. Though considerably more formal and deliberate in manner than Kennedy or Reagan (or Bill Clinton), Nixon on television successfully projected an air of seriousness, sincerity, competence, and hard work. He spoke easily, and from the very first he mastered the slightly understated style that was essential for success on TV but that often came hard to politicians trained in the wilder, more hyperbolic theatrics of the stump. He was always able to project the studious intelligence that he did actually possess, and was excellent at never appearing uncertain or out of his depths—perhaps the most fatal public impression for anyone contending for high political office. Nixon rarely excited (especially after toning down his more emphatically demagogic style of the late 1940s and early 1950s), but he did re-assure. (The superlative genius of Roosevelt and Reagan was to do both simultaneously.) In 1960, when many Americans felt that Eisenhower had let the country get too boring, excitement was at a premium. But in 1968, a year of more intense domestic turbulence than any, perhaps, since the era of the Civil War, when boredom was the last thing that anyone was complaining about, re-assurance was the more politically valuable quality. In that year Nixon invented the modern media campaign.

This campaign was, of course, the "selling of the president" that Joe McGinnis wrote about to such acclaim the year following the election. But McGinnis's book, effusively praised in its time by such luminaries as John Kenneth Galbraith, Murray Kempton, Jimmy Breslin, Joseph Heller, and Alistair Cooke, has not held up very well. This is not only because the innovations of the Nixon campaign that shocked McGinnis have since become standing operating procedure for all serious presidential efforts; and also not entirely because of the rather patchy knowledge that McGinnis sometimes displays of Nixon and of American politics in general (for example, he imagines that Nixon's chief of staff in 1968 was someone named "R. W. Haldeman"). The most important flaw in *The Selling of the President 1968* is its implication—which seems to have been responsible for the biggest impact the book made on the public—that Nixon was deceptively "packaged" by media advisers like the former advertising man Harry Treleaven and the former CBS television producer Frank Shakespeare: who, we are meant to believe, "sold" Nixon to the electorate like an inanimate commodity. The idea is that the candidate was as passive and as subject to manipulation as soap or cornflakes (indeed, Nixon is pictured on the cover of the best-selling Pocket Books paperback edition of McGinnis's book as a box of laundry detergent). There are at least two fundamental errors here, which need to be cleared up in order to understand what Nixon really did in 1968.

In the first place, the whole notion of "packaging" is philosophically shoddy, at least in the sense that, as normally employed, it operates in implicit opposition to some supposedly pristine or "authentic" presentation of human personality. As Nietzsche was, perhaps, the first to point out with full clarity, *all* presentations of the self are "packaged" in one way or another. There simply *is* no level of "true" selfhood that, pre-existing all language and ideology, is innocent of them and waits to be represented, truly or falsely, by the various arts and techniques of communication.

No better set of examples could be offered than those supplied by the history of political speech. For instance, to complain that the Nixonian innovations of PR politics put paid to a more honest era when politicians offered themselves to the public as they "really" were is to ignore the highly wrought, *artificial* nature of classical rhetoric itself—something that was not only freely admitted but virtually taken for granted by the ancient Greeks who invented it. Insofar as one can judge from reading his speeches and studying the impact they had on his contemporaries, William Jennings Bryan was quite likely the most gifted political orator in American history. Even H. L. Mencken, who despised most American politicians but despised Bryan more bitterly than perhaps any other, granted him excellence in this particular department. It would be difficult to name any specific example of political rhetoric that has had a bigger immediate practical impact than Bryan's most famous oration, the Cross of Gold speech at the 1896 Democratic National Convention. Bryan entered the convention as a very young, relatively little-known Midwesterner who had served two terms in the US House of Representatives. His keynote address so electrified the audience (one reporter on the scene wrote that some delegates, "like demented things, divested themselves of their coats and flung them high in the air") that Bryan left the convention as its presidential nominee.

Yet it would be absurd to claim that the artfully constructed and roaringly delivered speech represented the "true" Bryan (whatever that might mean); and few historians, even those more sympathetic to Bryan's general point of view than to that of the McKinley Republicans he opposed, would conclude from Bryan's rhetorical genius that he would have necessarily made a good president. When FDR's fireside chats began to replace formal public oratory with a more casual form of political speech, many listeners doubtless felt that they were being granted a privileged access into the president's "authentic" consciousness. But that was of course an illusion, one that Roosevelt very carefully devoted his formidable literary and forensic skills to producing. His art was *ars celare artem*, as the Romans put it, the art to conceal art—which may well be the highest, most polished kind of art there is. McGinnis's unique access to Nixon's 1968 media operation enabled him to reveal many interesting details of the way that the candidate's screen persona was constructed. But that a persona *was* being constructed should have been truly shocking only in the way that Captain Renault, in *Casablanca,* is "shocked, *shocked,*" to discover gambling at Rick's place. Constructing a political persona is simply what politicians (especially, perhaps, democratic politicians) do.

A possibly even more fallacious notion encouraged by *The Selling of the President 1968* is that Nixon allowed himself to be manipulated and sold while contributing little more to the effort than a box of detergent contributes to the ad campaigns for it. In the first place, the thing is intrinsically impossible: a human being is not like an item on the supermarket shelf. Speaking is the most fundamental act of human communication, and no amount of coaching or "handling" can produce (though of course it may help to refine and improve) the ability to do it well. Moreover, no politician has ever been more aware of this than Nixon, who always (as he himself bragged) remained firmly in control of his own campaigns. In 1950 it may have been Murray Chotiner who first thought of printing Helen Gahagan Douglas's voting record on pink paper. But, even at that early stage, and even when being assisted by someone as considerably more experienced in politics as Chotiner, Nixon deferred to no one. Shakespeare and Treleaven doubtless contributed technical expertise here and there, but on fundamentals they had little or nothing to teach Nixon. It was Nixon himself who incorporated the arts of modern public relations into presidential campaigning in ways that help to structure our politics to this day.

The most important innovation here was the one-hour question-and-answer sessions between the candidate and members of the general public that the Nixon campaign produced as paid television commercials and splashed lavishly around the nation's airwaves. This format allowed Nixon to employ all his great skill at speaking directly to a television audience, as with the Checkers speech, while the give-and-take with rank-and-file citizens made the whole thing seem more authentic, more spontaneous, more "interactive" (to use a somewhat anachronistic term). The success of the project depended crucially on Nixon's considerable ability to think and talk on his feet. When these programs first aired, many naïvely cynical Nixon-haters assumed that the sessions were well-rehearsed and that the ordinary voters were actually paid professionals working for the Nixon campaign. But no such scripted sessions could have possessed the air of suspense, of vitality, of *reality* that Nixon desired and that was enhanced by the rather daring move of airing the programs live—unless, indeed, the audience personnel had all been Oscar-caliber actors, whose fame would, of course, have defeated the whole purpose of showing Nixon responding to average Americans.

It was not just that Nixon responded fluently and without hesitation (yet not too glibly either) to each questioner. Doing so in response to inexperienced amateurs, for whom even the hot lights were a novelty, could hardly have been difficult for someone who had been more than holding his own for twenty years with the toughest, best-trained professionals of the national press corps. It was also that Nixon modulated his style with each answer, consistently conveying just the right tone. Asked, for instance, about whether his views had changed over the years, Nixon actually *toughened* the question to one about a supposedly "new Nixon" (a common journalistic term of the year), and replied that he had indeed formed new ideas in response to new world realities, though his underlying principles had remained constant. Faced with a rambling statement to no particular point about Eastern Europe, Nixon smoothly expressed sympathy for the problems of the East Europeans (thus pleasing a significant anti-Communist constituency at home). On one occasion, Nixon (perhaps taking a page from John Kennedy's book) even winningly laughed at his own ignorance when a farmer asked a highly specific question about a particular kind of parasite damaging to some crops. But he also assured the questioner of his deep concern for the nation's farmers.

Above all, Nixon managed to present himself consistently as a *re-assuring demagogue*—not the easiest sort of balance to maintain. He kept the racial theme alive (mainly through the universally understood code phrase, "law and order"), while maintaining a visible stylistic distinction between himself and the crude, ugly, untelegenic Wallace. It should be recalled that, in the most practical terms, Wallace, with his rival bid for racist votes, was in many ways more urgently Nixon's competitor that year than Humphrey. It was, indeed, because of Wallace that in 1968 there were no 1960-style debates. Nixon was perfectly willing to debate Humphrey one-on-one. There was little danger that the hapless vice-president (who later said that the greatest mistake of his political career had been not learning how to use television effectively) could do to him what Kennedy had done eight years earlier. But the Democrats insisted that Wallace be included in any such debates, and this Nixon could not allow: for he might then be forced to make the political difference between Wallace and himself clearer than he wished it to be. His advertisements for himself kept that distinction precisely as vague as he wished.

That was, indeed, perhaps *the* key point, at the time, of the whole advertising campaign—since competing successfully with Wallace for racist popular votes was the main thing Nixon had to do in order to amass the 270 or more Electoral votes needed to win the White House. But a longer perspective suggests a larger significance of the Nixon commercials. Though there was no innovation in the mere fact of Nixon's "packaging" himself—since politicians had been doing that, with great elaborateness, at least since Periclean Athens, and probably much longer—there *was* a real novelty in the form of the 1968 media campaign, one of which Joe McGinnis never seems to have been quite aware. Nixon not only presented himself with consummate skill, but he also presented himself, as it were, somewhat in the third person. The question-and-answer sessions were based in format on political press conferences held with professional reporters, and implicitly offered themselves as alternatives to normative journalism—precisely the reason that the campaign reporters following Nixon in 1968 tended to hate the commercials and to love McGinnis's "exposé" of them. The reporters sensed, without quite realizing what was happening, that the ground was shifting under their feet, as the Nixon team produced a simulacrum of "the news" that could well emerge as a serious rival to the real thing. Nixon was not only presenting and re-presenting himself to the electorate with great skill. Nixon was re-presenting presentation itself. He not only spoke to the voters face-to-face, so to speak, but also appeared with the apparent "objectivity" of profile. The content of the 1968 commercials was specific to the concerns of that election year. But the form held great promise (or a great threat) for the future of American politics.

3

The attack on journalism. If there is one myth (aside from white racism) that, for more than four decades, has served the electoral right wing in America more consistently and profitably than perhaps any other, it is the notion of the "liberal media." The notion that what Republicans today call the "mainstream media" (or "MSM" for short)—that is, the news divisions of the three major commercial networks, the news programs on public television and public radio, CNN, the major wire services, prestige newspapers like *The New York Times* and *The Washington Post,* and major news magazines like *Time* and *Newsweek*—promulgate a left-of-center ideology is so preposterous that it almost seems incredible that anyone has ever been made to believe it. To those familiar with the work of investigators who have examined the matter systematically and honestly—such as Jeff Cohen and the other researchers at FAIR (Fairness & Accuracy in Reporting), or press critics like Michael Massing and Eric Alterman—it is obvious enough that, insofar as the mainstream national press can be characterized as a whole, its orientation is overwhelmingly center-right: with some concessions to mild liberalism, occasional concessions to right-wing extremism that are a good deal more frequent than is commonly discussed (a notorious example is Ted Koppel's sympathetic treatment, on his popular *Nightline* program, of the idea of murdering physicians who had performed abortions), and almost no representation of any genuinely left viewpoint. Probably most journalists do vote Democratic (though this seems decreasingly true of the most visible national reporters, with their unprecedentedly huge salaries). But the stance of any organization is almost always determined not by its employees but by its bosses; and reporters, like most employees, are extremely sensitive to the views of their corporate superiors, the great majority of whom have always been conservative Republicans. Furthermore, most American journalists are trained not in substantive fairness but in the shibboleths of a formal, procedural "objectivity"—an indoctrination that often results in people who, as G. K. Chesterton might have put it, would never be so dogmatic as actually to agree with their own views.

The generally conservative orientation of the nation's press was widely recognized until relatively late in the Age of Nixon. Franklin Roosevelt, who described the press as "200 per cent Republican," designed his fireside chats—as people at the time clearly understood—in order to speak directly to an electorate that was being daily bombarded by the overwhelmingly anti-Roosevelt and anti-New-Deal editorializing of the country's newspapers. Joseph McCarthy had complaints about a few individual reporters, but on the whole enjoyed excellent relations with the journalists who covered him. He needed headlines, which they supplied, and they needed good copy, which he supplied; and it would not have occurred to McCarthy to regard the press in general as the enemy. Admittedly, the national media did drift somewhat left in the 1950s and 1960s, as such right-wing press barons as William Randolph Hearst, Colonel Robert McCormick, and Henry Luce passed from the scene. But this drift only meant a gradual modulation from the extreme right to the center-right. Where did the weird notion of a general left-of-center press bias come from?

It came primarily from the Nixon presidency—though not entirely so. Like the appeal to white racism, this aspect of Nixonian strategy was foreshadowed in the Goldwater campaign of 1964. The steady moderation of Lyndon Johnson—who, in the Senate, had been one of the most reliably pro-business and pro-military leaders in the history of that chamber—combined with widespread fears that Barry Goldwater, if elected, might incinerate the planet in a nuclear holocaust to produce a genuine and almost unique press bias in favor of the Democrats that year. The Goldwater campaign responded with reciprocal hostility, though not in any very systematic or effective way. When Eisenhower addressed the 1964 Republican Convention in San Francisco, the Goldwaterites in the audience (who generally despised Ike but tried to be publicly polite to the venerable war hero) responded with real enthusiasm only to a sentence in which the former president criticized "sensation-seeking columnists and commentators." At that line the audience went wild. Delegates jeered and shook clenched fists at the press sections, and some reporters on the scene felt physically threatened. Later, when it was all over and the Goldwater effort had been buried under one of the most crushing landslides in US history, Goldwater himself bitterly wondered aloud where Christianity would be if Matthew, Mark, Luke, and John had been like the journalists covering him. Walter Lippmann, then the undisputed intellectual doyen of mainstream American journalism, acidly replied that the authors of the Gospels had had a more inspiring subject to write about.

So the Goldwater grudge against the press amounted to little. But it seems reasonable to suppose that Nixon, who always followed American politics closely and who, as we have seen, studied the whole Goldwater phenomenon with special care, took some mental notes for future reference. The spontaneous upsurge of anti-press feeling at the San Francisco Cow Palace—though it achieved nothing in the short run except to make the Goldwaterites look even more unbalanced and dangerous than the television audience was already inclined to think them—contained (as one suspects Nixon saw) the germ of something that could later be put to good political use. Furthermore, Nixon had his own reasons, unrelated to the 1964 political season, to be thinking in terms of a war against the news media. Though his own coverage, unlike that of the hapless Goldwater, had been quite favorable on the whole—and would remain such until the Watergate crisis entered its terminal phase—Nixon's *ressentiment* and virtually anal-erotic need for order and control meant that, however favorable, the coverage could never be favorable enough to suit him. Convinced of his own self-sacrificing moral excellence, how could he regard anything short of hagiography as truly fair?

And Nixon knew what hagiography was like. During his House and Senate campaigns, *The Los Angeles Times,* by far the most powerful newspaper in southern California, had functioned practically as an adjunct of the Nixon campaign—thus setting a standard for pro-Nixon fervor that Nixon forever expected all journalism to adhere to. Whenever the coverage of him was slightly critical or even neutral, he became furious. His rambling (and perhaps drunken) attack on the press following his 1962 defeat in California passed instantly into American political legend. There was also, as usual, the matter of Nixon's deep Kennedy-envy. Contrary to a widespread myth for which Nixon himself was largely responsible, Kennedy, in 1960, had generally *not* gotten any special breaks from the press. As noted above, even *The New York Times,* though it editorially endorsed Kennedy, judged him a loser on the night that Kennedy's partisans have always regarded as the most glorious of the campaign. But Nixon did not see matters that way, and, besides, he knew that, whatever editors and publishers might have allowed to appear in print, the working reporters on the campaign trail personally liked Kennedy much better than they liked him; and that hurt. It was in neither Nixon's nature nor his interest to allow such hurts to go unavenged.

But Nixon was sensitive to the political damage he had caused himself by his "last press conference" in 1962, in which he sarcastically invited the reporters to "think how much you're going to be missing," because, "you won't have Nixon to kick around anymore." He came to understand that the press *could* be undermined, but not by such peevish frontal attacks that made him sound like a weakling and a whiner. The assault on journalism must be a little subtler, and ideally should be launched from a position of massive strength, like the White House. Furthermore, after winning the presidency, Nixon found that he had to hand the perfect instrument for the anti-media offensive: namely, his singularly unprepossessing vice-president, Spiro T. Agnew.

It is worth recalling a few things about this now mostly forgotten figure, whose name was for several years intimately linked to Nixon's in the public mind and who sometimes seemed almost *more* prominent on the national scene. Agnew had been a surprise choice as Nixon's running mate at the 1968 convention. His name was "not a household word," as a reporter commented shortly after Agnew's selection, and Agnew himself laughingly agreed—and no one really believed that the somewhat oafish and not very bright Agnew was (in the formula that all presidential nominees repeat about their running mates) the person best qualified to take over as president if the need should ever arise. But Nixon's political calculations in picking him were, as usual, impeccably shrewd. Odd though it may seem, Agnew, with his brief yet complicated political history—he had served less than two years as governor of Maryland when he joined the national ticket—was almost uniquely qualified to help keep Nixon's party unified behind him, and to allow him to pursue his general-election strategy as the "moderate" alternative to George Wallace. Agnew had been elected Maryland's governor as a comparative racial liberal running against a notoriously racist Democrat; and he had firmly identified himself with Nelson Rockefeller's brand of liberal-to-moderate Republicanism. But more recently—specifically, in the wake of the race riots in Baltimore and elsewhere that followed the assassination of Martin Luther King in April 1968—Agnew had taken to attacking civil-rights leaders and to using (codedly) racist rhetoric himself. He eventually dropped his once enthusiastic support of Rockefeller in order to endorse Nixon for the Republican nomination. The common journalistic wisdom of the day naively expected Nixon to choose as his running-mate one of the attractive young Republican moderates known for opposition to racism. Senator Mark Hatfield of Oregon, Senator Charles Percy of Illinois, Governor John Chafee of Rhode Island, and Mayor John Lindsay of New York City were all widely mentioned as possibilities. But such a pick would probably have shattered Nixon's all-important alliance with Strom Thurmond and undermined his Southern strategy. On the other hand, selecting an out-and-out racist like Thurmond himself would have fatally compromised Nixon's own appearance of moderation. Agnew was just ambiguous enough to pass muster with all concerned.

Nor did Agnew's usefulness to Nixon end on election day. As one suspects Nixon foresaw, Agnew made up in loyalty and gusto what he lacked in brains or subtlety. The new Veep was happy to deliver the sort of fierce partisan attacks that might seem beneath presidential dignity, and to serve as a lightning rod for criticism that might otherwise have been directed at Nixon. Nixon, of course, had performed a similar function as Eisenhower's VP, and Eugene McCarthy described Agnew as "Nixon's Nixon." Probably Agnew's most famous blast against Nixon's adversaries was his 1970 attack in Houston on antiwar student protesters as "an impudent core of effete snobs who characterize themselves as intellectuals." The line became the signature phrase of the Nixon Administration's stance towards its antiwar opponents. Young student protesters defiantly wore buttons that said, "I'm An Effete Snob For Peace," and Agnew became a national monster to many Americans, a national hero to many others. Of course, Agnew's speeches (as is always the case with vice-presidents) were carefully planned at the White House; most of his famous lines were authored by the Nixon speechwriters William Safire and Patrick Buchanan. Nonetheless, some mainstream political analysts of the more naïve sort (which is to say most of them) began to speculate about an ideological rift within the administration, with Agnew seen as the right-wing alternative to the more centrist, "moderate" Nixon—precisely the impression that Nixon desired.

Agnew's most enduring legacy, however, was established a bit earlier, by a speech in Des Moines to the Midwestern Regional Republican Conference on 13 November 1969. Nixon had taken to using his skill as a television performer in order to make more frequent national addresses on TV than any of his predecessors had ever done. The three networks all routinely donated to him, free of charge, as much of their extremely expensive airtime as he wished—thus providing Nixon, in those pre-cable days, with a virtual monopoly of television viewers—and usually provided commentary by their own or guest analysts afterwards. The comments were always respectful and frequently positive, but not always completely uncritical; and even the merest whisper of criticism, especially on the subject about which he was most sensitive—the Vietnam War—was more than Nixon could tolerate.

Agnew began his Des Moines speech by referring to a recent presidential address on Vietnam, and bitterly condemned the "querulous criticism" that he (or, actually, Nixon) found in some of the commentary on it. The attack on the network analysis continued at some length, and even included condemnation of "the expressions on their [the analysts'] faces," which Agnew deemed insufficiently respectful (readers of George Orwell's *Nineteen Eighty-four* will recall the grave offense called *facecrime*). More remarkably still, Agnew made the breathtaking claim that "the President of the United States has a right to communicate directly with the people who elected him, and the people of this country have the right to make up their own minds and form their own opinions about a presidential address without having a president's words and thoughts characterized through the prejudices of hostile critics before they can even be digested." Perhaps never, before or since, has a representative of the White House explicitly asserted such despotic powers. Agnew was maintaining that Nixon not only had the *right* to commandeer the networks' private property—the airtime they were voluntarily giving up—but also that other Americans appearing on television had no right to offer their own thoughts, at least until the president's words had been "digested," however long that might take. The claim, logically, was that, at least insofar as television was concerned, the presidency amounted to elective dictatorship.

Nor was that all. Agnew also attacked the network journalists personally. He called them "a small unelected elite," who, shockingly, "wield a free hand in selecting, presenting, and interpreting the great issues in our nation." He repeatedly characterized them as an isolated clique that was unrepresentative of the nation as a whole, noting that they tended to live in Washington, DC, or in New York City, the latter of which he condemned as "the most unrepresentative community in the entire United States." Accordingly, said Agnew, "the views of the majority of this fraternity do *not*—and I repeat, not—represent the views of America." Perhaps most ominously, Agnew suggested that "perhaps it is time that the networks were made more responsive to the views of the nation and more responsible to the people they serve."

Interestingly, Agnew did not overtly dwell on the putative ideology of the journalists he attacked so bitterly; the words *liberal* and *left* do not even occur in the Des Moines speech. But then, he didn't really have to. His speech condemned the television journalists for criticizing Nixon, and—even leaving aside such specific touches as the reference to New York City, which was, then as now, widely considered the *de facto* capital of American liberalism (and of American Jewry)—the entire context made it clear that he was not talking about criticism from the right. Reading words originally composed by the skilled rhetorician Buchanan, and then revised and polished by Nixon personally, Agnew constructed the network news organizations not as "objective" purveyors of truth but as a political and intellectual faction well to the left of the Nixon Administration and determined to oppose it mercilessly. Indeed, the Des Moines speech very nearly insinuates that it was *only* the journalists who really opposed Nixon. For Agnew claimed emphatically that the American people and their elected representatives in Congress differed sharply from the networks in warmly approving of Nixon's policies.

The Des Moines speech was, almost certainly, the most successful and consequential ever delivered by an American vice-president, at least during the twentieth century or since. Reaction to it was strong and immediate. The networks themselves were plainly terrified by this unexpected assault. They responded with characteristic timidity, eliminating or scaling back their commentary on future presidential addresses to the nation, and giving less airtime to coverage of antiwar protests. Sensing weakness, the Nixon Administration intensified its attacks and expanded them beyond the network news divisions to "the media" in general. Agnew happily continued as the nation's leading press-basher, but others of the president's men joined in too—while the president himself, still mindful of the disaster of 1962's "last press conference," maintained a dignified public restraint on the issue.

Some journalists tried to rebut the charges against them. But, even apart from the generally prevailing cowardice, the mainstream media were, in a way, caught in a trap of their own making. Since "objective" journalists were professionally committed to the ludicrous notion that they had *no* viewpoint, at least none that could be reasonably inferred from their work, they could hardly reply with the truth: namely that their coverage of the president was, in fact, generally favorable and that their organizations maintained a basically center-right political orientation. Indeed, much of what Agnew said in Des Moines, when stripped from its partisan context, was actually true. Most mainstream journalism *was* (and is) produced by a relatively small group of generally like-minded individuals, whose collective point of view was (and is) by no means necessarily identical to that of most Americans. The genius of the Nixon (or Nixon-Buchanan) strategy that emerged in Agnew's speech was to begin with this irrefutable point and then to claim that the most influential national journalism, far from being (as it usually was) somewhat more conservative than the hypothetical middle point of American opinion, was actually well to the *left* of it.

In the absence of convincing, wholehearted counterclaims by the media under attack, the inevitable effect was to shift the entire spectrum of respectable opinion measurably to the right.

Bullied into submission, the media could appear less "biased" in the ways that Agnew had charged only by becoming still more conservative and, in particular, by becoming more pro-Nixon. In the wake of the Des Moines speech, most coverage of the president modulated from generally favorable to almost worshipful. By the end of 1969, David Broder, the influential political analyst for *The Washington Post*, was praising Nixon for having "restored confidence in government's ability to govern." Even John Osborne at *The New Republic*—who, atypically, made little pretense of "objectivity" and was widely considered to be seriously critical of Nixon—wrote that "Nixon the President seems to me to have become a stronger man, a more decent and credible man..." These lines, it is worth recalling, were composed only a few months after Nixon had expressed his contempt for the United States Supreme Court (and for the United States) by nominating to it one Clement Haynsworth, a judge of dubious financial probity and obvious intellectual mediocrity—only to have the nomination rejected in an unusual display of statesmanship by the Senate.

The Nixonian assault on journalism continued to pay big dividends for the administration—most importantly during the summer and fall of 1972. Facing re-election, Nixon could potentially have been hurt by the reports that *The Washington Post* published about the involvement of his subordinates in the Watergate burglaries and the cover-up of them. Yet the offensive begun in Des Moines worked to shield Nixon from political damage. Most of the press remained so frightened of appearing anti-Nixon that they simply ignored the story, leaving the general impression that there couldn't be much to it. Despite a very few exceptions—most notably a special investigation that Walter Cronkite undertook on his *CBS Evening News* program (though it was truncated at the insistence of network executives after complaints from the White House)—the national media in general tacitly co-operated with the administration's efforts to depict the *Post* as a rogue newspaper pursuing a political vendetta against the president. Of course, this depiction was rendered all the more plausible by the success Nixon had achieved in constructing the press generally as a "liberal" and anti-Nixon political faction. As Nixon put together his landslide re-election, Watergate registered hardly at all as an electoral factor. Even the *Post* itself sharply reduced its Watergate coverage during the campaign's final days.

Eventually, of course, Nixon's endless series of lies and cover-ups caused Watergate to overwhelm him anyway. The anti-Nixon cause could hardly be portrayed as a merely left-of-center one when it came to include such staunch conservatives as Senator Sam Ervin of North Carolina and, finally, Barry Goldwater himself. Yet, even as Nixon fell into the unprecedented disgrace of forced resignation, the still traumatized press remained wary of appearing too "liberal." Nixon was succeeded by the deeply conservative Republican Gerald Ford, and Ford's assumption of the presidency was celebrated in the national media by an astonishing orgy of adulation. The height (or depth) of this spate of president-worship was reached, perhaps, when the *CBS Evening News*—the same program that had displayed a measure of courage and journalistic responsibility during Watergate—one morning sent a camera crew into the family living quarters of the White House in order to film Ford toasting and buttering an English muffin, then sitting down to eat it with a cup of coffee. Thus did CBS News, at that time the most respected organization in broadcast journalism, devote a few precious minutes of its evening news program to confirming (out of all the stories in the world that it might have covered) widely circulated reports that the new president was in the habit of making his own breakfast. Agnew himself was gone by this point—forced to resign the vice-presidency in a deal to avoid prison time for some tawdry financial corruption—but, in America's newsrooms, his soul went marching on.

Nor has that march halted to this day. Nixon's construction of the mainstream media as a left-of-center monolith proved far too valuable for the right wing to abandon it after its author's fall. If anything, indeed, the attacks launched in Des Moines have only become shriller and more persistent over the years and decades, continuing to intimidate most of the national press and driving them further and further right—though they have generally remained within the broad confines of a center-right orientation. (They have also responded by scaling back political reporting altogether, in favor of innocuous, uncontroversial "lifestyle" stories and "news you can use.") Probably the greatest neo-Nixonian innovation in the attack on mainstream political journalism is one that Nixon himself, dying in 1994, didn't quite live to see and that he could only have admired mightily: namely, the building of what might be called a counter-mainstream media establishment devoted to providing "balance" in the face of the older media's putative "liberal" bias. This counter-establishment includes such newspapers as *The Washington Times* and the long-established *Wall Street Journal*, but is much more consequentially represented by Fox News on television, by the majority of talk radio, and by some of the Internet blogosphere. This interlocking set of organs—reasonably coherent in political stance though not entirely homogeneous—promulgates, with varying degrees of forthrightness, a militantly reactionary ideology sharply to the right of the more moderate formation of the older media establishment: thus helping to define the spectrum of permissible opinion in US public discourse as ranging from center-right to hard right. Fox News is by long odds the single most influential component of this right-wing counter-establishment; and it is neither surprising nor accidental that its founding genius, Roger Ailes, got his start in the political big time as a media adviser to Nixon's 1968 campaign.

Ailes was deeply involved in the production of Nixon's

campaign commercials that year, and so suggests in his very person the congruence between the Nixonian assault on the normative presentation of the national news and the Nixonian construction of political PR as a simulacrum of the news. They were—and are—twin projects. On the one hand, Nixon sowed distrust of the version of reality presented by the news organizations that had generally been considered relatively trustworthy and uncontroversial: while, on the other hand, he offered to the public his *own*, simulated version, a simulacrum of the news typified not only by the 1968 question-and-answer sessions but by many other productions as well (for example, the excellent documentary-style films about him shown at the 1972 Republican Convention, which were produced by David Wolper, one of the most prestigious makers of genuine documentaries). In a sense, the ultimate target of this blurring of the boundary between news and advertising was the concept of objectivity itself. There is a straight line between Nixon's innovations and the attitude famously typified by an anonymous and widely quoted official of the George W. Bush Administration, who scorned mainstream journalists for being "reality-based," and for failing to understand that the president and his people were capable of "making their own reality."

In strictly intellectual terms, to attack the concept of pristinely objective reality is, as we saw in chapter 2, like kicking through a rotten door. Philosophically, the concept was effectively killed by Kant in the eighteenth century, and then buried with elaborate funeral rituals in the nineteenth century by Marx, and, especially, Nietzsche. Even within the natural sciences, simplistically "objective" empiricism did not survive quantum mechanics, relativity theory, and other advances of modern physics. But, as Nietzsche explained more clearly, perhaps, than any other thinker, the ultimate issue raised by the hopelessly problematic character of objectivity as a theoretical concept is simply *power*. Nixon thought and wrote less elegantly than

Nietzsche but had just as sure a grasp of this very point. Indeed, we might almost say that, what Nietzsche and others have done in philosophy, Nixon—more than any other single individual—did in American electoral politics. The attack on mainstream journalism combined with the new techniques of political salesmanship to create new opportunities for the production and circulation of Nixonian—and post-Nixonian—cultural power. The question, as that proto-Nietzschean, Humpty Dumpty in *Alice in Wonderland,* said, is who is to be master. Lewis Carroll's Alice does not seem to understand the point, but Nixon understood it perfectly. And *he* determined to be master.

4

The presidential imperium. Although the once-conventional wisdom that held Nixon (at least prior to his White House years) to be relatively unconcerned with money has had to be modified in the light of Anthony Summers's detailed biographical research—which establishes that Nixon took an active interest in the pursuit of wealth from the beginning of his political career, not scrupling even to become financially involved with organized crime—yet the older image should not be discarded as entirely misleading. Nixon himself, of course, frequently and emphatically promoted (perhaps most memorably in the Checkers speech) the notion that he was a man free from material avarice. Though, as usual with Nixon, this self-presentation involved a good deal of hypocrisy, it also contained a significant amount of psychological and symbolic, if not strictly literal, truth.

The clearest evidence here is to be found simply in the overall trajectory of his career. Entering politics in 1946 was doubtless a smart career move in all respects for Nixon, whose earlier work as a practicing attorney had displayed little promise of brilliance or future wealth. It made similarly good sense to move up to the Senate in 1950 and to join Eisenhower's ticket in 1952. But, after losing the presidency to Kennedy in 1960, Nixon could easily have enjoyed a comfortable, affluent life as a well-connected Republican lawyer in Los Angeles. The law firm he joined after his move back home from Washington was happy to give him good pay for undemanding work, since, of course, the payment was in large part simply for the prestige of having a former vice-president's name on the firm's stationery. Nixon himself notes in *Six Crises* that his income *tax* for the first year back in California was double his vice-presidential salary. Yet, instead of continuing on this pleasant path, he soon plunged back into the world of political competition, running for an office—governor of California—that he later admitted had little intrinsic appeal for him. After being defeated by Pat Brown in 1962, he joined a New York law firm that was even wealthier and more high-powered than his Los Angeles one. Once again, he had the opportunity to live a life of material ease, doing as much or as little legal work as he chose, while pulling down a huge income and enjoying the best of everything in sumptuous Manhattan style. This was precisely the course that his wife, by all accounts, desired. But once again Nixon chose the bitterness, grinding hard work, and uncertainty of politics. Why?

The question nearly answers itself. As much as Nixon may have desired wealth, he desired political power even more. In Freudian terms, the love of order was a stronger component than monetary acquisitiveness in his particular anal-erotic personality. But the most interesting point here is that, for Nixon, this preference was not merely a personal taste but seems—as we might expect in such a strenuous moralist—to have been shot through with profound ethical significance. Early and late, Nixon genuinely bristled at imputations of financial corruption, which he always regarded as deeply shameful in a way that, for him, did not apply at all to the corruptions of power. Indeed, it is not clear that the latter concept even truly existed in his mind. The Checkers speech was not only a brilliant bit of political strategy but also a heartfelt, agonized denial of the charges of venality that had been laid against him. Much later, there were, among the myriad scandals commonly grouped under the single rubric of Watergate, a few that were financial in nature—and it was these, and even these alone, that appeared to wound Nixon personally. To other people, in the main, they seemed almost laughably minor: e.g., his illegal backdating (for the sake of a hefty tax break) of the contribution of his vice-presidential papers to the government; or the public funds spent on improving his private homes in San Clemente and Key Biscayne for "security" purposes that turned out to require items like a shuffleboard court and an automatic ice-maker. What did such things matter in comparison to his assaults on the Constitution? Yet it was primarily the tax cheating—not, say, the cover-up of the burglaries of the Democratic National Committee offices in the Watergate hotel—that Nixon was referring to when he made his infamous denial, "Well, I'm not a crook" (a claim that became probably the most widely ridiculed statement by any US president in history). "I made my mistakes," he went on to the amazed audience of Associated Press editors that he was addressing in a televised news conference, "but in all of my years of public life I have never profited from public service."

Profit? *Crook*? The irony is that, for Nixon's opponents—a category that came to include the great majority of the American people—Nixon's crookedness, though certainly not laudable, was nearly the most normal, the most human, the most forgivable thing about him. For one thing, monetary greed is more normal than power-lust in the straightforward statistical sense. Nearly all of us would like to have more money in our pockets, but the desire to be able to tell large numbers of people what to do is a considerably more specialized taste. Then too, material avarice is more self-limiting—in large part because it is only extrinsically competitive, whereas the compulsion to amass power is constantly and intrinsically so. We desire more money but, with most of us, only somewhat more; and my capacity to buy the things I want is in no *direct* way impaired by the capacity of others to do the same. But power-lust is absolute, and by its very nature insatiable. My neighbors' power to do things—even if it is only the power to organize their own lives as they choose—even, indeed, if it is only the power to continue living at all—is a direct limitation on my power to do whatever I want with them and to them. The fact that Nixon stole an infinitesimal amount of my money to buy himself an ice-maker is, no doubt, annoying. But it essentially wounds me no more than being very slightly overcharged at the store. I am wounded in a much more serious way by the Nixonian conspiracies to render my right to vote effectively meaningless. The prototypical extreme of material greed is instanced by someone like J.P. Morgan: hardly a benign social presence by any sane standards, but, in his direct effects on those around him, considerably less destructive than someone like Hitler, the type of the absolute drive for political power.

But Nixon was, by all the evidence, genuinely incapable of grasping the corruptions of power. Indeed, this incapacity may well have been the main reason why his political instincts—which had hitherto been so close to pitch-perfect—failed him so disastrously during Watergate. Himself unable to take seriously the most important charges against him, he found it hard to believe that *others* would take them seriously either—let alone seriously enough to force the unprecedented step of impeaching and removing from office an American president. Even when it was all over, and when, on the ninth of August, 1974, he was addressing his White House staff on his last morning in office, Nixon could still think of no better way to defend his presidency than to issue yet one more denial of petty financial corruption. The following passage represents but one sounding of the theme:

> No man or no woman came into this administration and left it with more of this world's goods than when he came

> in. No man or no woman ever profited at the public expense or the public till. That tells something about you. Mistakes, yes. But for personal gain, never. You did what you believed in. Sometimes right, sometimes wrong. And I only wish that I were a—a wealthy man—at the present time I've got to find a way to pay my taxes—and if I were, I'd like to recompense you for the [financial] sacrifices that all of you've made to serve in government.

The tone is virtually identical to that of the Checkers speech—the same mawkish self-revelation, the same bragging about his supposedly straitened monetary circumstances, and of course the same flat denial of monetary wrong-doing.

Nor is that all. The real, though usually forgotten, center-piece of the speech is a long quotation from Theodore Roosevelt, describing his feelings upon the death of his first wife, who died when they were both in their twenties. ["W]hen my heart's dearest died," said TR, "the light went from my life forever." But, comments Nixon, it was not so. He notes that Roosevelt went on to a brilliant political career that included not only the presidency but also an unusually active ex-presidency—while, significantly, *failing* to note that the bereaved widower was remarried (to his childhood sweetheart) two years after his loss. "We think," Nixon goes on, "that when someone dear to us dies, we think that when we lose an election, we think that when we suffer a defeat, that all is ended….Not true. It's only a beginning—always." The equivalence assumed between the death of a loved one and the loss of a political office is staggering enough. But even more so, perhaps, is the implied positive side of the equation: namely, the notion that the possession of political power is like married love, at once sanctified and passionately consuming. Unlike the love of money, the love of power, far from being potentially corrupting, is, for Nixon, as noble as the love of a loving wife.

And power, for Nixon, should be not only loved but—again

the erotic parallel seems plain—*enjoyed*. In *Leaders*, the most self-revealing of all Nixon's books outside the strictly autobiographical ones—and composed when his emotions had had nearly eight years to calm down after the harrowing events that culminated in the resignation of August 1974—enjoyment is the precise category that Nixon repeatedly and explicitly invokes in outlining the attitude that the true leader should take towards power. He admits, indeed, that it takes "a particular kind of person" to enjoy power properly. "Power," after all, "is not for the nice guy down the street or for the man next door." "[T]he qualities required for leadership," he goes on, hammering the point home, "are not necessarily those we would want our children to emulate." But they are clearly the qualities he values most in himself and in others. Nixon frequently praised himself but never, perhaps, more ardently than on the occasion when the White House taping machine heard him listing himself as one of only three men in America "who really understand the use of power" (the other two admitted into this august company were John Connally and, more grudgingly, Nelson Rockefeller). To understand the use of power is the *ne plus ultra* of Nixonian compliment—when combined, of course, with the will actually to make such use happen. In the final chapter of *Leaders*, the particular quality that Nixon singles out for praise in Lincoln, the ultimate leader, is his willingness to gather in his hands the maximum amount of untrammeled power. The sixteenth president, writes Nixon admiringly, "broke laws, he violated the Constitution, he usurped arbitrary power, he trampled individual liberties"—always for good reason, to be sure.

Nixon's motives in composing that sentence surely included more than a little self-justification: for he was unlikely to have forgotten that the actions he finds so commendable in Lincoln were the same as those for which his own adversaries drove him from office. Once condemned by many as a tyrant, Lincoln eventually became the most widely and exuberantly admired of all American heroes. Could not Nixon hope for a similar fate? Though this hope may seem like a pathological delusion, it is important to recognize that Nixon's love of power was *not* a mere pathology. If it was pathological at all, it was but the pathological extreme of something as "normal" and as deeply American as the cult of Lincoln itself: namely, the closely related cult of the "strong president."

Here, indeed, we find another filiation between Nixon and the American tradition of procedural liberalism. For—at least up until Nixon's own administration—few assumptions had been more securely lodged within liberal political science in the US than the notion that the most powerful presidents in our history have been, almost by definition, the best. In this understanding, the "weak," or bad, president is the one who leaves Congress more-or-less to its own devices and lets the country drift where it may. By contrast, the "strong," or good, president bends both the country and its elected representatives to his own will. Such criteria can result in grotesque judgments on particular individuals. The virulently anti-labor Grover Cleveland (conventionally ranked as "near-great") and the repressive, racist, bellicose Woodrow Wilson (conventionally ranked as "great") are absurdly overrated because, at any rate, they *did* things. On the other hand, Ulysses S. Grant is commonly dismissed as a (rare) instance of outright presidential failure because of the way his presidency got bogged down in financial corruption—despite the fact that the Grant Administration, for all its faults, did (in partnership with Congress) make a serious, partly successful, and (prior to the presidency of Lyndon Johnson) unique effort to establish a measure of racial equality for black citizens.

Still other presidents are simply misunderstood by the cultists of presidential strength. George Washington, for example, is praised for being strong and great. Yet, in his own time, Washington was particularly admired, especially in Europe, for the way he *declined* to "enjoy" (as Nixon would say) power and strength. Twice he stunned the world by renouncing executive power: first when he resigned his military command at the end of the Revolutionary War, refusing to overthrow the Continental Congress and establish a Cromwell-style military dictatorship, as most of the Continental Army wished and expected him to do; and then again when he retired from the presidency after serving only two terms. Even when serving as general or president, Washington frequently exercised a good deal more restraint in the use of power than circumstances required.

The liberal misunderstanding of Washington points to a more general discrepancy between the cult of presidential power and the more traditional view of such things. "Power tends to corrupt and absolute power corrupts absolutely"—Lord Acton's famous aphorism describes a certain classical wisdom whose adherents have ranged from Aristotle, to Thomas Aquinas, to Washington himself, to the Lenin of *State and Revolution*. But the celebrants of the "strong" American president have not only rejected this view but turned it on its head. For them power tends not to corrupt but to *ennoble* and even to sanctify. This can be seen most clearly, perhaps, in the once largely taken-for-granted—but, when one comes to think of it, almost unspeakably weird—idea that a man (and of course it always has been a man) who assumes the US presidency, whether by election or direct succession, tends to "grow in office." Power is assumed to exercise such fantastic intellectual and moral alchemy as to transform, almost overnight, an ordinary hack politician into a visionary statesman. Like a religious relic, the Oval Office works miracles.

Perhaps this grotesque and almost entirely counterfactual notion—from which Nixon himself, until overwhelmed by Watergate, mightily benefited in the press coverage of him—is at least partly an effect of the Constitutional accident that the US president combines in a single person the functions of both head of government and head of state: so that the grandeur and glory often held to inhere naturally in the latter are inevitably attributed to the former as well. During Watergate, certainly, many British observers suddenly found themselves becoming ardent royalists, grateful that their own country's political system separated the majesty of the monarchy from the more humdrum and, by US standards, fairly limited governing powers of the prime minister. Be that as it may, Nixon's own glorification of power, and his determined expansion of his own presidential power to the maximum, was very much in the (liberal) American grain. Liberal American political theorists like Arthur Scheslinger (who seems to have had some influence in instructing his hero John Kennedy in the virtues of the "strong president") may have been horrified by the arrogant imperium into which Nixon made, or tried to make, the US presidency. But what horrified them was the sight of their *own* chickens coming home to roost.

Not, of course, that the increasing power of the White House in American politics began—or ended—with Nixon. The longstanding cult of presidential strength reflected, in part, precisely this increase, which can be traced back at least as far as Andrew Jackson (another of Scheslinger's heroes) and which became especially marked with Nixon's beloved Lincoln. The growing magnification of the presidency is closely related to—indeed, at some points coterminous with—the larger pattern of national centralization that we have already discussed. Both trends are doubtless attributable—"in the last instance," as Marxism has it—to the changing needs of American capitalism as the latter passed from its relatively laissez-faire nineteenth-century stage to its modern or monopoly phase, when the reproduction and expansion of US capital came to require much more extensive intervention into the economy by the state.

But Nixon's personal contributions to the growth of the presidential power he loved so much in both theory and practice should not be underestimated. Indeed, this growth can be seen as, in many ways, the ultimate aim of his entire political career—

more than the war on cancer, more than the opening to China or the détente with the Soviets—and it is deeply connected to the other long-term trends discussed in this chapter that Nixon did so much to further. The continuing centralization of power in the nation's capital helped to enhance the authority of the White House by diminishing the persistence of rival power elites centered in regions, states, or large municipalities (a factor that had often limited Franklin Roosevelt, though he was by long odds the most powerful president up to his own time). The undermining of the mainstream national press largely emasculated its ability to function as a true "fourth estate" that could meaningfully check the power of the presidency, while the construction of new forms of political communication designed to simulate journalism carried the fight to the press's own territory.

Sometimes, to be sure, Nixon expressed his lust for power in ways that were unintentionally comical, though certainly not any the less revealing of the man. The most (in)famous example remains his order that the White House guards be dressed in fancy uniforms that looked as though they had been designed for Balkan military officers as represented in an Italian comic opera. The public ridicule was sufficiently robust that Nixon felt compelled to abandon the plan. But there was little funny about most of Nixon's grabs for more power, which, of course, came to include the high crimes that ultimately brought him down. The Watergate felonies, it should be remembered, were aimed not only at centers of electoral opposition like the McGovern and Muskie campaigns and the Democratic National Committee, nor even only at more pointedly ideological enemies in the antiwar movement like Daniel Ellsberg. In Nixon's drive to accumulate as much power as possible in the White House, Watergate—in the largest sense—also represented an assault on other organs of the executive branch of the national government, including the two most important repressive apparatuses, the FBI and the CIA.

Indeed, the Plumbers—the secret White House unit designed to plug leaks by burglary, wiretapping, and any other means necessary—was established by Nixon precisely because he felt he could not trust the FBI (then headed by the uniquely powerful J. Edgar Hoover) to be sufficiently subservient to him.

Eventually, of course, Nixon *was* brought down, and his power—specifically his presidential power—reduced to zero. Should, then, his augmentation of the imperial presidency be considered an ultimate failure? Yes and no. It is clear that Nixon overreached, especially in picking a fight with the CIA, which he attempted to use to its own detriment in managing the Watergate cover-up. A persistent though never quite proven hypothesis in Watergate scholarship has long held that Alexander Butterfield, the Nixon aide who publicly revealed the existence of the taping system that played an indispensable role in Nixon's downfall, was actually the CIA's man in the White House: and that, more specifically, Butterfield, in informing Congress and the public of the taping system, was taking orders from Richard Helms, the former Director of Central Intelligence, who, defending his agency and himself, schemed to get rid of the president. If this interpretation is true, then Nixon's forced resignation was almost a kind of historical accident. If only he had been willing to work *with* rather than against and in competition with the FBI and the CIA—which were, after all, organs of his own executive—perhaps he might have survived. In that case, the Watergate narrative can hardly be considered a simple case of the good guys finally winning, to invoke the title of Jimmy Breslin's book on Nixon's political downfall. In that case too, the outcome of Watergate, far from proving that "the system worked"—as the favored journalistic cliché of the 1970s had it—only proved the wisdom of the (presumably) fictional lines spoken by Nixon in the Oliver Stone film: "You don't fuck with Dick Helms, period."

This is speculation. But the articles of impeachment against Nixon that the House Judiciary Committee passed (and that the full House eventually accepted with only three dissenting votes—though Nixon, foreseeing the certain outcome, had resigned in the meantime) are a matter of inarguable public record. The committee passed three articles (though it considered others), all of them concerned with matters of political and legal *process*. Nixon was condemned for obstructing justice by impeding the criminal investigation into the Watergate burglaries; for improperly using such federal agencies as the CIA, the FBI, the IRS, and the Secret Service in ways that violated the Constitutional rights of US citizens; and for defying the committee's own subpoenas in its investigation of the impeachment issue. These were serious enough crimes by any reasonable standards. But it is interesting that the committee expressly *rejected* a number of other charges no less provable and in some cases even more serious: most notably Nixon's secret bombing of Cambodia, an entirely illegal and unprovoked attack on a helpless neutral nation. Especially since it led directly to mass murder and the devastation of Cambodian society during the rule of the Khmer Rouge, Nixon's assault on the country must be accounted one of the great war crimes of the twentieth century. Yet Congress refused to make it a formal charge against Nixon, even in the act of ousting him from the presidency. The motive seems to have been *not* actual approval of Nixon's actions in Southeast Asia, but rather a reluctance to interfere with presidential power itself, specifically the presidential power of warmaking, however illegally or immorally it may have been exercised. Congress, in its move against the thirty-seventh president, felt secure only when staking its case on his violations of generally accepted legal and political processes. If, on one level, Nixon may have been brought low by the brilliant bureaucratic maneuvers of Richard Helms, on another he was certainly felled—paradoxically enough—by one of the more statesmanlike and courageous expressions of the liberal proceduralism that he himself in so many ways exemplified.

In any case, the defeat of Nixon halted the growth of the presidential imperium only temporarily. Probably the Ford and Carter Administrations were somewhat more restrained than they might otherwise have been in their "enjoyment" of power because of the aftereffects of Watergate. But, at least from 1980 onwards, the Nixonian concept of the presidency has again been in the ascendant. This is not the place to discuss the exceedingly complex high crimes and misdemeanors of the Reagan White House that were (somewhat) revealed in the Iran-Contra scandal—not to mention those that the George W. Bush White House, in its determination to attack and occupy Iraq, seems to have committed and that have yet to be more than very partially exposed to public view. It seems a safe guess, however, that, as we learn more about presidential adventures in illegal and unprovoked warfare, we will find that, in the matter of presidential power as in so many other ways, our age remains the Age of Nixon.

Epilogue: Nixon in Art

1

There have been a good many works of art based on the character and career of Richard Nixon—more, probably, than about any other American president since Lincoln, Nixon's own chief role model—and among them are at least three items of major aesthetic significance: Robert Coover's novel *The Public Burning* (1977), John Adams's opera *Nixon in China* (1987), and Oliver Stone's film *Nixon* (1995). Stone's film is, inarguably I think, his own masterpiece to date, and it is at least arguably the finest biographical film in English since David Lean's *Lawrence of Arabia*. *The Public Burning* is—along with Joyce's *Ulysses*, Thomas Pynchon's *Gravity's Rainbow*, and perhaps two or three others—one of the most successful modern novels in English of truly epic scope and achievement. *Nixon in China* seems to have pretty securely established itself as the most popular modern opera among both professional music critics and the opera-going public. It is perhaps no real paradox that a man so distrustful of the arts should have proved such a great inspiration to artists.

Though Coover's novel seems to me far and away the most important literary treatment of Nixon, there are a number of other works of prose and poetry worth mentioning. Among them are two neo-Swiftian satires, Philip Roth's *Our Gang (Starring Tricky and His Friends)* (1971)—a fable written in a white heat of savage indignation directly reminiscent of Swift himself—and Gore Vidal's *An Evening with Richard Nixon* (1972), a more urbane text that condemns the thirty-seventh president largely through his own words taken from the public record. (One might also mention here Vidal's other notable representation of Nixon, namely the thoroughly Nixonian character Joe Cantwell in his play *The Best Man* [1960], made into a good film of the same title in 1964 by Franklin J. Shaffner). In a different genre, Philip K.

Dick, the finest American science-fiction writer, memorably expressed a life-long antipathy to Nixon's politics in *Radio Free Albemuth*, in which Nixon appears as President Ferris F. Fremont. The novel was written in about 1976 but (uniquely among the author's science fiction) remained unpublished until 1985, three years after his death. Another memorably science-fictional treatment of Nixon is Eileen Gunn's widely admired short story "Fellow Americans" (1991). Mark Maxwell's much underappreciated novel *NixonCarver* (1998)—which for me is second in quality only to *The Public Burning* among these works of prose fiction—might also be classified as science fiction, for it is set in an alternative historical line in which Nixon and the short-story writer Raymond Carver developed a quirky but close friendship during their later years. It is one of those works whose premise, stated in the abstract, sounds peculiar and unpromising but whose execution redeems the design with rare persuasiveness and brilliance. Finally, we should not overlook *The Company* (1976), John Ehrlichman's best-selling *roman à clef*. Nixon's chief domestic-policy adviser, like so many others of the president's men, found himself seriously embarrassed by legal bills shortly after leaving Nixon's service. To help rebuild his finances, Ehrlichman published this surprisingly taut and well-constructed thriller. The portrait of Nixon, as President Richard Monckton, seems to be based on close personal observation.

Poets appear to have been less frequently inspired by Nixon than prose writers, but mention should certainly be made of Lawrence Ferlinghetti's *Tyrannus Nix?* (1969), one of the author's "political-satirical tirades," a verse form he invented with his earlier and better-known *Tentative Description of a Dinner Given to Promote the Impeachment of President Eisenhower*. There is also a whole series of remarkable Nixon poems by the far too little-known contemporary poet Rachel Loden.

In film and video, Stone's *Nixon* clearly commands the field, but it was preceded by Robert Altman's one-man show *Secret*

Honor (1984), in which Nixon (Philip Baker Hall, then almost unknown) delivers a rambling and furious monologue about (among other things) the "true" and even treasonous facts behind Watergate. It is curious that, though Altman was long one of Hollywood's most respected directors, and though this film was highly praised by influential reviewers when it came out (Roger Ebert called it "one of the most scathing, lacerating and brilliant movies of 1984"), it became for many years almost impossible to see. It is now available in DVD format. Much lighter (and more recent) is Andrew Fleming's *Dick* (1999), in which Dan Hedaya, who had played a minor role as a Nixon associate based on Bebe Rebozo in Stone's film, does an excellent job as the great man himself. Its success at the box office seems to have been hurt by the fact that full enjoyment of the film requires both a taste for teenage romantic comedy and a detailed knowledge of Watergate; but, as one of the few, perhaps, to possess both, I find the movie brisk, effective, and funny. Also worth mentioning here is the somewhat historically misleading but genuinely entertaining *Frost/Nixon* (2008), Ron Howard's cinematic reworking of the highly successful play of the same title by Peter Morgan, who wrote Howard's screenplay. In both the play and the film—which center on the post-presidential interviews with Nixon conducted by David Frost—Frank Langella's starring role as Nixon is noteworthy (though I found Langella more powerful on stage than on screen). Nixon is also the center of interest in two above-average television miniseries, *Washington: Behind Closed Doors* (1977), based on Ehrlichman's *The Company*, and *Blind Ambition* (1979), based on John Dean's memoir of the same title; here Jason Robards and Rip Torn, respectively, give first-rate performances as the president.

Indeed, Nixon's awkward body language and sometimes over-earnest oral delivery have helped to make him a subject of considerable fascination for creative and intelligent actors—as the work of Hall, Hedaya, Langella, Robards, and Torn (and above all Anthony Hopkins in Stone's film) illustrates. We might also include here two arguably Nixonian performances in films with no explicit connection to the thirty-seventh president. F. Murray Abraham has stated that his highly acclaimed performance as Antonio Salieri—the bitter, resentful, ultimately murderous composer in Milos Forman's *Amadeus* (1984)—was partly based on his study of Richard Nixon. I am not aware that Humphrey Bogart ever said anything similar about his role as the paranoid, neurotic Capt. Queeg in Edward Dmytryk's *The Caine Mutiny* (1954). But Bogart is known to have detested the Red-baiting in which Nixon played such a prominent part, and I am not the only admirer of Bogart's performance who has seen evidence of a Nixon connection on the screen.

If Nixon's physical posture and speaking style have helped to fire the imagination of actors, much in Nixon's facial appearance—such as the heavy jowls, the hooked nose, and the frequent five o'clock shadow—have done the same for visual artists, especially those skilled in caricature. Here the chief example is probably Philip Guston's neglected masterpiece *Poor Richard,* an extraordinary series of drawings that the artist composed in the summer of 1971. The project grew partly out of Guston's friendship with Philip Roth, who was composing *Our Gang* at the same time, but remained unpublished until twenty-one years after Guston's death, when the art curator Debra Bricker Balken printed the caricatures, along with her own extensive commentary, as *Philip Guston's Poor Richard* (2001). The wordless minimalism of Guston's art provides an interesting counterpoint to the much better-known captioned cartoons of Herbert Block, the political cartoonist for *The Washington Post* who signed himself "Herblock" and whose art chronicled Nixon's career for more than a quarter century. Many of his Nixon cartoons, along with a running prose commentary by the artist, were collected as *Herblock Special Report* (1974) shortly after Nixon's departure from the White House. They provide ample evidence as to why Nixon, at least at one point in his career (and long before Watergate), refused to have *The Washington Post* delivered to his home.

There are other Nixonian art works that might properly be mentioned here, even without allowing for the aesthetic element in works of creative nonfiction, e.g., Emile de Antonio's documentary film *Millhouse* (1971), or the journalistic coverage of Nixon by such brilliant stylists as Norman Mailer, Hunter S. Thompson, and Mary McCarthy—not to mention Mary McGrory, whose columns in *The Washington Star* provided the best written, most intelligent, and wittiest commentary on Watergate by any newspaper journalist. Furthermore, I should stress that the foregoing account has been concerned only with direct *representations* of Nixon. There is a virtually uncountable number of artistic works in which Nixon is present in more subtle ways. Movies are especially important in this connection, for, as Mark Feeney has shown in fascinating detail, Nixon had a surprisingly powerful impact on Hollywood (as Hollywood did on Nixon). The most notable works of cinematic art in which Nixon is not represented in any direct way but that nonetheless register the cultural importance of Nixon begin, perhaps, with classics from the 1970s like Hal Ashby's *Shampoo* (1975), much of which is set on the night of Nixon's 1968 victory, and Alan J. Pakula's *All the President's Men* (1976), which is based on the Bernstein-Woodward bestseller about Watergate. But they also include such more recent films as Terry Gilliam's *Fear and Loathing in Las Vegas* (1998), which is based on the comic masterpiece by Thompson, most Nixon-obsessed of journalists, and—perhaps most brilliant of all—Niels Mueller's *The Assassination of Richard Nixon* (2004), in which Sean Penn gives a shattering performance as Sam Bicke, who attempted to crash a commercial airliner into Nixon's White House. And there are many, many others.

But my chief aim in this epilogue is not to provide an

exhaustive survey. It is rather to examine the representation of Nixon in three works that seem to me not only of major artistic value but also especially illuminating from the viewpoint of Nixon studies. I take it as axiomatic that, as the Roman poet Horace wrote many centuries ago, the aim of art is to instruct as well as to delight. In the several views of Nixon discussed below, the reader will notice many parallels with the view I have developed in the pages above—and also, to be sure, some discrepancies. With an eye on the precedent provided by Marx—who claimed to have learned more about the social structure of France from the novels of Balzac than from all the historians, economists, political analysts, and other such nonfiction writers put together—I happily admit to having learned more about Nixon, in some ways, from Robert Coover and from Oliver Stone than from any *particular* journalist, biographer, or historian, with the single exception of Garry Wills. Conversely, the most powerful challenge to my own view of Nixon has come from certain elements in the music of John Adams. Critics of many different schools have agreed that the great creative artists often provide the deepest insights into the ages in which they live; and that is certainly true of the Age of Nixon.

2

Of the works by Stone, Adams, and Coover, Stone's *Nixon* is the most widely known, and it is also in many ways the most straightforward. It has several times been mentioned in passing in the pages above. Simply put, *Nixon* is a tragedy; and one way to approach it as such is to understand how it thus contrasts, sharply, with Stone's earlier film about Nixon's pre-eminent rival and antagonist, *JFK*.

Actually, Stone takes considerable pains to guarantee that the respective reconstructions of American history in these two companion pieces do not directly contradict one another on the plane of fact. But in genre, in overarching assumptions, and in their general "feel," the two movies are not only different but virtually opposed. For *JFK* is (in a way that created no little political scandal when it was released in 1991) a work of conspiracy theory; and there could hardly be a view of the world more antithetical to the tragic view than the conspiratorial one.

For the power of conspiracy theory is its ability to explain everything by a single hypothesis, which is usually complex in its particulars but simple and lucid in its overall design—and which is capable of accounting for the most varied details within one grand scheme. Tragedy, by contrast, normally insists that *not* everything can be fully explained. Tragedy implicitly (or, more rarely, explicitly) maintains that, at least in some instances, the world is, somehow, such that an irreducible margin of mystery will remain even after every attempt at explanation has been exhausted. Much of this irreducible mystery is generally held to exist in the character of the tragic protagonist; and it is on this protagonist, this single individual, that the tragic work of art is wont to focus most of its energy—hence the tendency of tragedies to refer in their very titles to specific persons, whether by name (*Oedipus the King*, or *Macbeth*, or *King Lear*) or more generically (*Death of a Salesman*). The work of conspiracy theory, on the other hand, usually invests in a huge cast of characters, as the very term *conspiracy* may be taken to imply (for the word has taken on connotations of a combination by a great many people, even though, in the technical legal sense, a conspiracy may be a combination by as few as two people). Finally, the two modes are generally opposed in their moral assumptions. Conspiracy theory most naturally takes a Manichean or dualistic view, setting the almost purely evil machinations of the conspirators against some individual or institution that is taken to be unproblematically, or at least fundamentally, good. Tragedy, with its concentration on the single protagonist, seldom presents its main figure as either simply virtuous or simply vicious. As commentators from Aristotle onwards have pointed out, the tragic hero is generally a person with some genuinely impressive and admirable qualities who, however, possesses an ineradicable flaw that ultimately helps to seal his (or, much more rarely, her) own doom—unlike the victim of conspiracy, who is usually brought low almost wholly by forces *outside* his or her own character.

Few aesthetically important contemporary works fulfill the pattern of conspiracy theory more exactly than *JFK*—which is, in a sense, misleadingly named, since the thirty-fifth president is not even really a character in the movie (one suspects that Stone already had *Nixon* planned, and desired a symmetry between the two titles). Yet the title is not without its logic, too. In the film's Manichean ethical structure, John Kennedy stands as the transcendent moral center. As such, he is, in the normal manner of representing transcendence, physically and visually absent (save for a few minutes of archival footage of the historic Kennedy scattered throughout the film's more than three hours). The qualities ascribed to this ethical paragon—such as vision, nobility, courage, and compassion—are inherited, in somewhat diluted form, by his symbolic son and the movie's actual protagonist, the New Orleans District Attorney Jim Garrison (who to this day remains, in historical fact, the only prosecutor ever to bring an indictment against anyone in the Kennedy assassination). In the film's long final scene—the summation that Garrison (Kevin Costner) delivers to the jury in his prosecution of the New Orleans businessman Clay Shaw (Tommy Lee Jones)—Garrison expressly casts himself as a crusading Hamlet trying to avenge the murder of his blameless father-king.

Dualistically opposed to the goodness of Kennedy and Garrison are the entirely malign conspirators, who include, alongside Shaw, countless others, from Dixie Mafia capos, to anti-Castro Cuban exiles, to small-time hustlers from the homosexual subculture of New Orleans—all the way up to Lyndon Johnson, J. Edgar Hoover (both named in Garrison's summation as "accomplices after the fact"), and high officials of the Pentagon and the CIA. A few of the conspirators are examined closely, others are seen in only a shadowy way, and some are never seen at all. But they all add up to an immense network of wickedness and corruption.

Indeed, one of the great cinematic strengths of *JFK,* with its more than 200 speaking parts, is that this very crowded canvas enables Stone to get first-rate performances from a remarkably large and diverse range of performers: to offer but two examples, Ed Asner as a far-right private detective with a violent temper, and Kevin Bacon as a psychopathically charming gay hustler (and fervent admirer of Nixon) whose sexual charisma irresistibly attracts Clay Shaw. Vast as the cast of evil-doers is, all of their motives and actions are made to fit neatly, in the classic manner of conspiracy theory, within one hypothesis that remains fundamentally simple, despite the almost endless complexity of its details and ramifications. This hypothesis—laid out for the viewer in the movie's two principal passages of exposition, namely Garrison's summation to the jury and the earlier tutorial that Garrison receives in Washington from the enigmatic "X" (Donald Sutherland), a renegade US intelligence operative with long experience at high levels of the Pentagon—is simply that President Kennedy had planned to liquidate not only US involvement in Vietnam but the Cold War *in toto;* and that, alarmed by this threat to their purpose and even to their very institutional existence, representatives of the various arms of the national-security state conspired to have him murdered. Though few serious historians are confident that the real-world Kennedy (who, after all, was a lifelong Cold War anti-Communist) had anything of the sort in mind, Stone's film presents the views of "X" and of Garrison as amounting to an entirely satisfying explanation of the assassination. There are many details that *JFK* leaves unexplored but nothing that it finds fundamentally mysterious.

Thus, though *JFK,* like many tragedies, is named after a

powerful leader who dies, the film is about as far from tragic as a narrative could be. Kennedy is not the protagonist of the movie, and he dies not from any tragic imperfections of his own but as the entirely innocent victim of conspiratorial evil. Garrison, the true protagonist, is also essentially blameless in his courage, intelligence, and determination (though the film levels some mild criticism at him for understandably neglecting his wife and children while pursuing his investigation). And Garrison does *not* die in the film. He lives to fight against a conspiracy of limitless malevolence and immense scope. Though he fails to bring down the conspirators on the plane of action (Shaw, of course, is acquitted), he does succeed, as a great conspiracy theorist, in unlocking the essential secrets that the evil-doers have worked so hard to keep hidden. The real-life Garrison plays a minor part in the film (that of Earl Warren) but died (of natural causes) shortly before *JFK* was released; and the film in effect asks its primary viewers, the American people, to continue Garrison's struggle. This didactic purpose, this implied challenge to political action, may, indeed, be taken as yet another quality that distinguishes the work of conspiracy theory from the work of tragedy. For tragedy normally invites the audience to reflection, not action.

As noted above, Stone's *Nixon* does not flatly contradict any of the factual particulars of *JFK*. Some of the conspiratorial concerns of the earlier film even maintain a marginal presence in the later one, especially as regards the Kennedy assassination itself (Stone does not represent Nixon as part of the conspiracy, but does suggest that Nixon knew some of the conspirators and may have received a subtle invitation to join them—which he tacitly declined). There are also some important technical affinities between these two films by this most technically versatile and resourceful, perhaps, of all current American filmmakers. The remarkable stylistic versatility of *JFK* and *Nixon* is made possible by Stone's use of an unusually large variety of photographic forms (video, still pictures, several different kinds of film stock), by the frequent intervention of black-and-white footage into these predominantly color films and of nonfictional archival footage into Stone's own fictional sequences, and by devices like elaborate flashbacks, cross-cuttings, cut-aways, superimpositions, freeze frames, slow-motion sequences, and the like. Such resources are skillfully deployed and unified in order to tell, in both films, a large and complicated story. Despite these similarities, however—and despite the obvious symmetry between two films named for the two dominant American political figures of the 1960s—*Nixon* leaves behind, for the most part, the conspiratorial vision of *JFK* in order to embrace an overwhelmingly tragic one.

Nixon is named for its tragic protagonist (played superbly by Anthony Hopkins), who, in the classic tragic manner, utterly dominates the action of the film. To be sure, there is here, as in *JFK*, a large cast of characters (and a large variety of brilliant performances). But in the earlier film the various characters exist for their own sake and for their different roles vis-à-vis the Kennedy assassination, not as mere satellites of Jim Garrison. In the later film the secondary figures exist for the sake of Nixon himself. He is the dark center of the movie, the black hole, so to speak, who, like Lear or Macbeth, holds the other characters within his gravitational field. Then too, the film, like nearly all tragedy, maintains a stubborn margin of mystery in its narration of historical events. On one level, this quality of the mysterious is condensed into the famous 18½-minute gap that appeared on a crucial White House tape released to the courts and the public during the Watergate scandal. In *JFK*, we would know, in essentials, what such a lacuna meant without having to ask for details. But in *Nixon* it remains genuinely inexplicable. Admittedly, there is a hint that the gap has something to do with the failed Bay of Pigs invasion of Cuba and also with the Kennedy assassination itself. But this hint (part of the faint residue of conspiracy theory that, as noted above, is not entirely absent in the film) amounts to no more than a vague possibility.

Furthermore, the mystery of the 18½-minute gap is ultimately a figure for the larger mystery of Nixon himself: the mystery of his own character and especially of the tragic flaw or flaws that precipitate his fall. True, Nixon, unlike the classic tragic protagonist, does not die during the action of the film. But his forced resignation of the nation's highest office is a symbolic (and indeed more than symbolic) death for this man who, throughout the movie, has been portrayed as utterly consumed by political ambition and as having no real life or interests outside the political arena. "If he's not this Nixon, he's nobody," as his old mentor Murray Chotiner (played by Fyvush Finkel) says while indicating a Nixon campaign poster in the aftermath of the 1960 loss to Kennedy. Though Nixon, in historical fact, lived for two decades after leaving the White House, Stone's film gives very short shrift to the post-presidential career of its hero. Having lost the presidency, Nixon is, in the film's terms, nearly as much "nobody" as the corpse of King Lear at the end of Shakespeare's play. Significantly, the only scene after Nixon's helicopter departs from the White House lawn in August 1974 is composed of some file footage of Nixon's funeral nearly twenty years later.

Stone's Nixon—not only obsessed by political success to the exclusion of everything else, but also bitter, paranoid, egocentric, vengeful, and repressed—is not a hugely attractive figure. But then, neither is Macbeth or Lear; and the Stone of this movie, despite his well-known personal antipathy to Nixon's politics, especially the prosecution of the Vietnam War (in which Stone fought and about which he made several films), by no means simply celebrates Nixon's downfall as the Stone of *JFK* certainly *would* celebrate the defeat of the assassins, if they could be defeated. Stone's Nixon, while manifestly no moral paragon like his Kennedy, is also not exactly a villain in the mold of Clay Shaw and the other conspirators. If Nixon's spiritual isolation, his inability to trust others and his certainty that enemies are everywhere, are among the qualities that doom him, there is nonetheless a genuinely tragic grandeur in the career and personality that are thus brought low. Nixon's story is, explicitly, a tragedy not only for the audience but for other characters within the film as well. Henry Kissinger (Paul Sorvino) tells a White House associate, "It's a tragedy, because he had greatness in his grasp. But he had the defects of his qualities"; and Kissinger later tells Nixon himself that his is "a fate of Biblical proportions." During a summit meeting at the White House, the Soviet Premier Leonid Brezhnev (Boris Sichkin)—Nixon's prime geopolitical adversary but also, in a strange way, his friend and colleague—speaks to a subordinate in language that (as the subtitles translate the Russian) is striking similar to Kissinger's: "Tragic, isn't it? He had the world in the palm of his hands."

On the policy level, the chief greatness that the film grants to Nixon is, rather conventionally, his mastery of foreign policy and global *Realpolitik*—as the words of both Kissinger and Brezhnev are clearly meant to imply. During the extensive black-and-white flashback sequences that dramatize Nixon's upbringing in Whittier, California, much is made of the fact that his mother, the saintly Hannah Nixon (Mary Steenburgen), expects great things of the brightest and most disciplined of her sons. Stone's view seems to be that Nixon fulfilled his mother's expectations mainly by opening US relations with China and, even more, by somewhat moderating the Cold War through the détente he established with the Soviet Union (so that, ironically enough, Nixon achieved a milder version of what Kennedy, according to *JFK*, was murdered for merely planning). At the end of the film, voice-over narration reminds us that, after Nixon was forced from office, the Cold War resumed with its old ferocity and arms spending by the US and the USSR soared.

But the film concentrates even more on the psychic and spiritual than on the geopolitical aspects of its hero's tragic greatness. Stone's Nixon is a profoundly dark figure. He is "the darkness reaching out for the darkness," as the Watergate burglar E. Howard Hunt (Ed Harris) tells the young White House counsel John Dean (David Hyde Pierce). Hunt's insight is ratified not only by Hopkins's stunning incarnation of Nixon's gloomy and malignant self-obsession, and by the lines that the script gives him to speak, but also in much of the film's cinematography. Few predominantly color movies give us so much blackness to look at. Heavily influenced by the black-and-white achievements of German Expressionism and American *film noir* (both genres remote, in most ways, from the tradition of the biopic or film biography in which Stone is working), the world of *Nixon* is visually one of darkness and shadow, especially insofar as its protagonist is concerned. For example, when we first set eyes on Nixon—after following Alexander Haig (Powers Boothe), Nixon's final chief of staff, through the White House gates and into the president's inner sanctum—we find Nixon sitting alone, drinking whiskey, in a dark room illuminated only by the dim, flickering light of a wood fire. When Haig, after asking permission, turns on an electric lamp, Nixon winces and shades his eyes almost like Count Dracula assaulted by a ray of sunshine.

Later, in a flashback (*all* of Nixon's pre-Watergate career is presented through flashbacks of one sort or another), the film achieves a similar but even more remarkable visual effect. As the camera cuts from an earlier (and black-and-white) flashback that has represented the death from tuberculosis of Nixon's older brother Harold when Richard Nixon was still a young man hoping to attend law school, we see, at first, only the middle-aged Nixon standing alone against a black background. His expression is grim, and his eyes dart around with paranoid watchfulness. A few moments pass before the viewer is allowed to realize that this is, in fact, the scene of the greatest public triumph of Nixon's life to that point. As the screen behind Nixon brightens and a band playing "The Battle Hymn of the Republic" is heard, we see that this is the 1968 Republican National Convention, with Nixon about to give his speech accepting the nomination for president. Hopkins looks around as though he has just realized where he is, and then flashes a precise duplicate of the real-life Nixon's weirdly mechanical smile. The point is vividly made that the darkness is Nixon's "natural" home, from which he emerges only for specifically calculated reasons.

Yet, for all the personal darkness and political evil through which Nixon moves (the latter, for Stone, represented most importantly by the mass death for which Nixon was responsible in southeast Asia), there is also a fearful sincerity about him as well. On a level beneath all the public lies and manipulations of Tricky Dick, Stone's Nixon displays a kind of awful, ragged honesty—and it is this quality above all others that distinguishes him, as a tragic hero, from the smooth hypocrisy and one-dimensional villainy of Clay Shaw and the other assassins in Stone's earlier film.

For Nixon *is*, finally, his mother's son. The time and emphasis that the film gives to Hannah Nixon—which might seem excessive insofar as the purely political story is concerned—are necessary in order to show the iron spiritual discipline in which Nixon has been raised, and to prepare for the maternal preoccupations that forever dominate his psyche. Throughout the film, even (or especially) after Hannah Nixon's death, he obsessively refers to his mother as his source of moral guidance. Sometimes she is even present, in apparent hallucination, before his eyes. Stone's Nixon has inherited a virtually impossible standard of moral rectitude from the Quaker saint Hannah, to whom his attitude is one of pure masochistic obeisance: "Think of me always as thy faithful dog," he tells her when still a boy. His own "long history of underhanded dealings" (as Howard Hunt aptly puts it) in no way liberates him from this terrible heritage but, on the contrary, only exacerbates the spiritual agony with which he strives and fails to live up to what he conceives to be his mother's ethical imperatives. When Nixon tells his wife that his country is "in deep, deep, deep trouble," the triple repetition (heavily emphasized in Hopkins's delivery) may be a deliberate echo of King Lear's famous "Never, never, never, never, never," and is in any case just as frightfully genuine in its psychic torment. Nixon's greatness depends on the fact that he *does* believe that the US is in trouble, and that, like Lincoln—an earlier small-town Republican lawyer born into modest circumstances, and, of course, Nixon's all-time political hero—he really believes himself to be the only person capable of serving as the nation's savior.

Of course, Nixon's brand of moral sincerity, in which everything depends on even the smallest of his own actions (such as his smoking—or not—the corn-silk cigarette for which Hannah mercilessly chides him during his boyhood), is inseparable from his paranoid pre-occupation with self. It is in certain passages that depart from the known historical record that the film presents with special force its protagonist's tragically egotistic combination of great ability and sincerity with bitter resentment and paranoia. Sometimes, indeed, the film's "objectivity" seems to dissolve, somewhat, as its own vision merges with Nixon's. For example, the film contains a good deal of voice-over that seems intended to represent the viewpoint of mainstream electronic journalism. There is the same generic (Midwestern or West Coast) American accent, the same tone of self-satisfied authoritativeness. Yet the voice is generally hostile to Nixon in ways that the actual mainstream media almost never were. Hardly any "objective" journalist, for example, would have described Nixon's Christmas 1972 bombing of North Vietnam as "without doubt the most brutal bombing in American history." Indeed, as we have seen, Nixon usually enjoyed favorable press treatment. Once he was in the White House and until he was overwhelmed by Watergate, many journalists positively fawned over him. Yet the hostile voice-over faithfully represents the way Stone's Nixon (and probably the historic Nixon) *feels* himself to be represented.

Even more important are the several extended scenes between Nixon and his wife Pat (played by Joan Allen in the most remarkable performance of the film next to Hopkins's own). There is almost no public record on which such *tête-à-tête* conversations could be based, so here Stone and his fellow screenwriters enjoy unusual freedom. They use it to display with particular vividness the cinematic Nixon's almost clinically unbalanced self-obsession and his terrible sincerity. Though one may wonder whether the actual Pat Nixon habitually spoke to her husband with such bluntness as the Joan Allen character employs, this forthright speaking enables the character to function as a sort of one-woman Greek chorus, questioning the tragic hero from a position of relative "normality." Again and again Pat begs her husband to calm down, to savor all he has achieved, not to take politics so personally—and perhaps to enjoy a beach vacation or some lovemaking with her. Invariably Nixon rejects such suggestions ("I'm not Jack Kennedy," is the revealing way he declines a sexual offer). He insists that his mother would have expected him to devote all his energy to the moral and political struggle, which he views as centered emphatically on his own person and personality. Despite the many years she has lived with him, Pat Nixon can still be freshly shocked by the degree of her husband's self-obsession:

> **Richard Nixon**: They're playing for keeps, Buddy. You know—the press, the kids, the liberals out there. They're out there trying to figure out how to tear me down.
> **Pat Nixon**: They're all your enemies?
> **Richard Nixon**: Yes!
> **Pat Nixon**: You personally?
> **Richard Nixon**: Yes! Listen: this is about me. Why can't you understand that—I mean, you of all people? It's not the war—it's Nixon! It's not Vietnam—it's Nixon! They

> want to destroy Nixon! If I expose myself just the slightest bit, they'll tear my insides out. You want that? You know? You want to see that, Buddy? It's not pretty.
> **Pat Nixon**: Sometimes I think that's what you want, Dick.

Later, Pat speaks even more bluntly and fulfills with complete precision her role as the chorus of Greek tragedy speaking to the doomed protagonist: "Dick, sometimes I understand why they hate you."

Like nearly all important modern tragedy, *Nixon*, as many comparisons noted above suggest, owes a great deal to the definitive tragic models established by the Greek tragic poets and by Shakespeare. A closer comparison, though—and one of which Stone is clearly quite conscious—is to Orson Welles's 1941 masterpiece, *Citizen Kane*. Conventionally ranked by film scholars as the most innovative and consequential work in the entirety of American cinema, *Kane* is beyond doubt the greatest and most influential movie ever to center exhaustively on the character and career of a single individual. As so many other directors have done before and since, Stone, in *Nixon*, pays a certain amount of specific homage to Welles. When *Nixon* was released, film buffs were quick to point out its various "quotations" of *Kane*—for instance, the way that Stone, like Welles, incorporates some mock-documentary footage in the style of the old "March of Time" series, or the scene where President and Mrs. Nixon, like Charles Foster Kane and his first wife, sit at opposite ends of a long dinner table in a state of mutual irritation and incomprehension. But the affinity of Stone's film to Welles's goes much deeper than such stylistic allusions—and deeper, even, than Stone's emulation (though not imitation) of the almost unprecedentedly complex temporal structure of *Citizen Kane*.

For Charles Foster Kane (played, of course, by Welles himself) is, like Stone's Nixon after him, a figure of tragic greatness. A man of vast inherited wealth, immense natural abilities, magnetic charm, and—at least at the beginning of his career—authentically progressive and populist impulses, Kane seems well qualified to achieve great things. But, again like Stone's Nixon, his greatness is poisoned by his paranoid obsession with self. His need to control, to make others satellites of himself, ruins his marriages and fatally compromises his political ideals as a champion of the people: "You talk about the people as though you *own* them," as Jedediah Leland (Joseph Cotten), Kane's oldest and closest (and soon to be estranged) friend, says to him. Kane dies of natural causes, and with much of his economic empire intact. But, as the film makes clear more than once, he dies after having lost nearly everything that was most precious to him.

Kane's is also a profoundly *American* tragedy—and with this category, I think, we come to the final significance of Stone's *Nixon* and perhaps the deepest of all its affinities with its Wellesian precedent. It is not just that Kane is a "can-do" optimist and an empire-builder in the classic American way. It is also that Kane himself repeatedly insists, both consciously and unconsciously, on the defining importance of his national identity. It is no accident that, when we see Kane at his youngest, as a little boy playing in the Colorado snow, the words we hear him casually singing to himself are, "The Union forever!"—the lyrics taken from a Civil-War-era song celebrating the endurance and triumph of the American nation. Later, as a middle-aged newspaper magnate of huge wealth and influence, Kane makes much the same point with full intent. As though replying both to a Wall Street financier who has described him as a communist, and a labor leader who has called him a fascist, Kane insists: "I am, have been, and will be only one thing—an American." The very title of *Citizen Kane* has not, perhaps, been sufficiently appreciated. The point is surely a specifically national one, namely that, in a republic with a Constitutional prohibition against patents of nobility, "citizen" is the loftiest designation that even the richest and most powerful can enjoy.

Stone's Nixon is just as deeply American as Welles's Kane, though not in quite the same way. Perhaps the most unexpected scene in the more than three hours of *Nixon* is the very first one. It is a black-and-white movie-within-the-movie that seems to be a training film for salesmen; it features an older and evidently more accomplished salesman giving advice to a younger one whose career is in trouble. "A good salesman can sell anything," the mentor advises. But he also warns, "You have to remember what you're *really* selling—yourself." It turns out that this unremarkable piece of celluloid is being played in a hotel conference room where the Watergate burglars are relaxing over drinks immediately prior to breaking into the offices of the Democratic National Committee. Though the content of the film is on the diegetic level purely contingent (in historical fact the burglars played a film in order to drown out conversation about the crime they were preparing to commit), it is not by carelessness that this short embedded film is the first thing Stone gives the viewer to look at.

For the training film announces (perhaps with a deliberate nod to what is arguably the most typical and enduring of all American tragedies, Arthur Miller's *Death of a Salesman*) the form of American identity and American optimism that will define the Nixon of the film, whom the viewer at this point has yet to see. It is not the hearty, confident optimism of a Charles Foster Kane, who from childhood enjoyed vast wealth and privilege, but the brittle, insecure optimism of the petty-bourgeois striver desperately attempting to better himself in the snake pit of a highly competitive society. The salesman is (as Miller—and, after him, David Mamet in *Glengarry Glen Ross*—shows) perhaps the purest instance of this quintessentially American pattern; and an electoral politician is, of course, a salesman too, one who is constantly selling *nothing but* himself. This is especially true of a politician like Nixon, who, beginning with no inherited fortune or network of social and political connections, must depend upon self-promotion for everything. The paranoid pre-occupation with self that Stone's Nixon so consistently displays is thus by no means a freely chosen outlook, nor one forced upon Nixon only by his personal upbringing and his resulting mother-complex. It is also integral to his entire social and national situation.

More than that even, the whole American pattern of petty-bourgeois insecurity analyzed in the third chapter of this volume, is, in Stone's telling, not only the matrix of Nixon's personality but also the social support network to which he clings. Consumed by highly vocal resentment of nearly all whom he sees as more privileged than himself—pampered college kids, Ivy League intellectuals, the "elite" generically, above all the Kennedys—Nixon repeatedly invokes the presumed support of "ordinary Americans" in social self-validation. At one point, particularly enraged when antiwar journalists continue to criticize him even after he has arranged for the withdrawal of US troops from Vietnam, he goes so far as to insist of his (American) opponents, "They don't trust Americans": thus equating his own person with the true body politic. This equation finds its most powerful expression in some dialogue we have encountered before but which (as perhaps the finest single line in *Nixon*) is worth quoting again—namely, Nixon's words to the portrait of John Kennedy: "When they [i.e., the American people] look at you, they see what they want to be. When they look at me, they see what they are."

The film suggests that there is much truth to these words. The tragedy of Stone's Nixon is a more generally American tragedy as well. Nixon's fall is one that, in the classic mode of tragedy, can leave no viewer—but especially no American viewer—entirely superior or untouched. It is worth noting that the failure of specifically American ideals and efforts is, after all, the major overriding theme of Stone's entire career as a director: whether the failure takes place under subfascist foreign dictatorship, as in *Salvador*, or in the malign chaos of the Vietnam War, as in *Platoon* and *Born on the Fourth of July*, or among the white-collar criminals of high finance, as in *Wall Street*, or in the weird symbiosis between sociopathic murder and a corrupt media establishment, as in *Natural Born Killers*—or, of course, in the Kennedy assassination itself. As *Nixon* ends, a lovely choral rendition of "Shenandoah" fills the soundtrack. There is perhaps no more thoroughly American song, and it is a song of irredeemable American loss.

3

Robert Coover's novel *The Public Burning* is in many ways a very different sort of work from Stone's film. Whereas Stone's approach and tone are tragic, Coover's are mainly satiric. Humor is almost never to be found among the many strengths of *Nixon*, whereas *The Public Burning* is among the funniest—as well as among the most genuinely epic in structure and most intellectually ambitious in substance—of modern American novels. Nonetheless, Coover's Nixon resembles Stone's at many points. Both works are informed by exhaustive historical research (Coover's being a bit more impeccable than Stone's), and both *Nixon* and *The Public Burning* present a Nixon who is regarded with ambivalence in many ways but who is consistently represented as American to the core.

The term "epic" is used so loosely nowadays to mean so many different things that the first point that needs to be made about *The Public Burning* is that it is epic in the strictest sense. In the tradition of such definitive models as the *Iliad*, the *Aeneid*, and *Paradise Lost*, Coover's novel is a vast book, crammed with historical and pseudo-historical detail, the action of which, however, takes place over a quite brief span of time: specifically, from Wednesday June 17th to Friday June 19th of 1953, when Julius and Ethel Rosenberg were executed by the United States government. Again in the authentic epic way, the action of the novel, despite its chronological brevity, is represented as being of awesome importance. From Coover's viewpoint, the electrocution of the Rosenbergs—condemned to death after being convicted, in what the text regards as an egregious miscarriage of justice, of passing American nuclear secrets to the Soviet Union—is an event fully comparable in importance to the Trojan War for Homer, the founding of Rome for Virgil, or the fall of man for Milton. This act of state murder is presented by Coover as emblematic of the whole process of anti-Communist repression that poisoned so much of American life from the onset of the Cold War until the "present" of 1977. The Rosenbergs regard themselves as "the first victims of American fascism," and *The Public Burning* ratifies the basic spirit of this phrase that it quotes from the actual historical record.

Despite the gravity of its subject-matter, however, the book is, as noted above, also hilariously funny in many places, though its humor is always black humor in one way or another. *The Public Burning* owes much to the *mock*-epic tradition of the eighteenth century (Alexander Pope's *Dunciad* remains the outstanding example in English) as well as to the classical epic tradition proper. Not the least *tour de force* of the novel is the way that Coover succeeds in deepening and underscoring the essential epic seriousness of his theme through a liberal use of the grotesque and outrageous. The largest example here is alluded to in the title. Though in real life the Rosenbergs were, of course, put to death behind prison walls, *The Public Burning* transfers the electrocution to New York City's Times Square, where it is represented as a vast public spectacle that combines human sacrifice with uproarious carnival, complete with band music, slapstick entertainment, refreshments, Disney characters, and the attendance of as many spectators as can fit into the square, including "everybody who's anybody in the above-board American Power Structure." The result is a kind of terrible farce: one which emphasizes Coover's conviction that the Rosenberg execution must be seen not, fundamentally, as a judicial proceeding, but as a lethal public ritual of the repressive, conformist anti-Communism that came to dominate American social and political life. The literal "public burning" of the condemned couple also provides the central example of the way that the text departs from the historical record about which it is so meticulously well-informed in matters large and small: namely, in ways so deliberately shocking and outlandish that the symbolic value of such departures will be evident, and the reader will hardly suspect them of being either inadvertent errors or deliberate falsifications.

In the character structure of *The Public Burning*, the two essential poles are the victims, Julius and Ethel, and the victimizer, Uncle Sam. The Rosenbergs are sincere American leftists—brave, sympathetic, somewhat inept (and legally represented by an even more inept defense team), and wholly innocent of the charges brought against them. Essentially, they are the Rosenbergs of the best historical scholarship as of 1977. (Since then, evidence has come to light that does seem to indicate the legal guilt of Julius Rosenberg, though not of his wife; this new evidence, however, also confirms Coover's assumption that the prosecution team committed ideologically driven criminal misconduct.) As for Uncle Sam, he represents, as is conventional, the United States itself: but the US as understood by the right-wing nationalistic patriotism dominant during the time present within the book. Sam is the very spirit of the Cold War, and opposes himself to the Phantom, his opposite number on the Soviet side. Composed of countless bits of rhetoric and imagery from American folklore (especially the folklore of the American snake-oil salesman of the Wild West), Sam is a fantastic character who stands "above" history and above the realistic level of *The Public Burning*. On the level of history and realism, the incumbent president of the United States is taken always to be the current "incarnation" of Uncle Sam; and in 1953 Dwight Eisenhower fulfills this role impeccably.

Two characters stand apart from the polar opposites of Sam and the Rosenbergs. One—relatively minor in terms of the amount of space devoted to him but nonetheless of major structural significance—is Supreme Court Justice William O. Douglas, to whom Coover also dedicates the novel. Douglas attempts to stay the execution of the Rosenbergs (in Coover's telling and in historical fact), and he is the only character in *The Public Burning* who argues forthrightly against Sam and speaks to him as an equal. He may be taken to represent a version of American patriotism alternative to Sam's, one that stresses individual liberty over social conformity and justice over anti-Communism: a brand of Americanism that Coover clearly endorses but which he also represents as completely marginalized in the ideological hysteria of the early 1950s. The other character who stands, as it were, between Sam and the Rosenbergs is none other than Richard Nixon himself.

Historically, of course, Nixon played no important direct role in the Rosenberg case, though he contributed massively to the general anti-Communist "great fear" that was ultimately responsible for their condemnation. Indeed, in Coover's book Nixon is represented as at least mildly irked by the way that the sensational circus atmosphere surrounding the burning of the Rosenbergs seems to have distracted attention from his own greatest anti-Communist triumph, the perjury conviction of Alger Hiss. But Coover makes a place for Nixon in the story through one of the most ingenious devices in contemporary fiction: Nixon functions as the *narrator* of alternate chapters, and thus in some ways becomes nearly as central to the novel as the Rosenberg execution itself. When we review the differences between *Nixon* and *The Public Burning*—between a tragic biographical film, on the one hand, and, on the other, a frequently satiric and grotesque epic, and mock-epic, novel—it may be that the most important single difference, insofar as the presentation of Nixon is concerned, is the difference between the third person and the first. In the novel, the major revelations about his character are all *self*-revelations in the most direct and overt way.

The half of *The Public Burning* narrated by Nixon thus amounts to an as-if-spoken, first-person novel in vernacular American English—a form that includes some of the most enduring and influential novels in American literature. Like nearly all such works, Coover's owes a large debt to the prototype of the kind, Mark Twain's *Huckleberry Finn*, the rhetoric of which leaves its imprint on *The Public Burning* in many ways. Like the other major works that have flowed directly or indirectly from Twain's masterpiece, the Nixonian side of *The Public Burning* is noteworthy largely for its creation of an utterly consistent, convincing, colloquial *voice*. As with Twain's Huck, or Hemingway's Jake Barnes in *The Sun Also Rises*, or Salinger's Holden Caulfield in *The Catcher in the Rye*, or Philip Roth's Alexander Portnoy in *Portnoy's Complaint*, we know Coover's Nixon primarily by the way he speaks: that is, by Coover's sustaining, over hundreds of pages, a highly individual vocal style that creates the sense, on the reader's part, of being admitted to the intricate recesses of an authentic human consciousness. So supple and distinctive is Coover's rhetoric, so ample is the consciousness that seems to be thus opened up for our inspection, that the novelist William Gass, comparing his colleague's prose with the voice of the actual Nixon as found on the White House tapes, has gone so far as to declare: "Coover's Richard Nixon is a rich and beautifully rendered fictional character. The real Richard Nixon is a caricature."

Yet Coover has done his homework on the "real" Nixon of the historical record well, and in many ways sticks closely to him. Unlike Stone, who is guilty of what seem to be a few factual mistakes (such as imagining that Helen Gahagan Douglas was a member of the U. S. Senate rather than the House of Representatives when Nixon defeated her in 1950), Coover, so far as I can determine, has flawlessly mastered the nonfictional work on Nixon available to him in 1977. Probably no one who has not slogged through thousands of pages of Nixon biography and autobiography can fully appreciate the erudition that Coover wears so lightly, the countless details that Coover's Nixonian discourse presents so naturally and unobtrusively: for example, Nixon's reputation as a studious "iron butt" in law school, or his habit, when a young Republican politician, of successfully ingratiating himself with elder statesmen of the party like Herbert Hoover. Indeed, anyone well versed in Nixon studies will recognize many phrases and sentences in the Nixon chapters of *The Public Burning* as embedded quotations or near-quotations from Nixon's own writings (mainly *Six Crises*) or from Nixon's statements quoted by journalists and historians. Sometimes, to be sure, Coover engages in deliberate anachronism. For instance, when Coover's Nixon remarks, in the 1953 of the novel, that it's "a hell of a thing—that the fate of a great country can depend on camera angles," he is echoing a comment that the real-life Nixon made to Garry Wills during the 1968 presidential campaign. But such prestidigitation with chronology only enhances the novel's persuasive three-dimensionality in its representation of Nixon. One might say that, on the plane of empirical detail, Coover's Nixon speaks not quite as the actual Nixon of 1953 could have spoken but as he *would* (or at least might) have spoken had he possessed accurate foreknowledge of the remainder of his political career.

The factual solidity of Coover's Nixonian discourse is finally a means toward an interpretation of Nixon's character and career. Coover's abomination of Nixon's politics is at least as emphatic as Stone's; and the novelist and the director agree in seeing their subject as insecure, ruthless, ambitious, and personally isolated in virtually every spiritual, psychological, and sexual way. In *The Public Burning* no less than in *Nixon*, Nixon's pre-occupation with himself rises to nearly pathological heights, though Coover's presentation of such self-obsession is far more casual and colloquial than anything in Stone's film, with all the tragic grandeur of the latter. The brilliant consistency of Coover's Nixonian discourse is perhaps nowhere better illustrated than in the way that a rigorously factual narration can shade, with not the slightest shift in tone, into the wildest flights of self-aggrandizement:

> I was Eisenhower's salesman in the Cloakrooms, that was my job, I was the political broker between the patsies and the Neanderthals, I had to cool the barnburners, soften up the hardshells, keep the hunkers and cowboys in line, mollify the soreheads and baby tinhorn egos, I was the flak runner, the wheelhorse, I had to mend the fences and bind up the wounds. Yes, bind up the wounds: I'm a lot like Lincoln, I guess, who was kind and compassionate on the one hand, and strong and competitive on the other.

Coover's Nixon elsewhere tells us that, had he chosen, he could doubtless have become a great comedian on the level of Jack Benny, or, probably, a great jazz pianist. "If I'd had time for theology," he also comments, "I might have revolutionized the goddamn field."

As such passages suggest, Coover's Nixon, despite his monstrous egotism, is a slightly more sympathetic character than Stone's. He is at least a shade less paranoid and vindictive, and he is considerably more genial (though the comparison does not, admittedly, place the bar very high). In part, to be sure, this contrast is the direct result of the difference between third-person and first-person presentation. Whereas in Stone's film we see Nixon's lack of intimacy with anyone, even (or perhaps especially) with his wife, the Nixon chapters of *The Public Burning* give the impression that Nixon is effortlessly available to and communicative with at least one person that the reader trusts, namely the reader herself (or himself). First-person narration tends to seduce the reader into taking the narrator on the narrator's own terms, at least to a considerable degree. But, of course, the use of the first person is Coover's aesthetic choice, and it seriously complicates and qualifies the withering satiric contempt to which Coover (unlike Stone, with his tragic seriousness) subjects Nixon. By the end of the novel (which is as surprising as the forced resignation at the end of Stone's film is expected), Nixon, while by no means tragic, has achieved a remarkable degree of pathos.

The central site of the ambivalence with which Coover thus regards Nixon is the latter's function as the mediating, or deconstructive, term between the Rosenbergs and the murderous forces of Uncle Sam (the latter represented, on the immediate political level, by the Eisenhower Administration, which gives the actual order to burn the victims). This mediating function is in turn the key to Nixon's deeply American identity. The acutely self-conscious Nixon is, in fact, fully aware of the in-between role he plays, and thinks of himself as supplying "the middle ingredient...the true America. My America. Dwight Eisenhower and Julius Rosenberg would never understand each other, but I could understand—and contain—both." Despite Nixon's fundamental Republican and anti-Communist loyalty to Eisenhower—and, behind Eisenhower, to Uncle Sam, whose "incarnation" Nixon, with his eye already on the White House, passionately desires to become—Nixon finds himself, in his musing, becoming surprisingly sympathetic to the Rosenbergs too.

It is not just that he comes to doubt both their guilt and (like Justice Douglas) the technical legality of the executions. He also recognizes a number of unexpected similarities between their story and his own: "Ethel was two years younger than I was, around Don's age [Donald Nixon, one of Richard's younger brothers], Julius was younger. We all probably went to the same movies, sang the same songs, read some of the same books. We were the Generation of the Great Depression." Like both Rosenbergs, Nixon was born into humble material circumstances. Like Julius, he had a strict religious upbringing, experienced a good deal of childhood illness, and developed an early interest in politics. Like Ethel, he was shy and studious in school and had a special love for books and the theatre. Even some of the obvious differences may point toward an underlying affinity: Julius had "become a left-winger in college, but ghetto Jews were *supposed* to be left-wingers at a time when most right-wingers were Jew-baiters, so in a way he was being just as conventional as I was back at Whittier College" (emphasis in original). The Rosenbergs' experience is after all just as American, in its own fashion, as everything that Uncle Sam stands for: so there could hardly be a finer proof of Nixon's all-encompassing Americanness than his ability to feel at one with the Rosenbergs while also being both a leader of the anti-Communist ideology ultimately responsible for their electrocution and a high official of the government that actually throws the switch.

Nixon's somewhat attractive ability to empathize with the Rosenbergs, who are, in a sense, his own victims, finds its most extraordinary—and most grotesquely humorous—expression in the way that, though normally asexual and with a pronounced hostility to the body, Nixon develops an intense sexual yearning for Ethel. His desire leads to one of the most outrageous departures from history in *The Public Burning*. Coover's Nixon makes his way from Washington to Sing Sing prison in upstate New York, and, trading on his status as vice-president, persuades the warden to allow him a private interview with Ethel Rosenberg on death row—where he manages to consummate a sexual encounter with her. Some of the rhetoric with which he attempts to woo her is characteristically "Nixonian" in its absurdly inflated emphasis on himself. For instance, Nixon tells Ethel,

"I've suffered a lot of smear attacks myself, you know!", as though being criticized while running (successfully) for office were comparable to being convicted of treason and sentenced to death. He later insists that he has suffered even *more* than she has. But the vice-president also shows, with some sincerity, a more romantic side as well: "You're an artist, Ethel, a poet! You know what love is, what it might be! All the rest is just lies!" They get physical when Nixon decides to overpower Ethel by brute force, but—in the usual way of a certain conventionally masculine fantasy—what begins as rape soon mutates into the most ecstatic and fully consensual lovemaking. By the end Ethel Rosenberg is overwhelmed with sexual bliss, and she is hopelessly in love with Richard Nixon.

This thoroughly bizarre episode—which seems brilliantly calculated to offend, in one way or another, virtually every reader, of any conceivable ideological viewpoint—amounts on one level to a typically Nixonian fantasy of self-aggrandizement. Sexual love has never been one of Nixon's particular interests (he's not Jack Kennedy, as Stone's Nixon might remind us). Yet, if he can win over Ethel Rosenberg herself, what could he *not* accomplish in this department of life too? Indeed, it is just possible that Nixon has hallucinated the whole thing. But the episode, for all its grotesque satire, also highlights what the novel presents as genuine ambiguities in Nixon's character: the character of the man who can love Ethel even as he is partly responsible for sending her to her death. He is a rapist, but also, at least briefly, a genuine lover. The erotic tenderness we see between Nixon and Ethel is by no means only on the latter's side: "I opened myself to her," he says, "as to no other woman in my life." The experience is so shattering for Nixon, so emotionally overwhelming, that he feels that he has "lost himself" in "one of life's mountaintop experiences" (the rhetoric here is lifted directly from *Six Crises*): to such a degree, indeed, that for a time he forgets his own name. When he turns up at Times Square, not knowing how he got there, his trousers are still down around his ankles: an extraordinarily uncharacteristic way to make a public appearance for a man so tightly controlled and buttoned-up (so *dressed*, as Garry Wills put it) as Nixon. He reflects, "I can't even let my *hair* down in public, much less my pants!" (emphasis in original).

But the comparatively sympathetic and, so to speak, untrousered side of Nixon proves far less powerful than the more essentially "Nixonian" side. Not only does Nixon manage to attend, as an approving member of the American power structure, the electrocution of the woman with whom he has recently been making love. He even succeeds in transforming his state of partial undress—an effect of his recent and extremely rare moment of self-forgetfulness—from a dreadful embarrassment into an entirely self-interested and highly effective trick of partisan demagogy. In what seems to be a sly parody of the real-life Checkers speech, Nixon tells the crowd that his dishabille is no matter of accident or carelessness but is deliberately intended to illustrate how America itself has been caught with its collective pants down in the face of the Communist menace. In the frenzied carnival atmosphere of the eagerly awaited execution, this suggestion proves wildly popular, and Nixon soon persuades his fellow Americans that *all* true patriots will drop their trousers right away. "*PANTS DOWN FOR DICK!*" the mob screams, and suits its actions to these words. It is a thoroughly Nixonian triumph.

But Nixon does not exactly have the last laugh. Caught up in his own oratory and demagogic power, Nixon goes so far as to impugn the patriotism of Uncle Sam himself; and this, as Sam says, is going too far. The electrocution of Julius and Ethel goes off as planned, much to the satisfaction of the crowd. Afterwards, however, at the very end of the novel's more than five hundred pages, Sam returns to settle accounts with Nixon, who knows, as Sam approaches, that something terrible is in the offing: "I felt like I used to feel whenever I'd hear my old man approaching in a rage, clutching his razor strap." As Sam seizes and partially strips him, Nixon again feels a pang of sympathy for the burned victims: "You didn't have to kill them! You just did it for fun! You're a...a butcher! a beast! *You're no better than the Phantom!"* (ellipsis and emphasis in original). What follows next is the anal rape of Nixon by Uncle Sam, and the reader is made to share Nixon's consciousness of excruciating pain:

> I was utterly gorged by him, he was slamming away in my belly, my chest, my very skull! I couldn't even breathe! I thought my heart would burst, my eyeballs would pop out. I was screaming and howling horribly but nobody came to my rescue.

Despite the darkly humorous grotesquerie, the pathos here is quite real too, and as impressive, in its way, as the tragedy of Nixon in Stone's movie. But the pathos soon dissolves into something stranger and more repellent. Just as Nixon's encounter with Ethel begins as rape but ends as lovemaking, so here too does the penetrated partner eventually give consent: only here it is a consent based on power-lust rather than erotic joy. Nixon comes to understand that being forcibly sodomized by Uncle Sam is the necessary prerequisite to becoming his incarnation: so that the torment that Sam puts him through means that someday he will be President Nixon. That makes it all worthwhile. Nixon confesses, *"I...I love you, Uncle Sam!"* (ellipsis and emphasis in original)—a precise echo of the last sentence of George Orwell's *Nineteen Eighty-four*, "He loved Big Brother."

Ultimately, then, the corruption of American ideals—represented in essentially *un*corrupted form, for Coover, only by the marginalized figure of Justice Douglas—is as thoroughgoing in *The Public Burning* as in *Nixon*. For both the novelist and the director, Nixon *is* America, more American, in Coover's terms, even than Uncle Sam himself; partly because, as we have seen, Nixon can encompass and mediate between Sam and the Rosenbergs. But his position between the executioner and the executed is not a matter of equidistance or equilibrium. The fundamental asymmetry between Ethel and Julius, on the one hand, and Sam, on the other, is of course the enormous power differential between two hapless leftists convicted of treason and the entire power structure of Cold War America, including but not limited to the executive branch of the federal government. For Nixon this power differential is decisive. Despite Nixon's moments of genuine fellow feeling with the Rosenbergs, despite Nixon's momentary capacity to lose himself in lovemaking with Ethel, the reader can never doubt that Nixon will finally choose Uncle Sam, the truer (at least in the sense of the more effective) side of the USA. To be sure, the reader may not guess that Nixon's choice will take the especially hideous form of accepting and even loving anal rape. But Coover suggests, in effect, that this is no more hideous—no more grotesque—than the choice that the American people made themselves when they twice elected Richard Nixon to be Sam's incarnation.

4

Nixon in China (which John Adams created in collaboration with his librettist Alice Goodman—though, as usual in opera, the words have comparatively little force apart from the music) is, like *The Public Burning*, set during the few days of a prominent public event: in this case, Nixon's ground-breaking visit to Beijing between the 21st and the 25th of February 1972. Like Coover's novel, Adams's opera is concerned with the epic significance of the event, which opened relations between China and the United States after a quarter century of almost complete estrangement. Again like *The Public Burning* and especially like Stone's *Nixon*, the opera focuses on the personal and psychological qualities of the principal historic figures. Unlike Coover, Adams does not enhance his presentation of Nixon with such fantastic devices as the character of Uncle Sam or the sexual encounter between Nixon and Ethel Rosenberg. Like Stone's film, Adams's opera employs more-or-less "realistic" modes of representation, though realism is doubtless a problematic category when applied to opera.

In its musical structure, Adams's opera fits well with his description of himself as "a minimalist bored with minimalism." The stylistic diversity and adventurousness that these words imply have doubtless been largely responsible for the nearly unique capacity of *Nixon in China* to transcend the normally very limited popularity that modern opera enjoys. To be sure, much of the music is composed in the tradition of austere modernism that dominates academic musical circles and that has been responsible for so much compositional innovation since the original breakthroughs of Arnold Schoenberg in the early twentieth century. But Adams does not display the resolute antipathy to C-major that characterizes many modern compositions. On the contrary, *Nixon in China* contains a number of lyrical and melodic passages that recall earlier musical forms; and it alludes at many points—partly in a parodic fashion, perhaps, but by no means entirely so—to styles and conventions from the "classical" operatic tradition of the nineteenth century.

In the opening scene of Act One, for instance, a chorus introduces us to the Communist setting ("The people are the heroes now"), and shortly thereafter Nixon's plane, *The Spirit of '76*, lands on the runway. The president makes an imposing entrance onstage, exchanges courtesies with his host, Premier Chou En-lai, and then sings an entrance aria, "News has a kind of mystery," with the first word repeated twelve times. The tune is jaunty and upbeat, and the effect is partly comic, but also genuinely grand in its epic invocation of the "eyes and ears of history." The final word is repeated several times, and the baritone singing the Nixon part is meant to articulate it with special clarity. There is, admittedly, not quite the same sort of pomp here that is found, say, in the triumphal entrance of Radamès near the beginning of Act Two of *Aida*, with the famous "Verdi trumpets"—perhaps the most spectacular entrance scene in all of opera. But it is difficult to believe that Adams is not thinking, and intending the viewer or listener to think, of that scene and of other great entrances in the repertoire of traditional opera.

Later, at the end of Act Two, when Chang Ch'ing sings one of the most famous arias in the whole opera—"I am the wife of Mao Tse-tung"—the partly atonal music also includes more melodic, crowd-pleasing Wagnerian bombast: appropriately enough, since Madame Mao is portrayed as a revolutionary personality of Wagnerian fanaticism. There is also an ominous hint of Wagnerian violence, as when the soprano playing Chang Ch'ing sings, "When I appear the people hang/Upon my words," and repeats the first line before moving on to the second. It is possibly worth remembering that Wagner, when a young man, was something of a revolutionary himself.

If *Nixon in China*, with its mixture of atonal and more melodic styles, is thus divided in its musical loyalties, much the same is true—though without implying any simple structure of one-to-one correspondence—of its representation of Nixon. To a certain degree, Adams's Nixon is not radically dissimilar to the Nixons found in Coover's novel or Stone's film, or in the main text of the current volume. This is especially true in Act One, where Adams intends, perhaps, to win the audience's attention and sympathy by giving them the sort of Nixon that he calculates them to expect and want. Crucial here is a running implied contrast between Nixon and the modest, dignified figure of Chou En-lai. Chou sings both the last and (except for the chorus) the first words of *Nixon in China*; he is the only character ever to express self-knowledge or self-doubt; and he is in general something like the moral center of the opera. In the first scene of the initial Act,

Nixon's aria about news is interwoven with an abortive dialogue with Chou, who vainly struggles to get in some simple points about details of the presidential visit. Nixon's own discourse, while sometimes genuinely impressive in its grasp of history, also descends into the familiar Nixonian self-importance ("My hand/Is steady as a rock") and paranoia ("Nobody is a friend of ours"); and such lines are sung with an especially austere atonality.

The contrast between Nixon and Chou is developed more amply in the third scene of Act One, the scene of the state banquet in the Great Hall of the People. After the third course of the elaborate meal has been completed, the premier rises to toast his American guests. He offers a quietly eloquent vision of human progress and harmony, the tune softly but powerfully modulated and recalling much in European romanticism. The end of Chou's aria ("All patriots were brothers once:/Let us drink to the time when they/Shall be brothers again") suggests a virtually Beethovenian idea of fraternity; and memories of *Fidelio* and the Ninth Symphony are inevitably encouraged. It is a difficult act for Nixon to follow in his return toast, and he does not acquit himself well. His words are banal (e.g., "never have I so enjoyed/A dinner") compared to the rich, frequently metaphorical imagery of Chou's toast. More important, the music is insistently angular, nervous, and jerky, seeming to express an inner (but never admitted) agitation that contrasts badly with Chou's perfect tranquility. Nixon here appears to be quite "Nixonian" as Coover, for instance, would understand the category.

Yet, as the opera develops, Nixon becomes considerably more sympathetic—and more *American* in a favorable way quite different from the kind of Americanness that concerns Coover and Stone. To be sure, Adams's own politics do not appear to have much in common with Nixon's. He has said that in 1968, the year that Nixon won the presidency, his own first-ever vote was cast in the New Hampshire primary for Eugene McCarthy, the antiwar candidate representing the left wing of the Democratic Party and thus the major-party candidate furthest removed from Nixon, ideologically, of all those running that year. But Adams declines to make Nixon the villain of his opera, reserving that role for the essentially European figure of Henry Kissinger. Kissinger sings few lines; but, especially during the Houston premier of *Nixon in China* directed by Peter Sellars in close collaboration with Adams, he hulked a good deal on stage in a distinctly sinister fashion. More important, most of the words that *are* sung by the baritone playing the role come in the ballet-within-the-opera staged by Madame Mao in the second scene of Act Two, *The Red Detachment of Women*. Here Kissinger doubles as Lao Szu—the sadistic factotum of a wealthy landlord—who hugely enjoys his task of whipping the poor peasant woman Wu Ching-hua, heroine of the ballet. He indulges in sexual fantasies about his victim ("That luscious thigh/That swelling breast/Scented and greased,/A sacrifice"), and the most clearly articulated line sung by the Kissinger/Lao character is "Whip her to death!". "Doesn't he look like you-know-who!" Pat Nixon comments of Lao Szu to her husband, as both Nixons sympathize with Ching-hua.

It is, of course, significant, that, whereas Stone, in his treatment of Nixon, focuses on the Watergate scandal (though the intricate network of flashbacks encompasses most of the rest of Nixon's life), and whereas Coover focuses on the Rosenberg execution, Adams chooses to focus on the trip to China—i.e., on the most widely *praised* episode in the entirety of Nixon's political career, even by many who otherwise regard Nixon's record with strong disapproval. Although, as we have seen, Adams acknowledges the Nixonian paranoia and pompous self-importance that largely define his hero's character for Stone and Coover, his own ultimate view of Nixon is much closer to Nixon's own. For Adams (or Adams and Goodman), the thirty-seventh president looms largest as an intelligent, well-informed, and highly skilled geopolitical statesman who, during his five days in Beijing, achieves a diplomatic feat beyond the capacity of any other American political figure—and, moreover, a feat that virtually nobody expected from a president whose early political career was forged by the fiercest sort of anti-Communist demagoguery. If Nixon's emphasis on his own role in history at times seems unintentionally comical, it is for Adams more a pardonable foible than a pathological symptom: because Adams's Nixon *is*, after all, achieving things of world-historical importance. True enough, the Nixonian statecraft requires the assistance of the cruel and power-crazed toady Kissinger (whom Nixon at one point describes as "[m]y right hand man"). But this seems to be in keeping with the general insistence of *Nixon in China* on the inevitably mixed nature of all movements and political sides. The side of Chinese Communism, after all, includes the wise and visionary Chou En-lai, but also the grimly fanatical and implicitly murderous Madame Mao—as well as the more ambiguous figure of Mao himself. Nixon may need a Kissinger, but the president is clearly shown to be smarter and more penetrating than his Harvard-trained subordinate; and Nixon is never completely limited or defined by Kissinger.

The comparatively sympathetic portrait of Nixon that the opera offers is constructed on the personal level as well as on that of global politics: most notably in the third and final act, where the major characters, exhausted by the rigors of the state visit, turn more to their private thoughts and words than to public diplomacy. The music is the most subtly melodic in *Nixon in China*, and beautifully expresses the characters' reminiscences of their earlier years (the dialogue is taken up largely by these reminiscences). Act Three immediately follows the embedded ballet in Act Two; and the favorable impression the audience receives of the Nixons when they are honestly appalled at Kissinger/Lao's cruelty to the beautiful Ching-hua is deepened by their frank, loving conversation here with one another (so different from the way the Nixons talk to each other in Stone's film!). They sing of the period early in their married life when they were separated by Nixon's military service in the Pacific theatre of the Second World War. The shared Far East setting is the nominal connection between this chapter of the past and the time present in Beijing. But the real point is the notably *un*ironic portrayal of the Nixons as an admirably all-American young married couple and, especially, the highlighting of Nixon's wartime role as the popular proprietor of "Nick's Snack Shack," which he founded on the Pacific island where he was posted in order to supply free hamburgers and beer to the American airmen passing through.

Here Adams and Goodman are, in fact, displaying a shrewd knowledge of the biographical literature on Nixon. When he first emerged as a national political figure, journalists (and, later, historians) naturally began to interview people who had known Nixon during various earlier stages of his life. With remarkable consistency, Nixon's associates from school, college, law school, and from his tenure as a young bureaucrat in wartime Washington reported a Nixon quite coherent with what might be called the Coover/Stone view: namely, a cold, distant, mistrustful boy or man, who was frequently respected for his brains and efficiency but not much liked by almost anyone. Yet there was one striking exception. Those who had served with "Nick" in the US Navy remembered a cheerful, friendly, gregarious Nixon who was almost universally popular with his fellows. Veterans who had been enlisted personnel recalled Nixon as one of the few officers they knew who seemed like a real human being. Several independently described him as "Mister Roberts," the likeable and thoroughly American eponymous hero of Thomas Heggen's once widely read novel that attained even greater popularity as a play and then as a film (with Henry Fonda, who specialized in playing likeable parts, in the title role). Such, finally, is Adams's own Nixon: sometimes a bit corny and banal in the Middle American way, but a man who fundamentally represents and serves his country well, whether as a young sailor in wartime concerned for his buddies, or as a mature statesman achieving an extraordinary feat of peaceful diplomacy.

It therefore seems likely that Adams would agree with Senator Dole's insistence, in his funeral oration, that the second half of the twentieth century deserves to be considered the Age of Nixon; and that Adams would mean it, at least to a large degree, in pretty much the eulogistic sense that Dole intended. Adams's ultimately sympathetic portrait of Nixon represents a distinctly minority view among serious observers, and, obviously, not one I share. But its presence in a great work of art places it permanently on the agenda of Nixon studies.

FURTHER READING: A HIGHLY SELECTIVE AND LIGHTLY ANNOTATED BIBLIOGRAPHY

As noted in the Preface, I have been reading about Richard Nixon for about half a century, and the following list by no means contains everything I have learned from. I have confined myself here to full-length works (and thus excluded newspaper, magazine, and journal articles) and also to ones that have had a direct, significant impact on this volume. I have also, for the most part—though not entirely—confined myself to books primarily or in large part about Nixon himself, even though I have certainly been influenced by many volumes mainly devoted to other, related subjects, such as Joseph McCarthy, John Kennedy, or the Cold War. Finally, I have confined this list to nonfiction only, even though some of the best writing about Nixon has been in fictional form; the Epilogue above gives an account of what I believe to be the most important literary and other artistic treatments of Nixon. Since I intend this list chiefly for the use of readers who, after finishing this book, wish to read more about Nixon, I have sometimes included a brief comment by way of guidance. When I began to compile this bibliography, I thought it might be convenient for the reader to divide it into a number of different thematic sections. But any attempt to do so seemed to leave so many books as dubious or borderline cases that I decided such divisions would probably be more misleading and distracting than useful: hence the following single list.

Where I have listed more than one book by the same author, they are placed in chronological, not alphabetical, order.

Abrahamsen, David. *Nixon vs. Nixon: An Emotional Tragedy*. New York: Farrar, Straus & Giroux, 1977.

Aitken, Jonathan. *Nixon: A Life.* Washington: Regnery, 1993. The most substantial and scholarly biography written from an enthusiastically pro-Nixon point of view; the author, a British politician, eventually spent time in prison for his own scandals.

Alsop, Stewart. *Nixon and Rockefeller.* New York: Doubleday, 1960.

Alterman, Eric. *What Liberal Media?: The Truth About Bias and the News.* New York: Basic Books, 2003.

Ambrose, Stephen. *Nixon.* Vol. 1: *The Education of a Politician, 1913-1962.* New York: Simon & Schuster, 1987.

———. *Nixon.* Vol. 2: *The Triumph of a Politician, 1962-1972.* New York: Simon & Schuster, 1989.

———. *Nixon.* Vol. 3: *Ruin and Recovery, 1973-1990.* New York: Simon & Schuster, 1991. This three-volume opus remains the "standard" biography. Only so-so on matters of interpretation and analysis, it is massively researched and engagingly written.

Bernstein, Carl, and Bob Woodward. *All the President's Men.* New York: Warner, 1974. Contrary to what most people seem to remember, Bernstein is the senior author of this famed account of the Watergate story.

Breslin, Jimmy. *How the Good Guys Finally Won.* New York: Viking, 1975. A useful account of the politics of Watergate.

Brodie, Fawn. *Richard Nixon: The Shaping of His Character.* New York: Norton, 1981.

Caute, David. *The Great Fear: The Anti-Communist Purge Under Truman and Eisenhower.* New York: Simon & Schuster, 1978.

Chester, Lewis, Godfrey Hodgson, and Bruce Page. *An American Melodrama: The Presidential Campaign of 1968.* New York: Viking, 1969. The best general journalistic account of the 1968 campaign.

Colson, Charles. *Born Again.* Old Tappan, NJ: Chosen Books, 1976. One of the more interesting of the so-called "books by crooks," i.e., by Watergate felons.

Crouse, Timothy. *The Boys on the Bus*. New York: Random House, 1973.

Crowley, Monica. *Nixon Off the Record*. New York: Random House, 1996.

——————. *Nixon in Winter*. New York: Random House, 1998. A good many fascinating Nixonian comments are preserved in these volumes by the thirty-seventh president's adoring granddaughterly Boswell.

Dean, John W. *Blind Ambition*. New York: Simon & Schuster, 1976.

Drew, Elizabeth. *Richard M. Nixon*. New York: Henry Holt, 2007. A deft and intelligent overview of Nixon's career, though somewhat scanty on the pre-presidential years.

Ehrlichman, John. *Witness to Power: The Nixon Years*. New York: Simon & Schuster, 1982.

Evans, Rowland, and Robert Novak. *Nixon in the White House: The Frustration of Power*. New York: Random House, 1971.

Feeney, Mark. *Nixon at the Movies: A Book About Belief*. Chicago: University of Chicago Press, 2004. An interesting and unusual attempt to understand Nixon in terms of American film, and *vice versa*.

Garment, Leonard. *In Search of Deep Throat: The Greatest Political Mystery of Our Time*. New York: Basic Books, 2000. An intriguing but wholly erroneous job of detective work.

Greenberg, David. *Nixon's Shadow: The History of an Image*. New York: Norton, 2003. The design of this book—to study Nixon through the varied public images of him—is somewhat stronger than the execution, but the volume is an interesting, original contribution to Nixon studies.

Haldeman, H. R., with Joseph DiMona. *The Ends of Power*. New York: Times Books, 1978. Haldeman eventually repudiated this memoir of his time with Nixon.

Haldeman, H. R. *The Haldeman Diaries: Inside the Nixon White House*. New York: Putnam's, 1994. The most detailed inside account of any presidential administration in American history. The printed version contains only about 40% of the entire nearly three-quarters of a million words, which can be found in CD-ROM form (Santa Monica: Sony Electronic Publishing, 1994).

Higgins, George V. *The Friends of Richard Nixon*. Boston: Little, Brown, 1975.

Hiss, Tony. *The View from Alger's Window*. New York: Random House, 1999. Though only tangentially concerned with Nixon, this memoir by Alger Hiss's son makes a powerful case—more moral and psychological than documentary—for his innocence.

Hoff, Joan. *Nixon Reconsidered*. New York: Basic Books, 1994.

Jaworski, Leon. *The Right and the Power: The Prosecution of Watergate*. New York: Reader's Digest Press, 1976.

Kissinger, Henry. *White House Years*. Boston: Little, Brown, 1979.

———. *Years of Upheaval*. Boston: Little, Brown, 1982.

Korff, Baruch. *The Personal Nixon: Staying on the Summit*. Washington: Fairness Publishers, 1974. A grotesquely interesting curiosity by Nixon's last prominent public defender during Watergate.

Krogh, Egil. *The Day Elvis Met Nixon*. Bellevue, WA: Pejama Press, 1994. The story (by a White House aide) behind the famous picture of the two shaking hands, which is today the most popular photograph in the National Archives.

Kutler, Stanley. *The Wars of Watergate: The Last Crisis of Richard Nixon*. New York: Knopf, 1990. The best scholarly treatment of Watergate.

———, ed. with an Introduction and Commentary. *Abuse of Power: The New Nixon Tapes*. New York: Simon & Schuster, 1997. The most useful single collection of Nixon's White House tapes (no complete edition exists).

Liddy, Gordon. *Will: The Autobiography of G. Gordon Liddy*. New York: St. Martin's, 1980. Interesting as a chilling (but sometimes unintentionally comical) self-portrait of a man whose ardent loyalty Nixon attracted.

Lukas, J. Anthony. *Nightmare: The Underside of the Nixon Years*. New York: Viking, 1976. Still the best journalistic account of Watergate.

Mailer, Norman. *Miami and the Siege of Chicago*. New York: New American Library, 1968.

———. *St. George and the Godfather*. New York: New American Library, 1972.

Mankiewicz, Frank. *Perfectly Clear: Nixon from Whittier to Watergate*. New York: Popular Library, 1973.

Matthews, Christopher. *Kennedy and Nixon*. New York: Simon & Schuster, 1986.

Mazlish, Bruce. *In Search of Nixon: A Psychohistorical Inquiry*. New York: Basic Books, 1972.

McCarthy, Mary. *The Mask of State: Watergate Portraits*. New York: Harcourt Brace Jovanovich, 1974. Valuably employs speculation and a novelist's insight into character to try to disentangle some of the mysteries of Watergate.

McGinnis, Joe. *The Selling of the President 1968*. New York: Trident, 1969. See discussion in the sixth chapter of this volume.

Mitchell, Greg. *Tricky Dick and the Pink Lady: Richard Nixon vs. Helen Gahagan Douglas*. New York: Random House, 1998.

Monsell, Thomas. *Nixon on Stage and Screen: The Thirty-Seventh President as Depicted in Films, Television, Plays and Opera*. Jefferson, NC: McFarland, 1998.

Morris, Roger. *Richard Milhous Nixon: The Rise of an American Politician*. New York: Henry Holt, 1990. The most detailed account of Nixon's earlier years.

The New York Times. The Watergate Hearings: Break-in and Cover-up: Proceedings of the Senate Select Committee on Presidential Campaign Activities. New York: Viking, 1973. The record of what is more commonly known as the "Ervin Committee" or the "Senate Watergate Committee."

Nixon, Richard. *Six Crises*. Garden City, NY: Doubleday, 1962.

Nixon's only pre-presidential book, and valuable for its clues to his thinking in the aftermath of the 1960 campaign.

——————. *RN: The Memoirs of Richard Nixon*. New York: Grosset & Dunlap, 1975. Nixon's longest, best-written, and most informative book.

——————. *Leaders*. New York: Warner, 1982. Nixon's account of some of those whom he saw as his peers.

——————. *In the Arena: A Memoir of Victory, Defeat, and Renewal*. New York: Simon & Schuster, 1990.

Osborne, John. *The Nixon Watch*. New York: Liveright, 1970.

——————. *The Second Year of the Nixon Watch*. New York: Liveright, 1971.

——————. *The Third Year of the Nixon Watch*. New York: Liveright, 1972.

——————. *The Fourth Year of the Nixon Watch*. New York: Liveright, 1973.

——————. *The Fifth Year of the Nixon Watch*. New York: Liveright, 1974.

——————. *The Last Nixon Watch*. Washington: New Republic, 1975. These volumes collect Osborne's highly celebrated columns from *The New Republic*, which were probably somewhat overrated at the time—Jonathan Schell was doing better such work with less fanfare at *The New Yorker*—but remain valuable as a contemporary chronicle of the Nixon presidency.

Perlstein, Rick. *Nixonland: The Rise of a President and the Fracturing of America*. New York: Scribner, 2008. A massively detailed and engaging narrative of Nixon and Nixon's America between 1966 and 1972.

Phillips, Kevin. *The Emerging Republican Majority*. New Rochelle, NY: Arlington, 1969. The most influential statement of the theory implicit in the practice of Nixon's 1968 campaign.

The Presidential Transcripts. In Conjunction with the Staff of *The Washington Post*. New York: Dell, 1974. The first collection of

Nixon's White House tapes (no complete edition exists).

Rather, Dan, and Gary Paul Gates. *The Palace Guard*. New York: Harper, 1974. An examination of the staff system of Nixon's White House. Anticipating Robert Dole and myself, the first chapter is called "The Age of Nixon."

Reeves, Richard. *President Kennedy: Profile of Power*. New York: Simon & Schuster, 1993.

——————. *President Nixon: Alone in the White House*. New York: Simon & Schuster, 2001.

Reeves, Thomas. *The Life and Times of Joe McCarthy*. New York: Stein & Day, 1982.

Rovere, Richard. *Senator Joe McCarthy*. New York: Harcourt Brace Jovanovich, 1959.

Safire, William. *Before the Fall: An Inside View of the Pre-Watergate White House*. Garden City, NY: Doubleday, 1975. An interesting account by the best writer among Nixon's men.

Schell, Jonathan. *Observing the Nixon Years: "Notes and Comment" from* The New Yorker *on the Vietnam War and the Watergate Crisis*. New York: Pantheon, 1989. See the comment on the Osborne entry above.

Scheslinger, Arthur. *Kennedy or Nixon: Does It Make Any Difference?* New York: Macmillan, 1960. Since Schlesinger was the quasi-official Kennedy historian, his answer, unsurprisingly, was yes.

——————. *The Imperial Presidency*. Boston: Houghton Mifflin, 1973.

Sirica, John. *To Set the Record Straight: The Break-in, the Tapes, the Conspirators, the Pardon*. New York: Norton, 1979. A first-hand account of Watergate by the conservative Republican judge who did so much to expose the scandal.

Strober, Gerald, and Deborah Strober, *Nixon: An Oral History of His Presidency*. New York: HarperCollins, 1994.

Summers, Anthony. *The Arrogance of Power: The Secret World of Richard Nixon*. New York: Viking, 2000. Based on extremely important new research, especially into Nixon's financial corruption and his ties to organized crime. Though the Nixon family hotly denounced the book, they did not actually deny any of its allegations save the assertion that Nixon regularly beat his wife.

Thompson, Hunter S. *Fear and Loathing on the Campaign Trail '72*. San Francisco, Straight Arrow, 1973.

——————. *The Great Shark Hunt: Strange Tales from a Strange Time*. New York: Summit, 1979.

Volkan, Vamik, Norman Itzkowitz, and Andrew Dod. *Richard Nixon: A Psychobiography*. New York: Columbia, 1997.

Voorhis, Jerry. *The Strange Case of Richard Milhous Nixon*. New York: Popular Library, 1973. Not exactly a disinterested account.

Weinstein, Allen. *Perjury: The Hiss-Chambers Case*. New York: Knopf, 1978. The most academically influential account, which argues for Hiss's guilt. It has been seriously challenged on a number of grounds.

Whalen, Richard. *Catch the Falling Flag: A Republican's Challenge to His Party*. Boston: Houghton Mifflin, 1972.

White, Theodore. *The Making of the President 1960*. New York: Atheneum, 1961.

——————. *The Making of the President 1968*. New York: Atheneum, 1969.

——————. *The Making of the President 1972*. New York: Atheneum, 1973.

——————. *Breach of Faith: The Fall of Richard Nixon*. New York: Atheneum, 1975.

Though their understanding of Nixon in particular and of American politics in general is often laughably naïve and inadequate, these once-celebrated books are crammed with interesting factual details.

Wicker, Tom. *One of Us: Richard Nixon and the American Dream.* New York: Random House, 1991.

Wills, Garry. *Nixon Agonistes: The Crisis of the Self-Made Man*. New York: Signet, 1969. Still the single most brilliant, indispensable work in the entirety of Nixon studies. See chapter 5 of this volume.

Witcover, Jules. *The Resurrection of Richard Nixon*. New York: Putnam, 1970.

Woods, John. *Watergate Revisited: A Pictorial History*. Secaucus, NJ: Citadel, 1985. Since so much of the Watergate scandal unraveled in news photos and (especially) on television, this volume usefully supplements purely print accounts.

Woodward, Bob, and Carl Bernstein. *The Final Days*. New York: Simon & Schuster, 1976. More gossip than political analysis, but very good gossip.

Index

The name of Richard Nixon has been omitted from this index.

C

R

S

T

Contemporary culture has eliminated both the concept of the public and the figure of the intellectual. Former public spaces – both physical and cultural – are now either derelict or colonized by advertising. A cretinous anti-intellectualism presides, cheerled by expensively educated hacks in the pay of multinational corporations who reassure their bored readers that there is no need to rouse themselves from their interpassive stupor. The informal censorship internalized and propagated by the cultural workers of late capitalism generates a banal conformity that the propaganda chiefs of Stalinism could only ever have dreamt of imposing. Zer0 Books knows that another kind of discourse – intellectual without being academic, popular without being populist – is not only possible: it is already flourishing, in the regions beyond the striplit malls of so-called mass media and the neurotically bureaucratic halls of the academy. Zer0 is committed to the idea of publishing as a making public of the intellectual. It is convinced that in the unthinking, blandly consensual culture in which we live, critical and engaged theoretical reflection is more important than ever before.